DATE			

ALSO BY GEORGE GILDER

The Party That Lost Its Head
(with Bruce K. Chapman)

Sexual Suicide

Naked Nomads

Men and Marriage

Life after Television

Microcosm

Wealth and Poverty

Recapturing the Spirit of Enterprise

VISIBLE MAN

A True Story
of Post-racist America

GEORGE GILDER

A copublication of the
INSTITUTE FOR CONTEMPORARY STUDIES
and

DISCOVERY
INSTITUTE

ICS PRESS
San Francisco, California

The copublishers and the author gratefully acknowledge the encouragement and generous support of Robert J. Cihak, M.D., in making *Visible Man* publicly available once again.

© 1995 George Gilder

Printed in the United States of America on acid-free paper. All rights reserved. No part of this book may be used or reproduced in any manner without written permission except in the case of brief quotations in critical articles and reviews.

First published in 1978 by Basic Books, Inc., Publishers, New York

This edition is a copublication of the Institute for Contemporary Studies, San Francisco, California, and Discovery Institute, Seattle, Washington.

This book is a publication of the Institute for Contemporary Studies, a nonpartisan, nonprofit, public policy research organization. The analyses, conclusions, and opinions expressed in ICS Press publications are those of the authors and not necessarily those of the Institute or of its officers, its directors, or others associated with, or funding, its work.

Discovery Institute is a nonprofit public policy center for national and international affairs. While our fellows cooperate and interact in developing their positions, opinions expressed in Discovery publications represent those of the individual author, not necessarily those of other fellows or of the Institute.

Inquiries, book orders, and catalog requests should be addressed to ICS Press, 720 Market Street, San Francisco, CA 94102. (415) 981-5353. Fax (415) 986-4878. For book orders and catalog requests, call toll free (800) 326-0263.

Cover design by Ben Santora. The book was set in Palatino type by ICS Press Composition Unit and printed and bound by Haddon Craftsmen, Inc., an R. R. Donnelley & Sons Company.

0 9 8 7 6 5 4 3 2 1

Library of Congress Cataloging-in-Publication Data

Gilder, George F., 1939–
    Visible man : a true story of post-racist America / George Gilder.
        p.   cm.
    "Copublication of the Institute for Contemporary Studies and Discovery Institute"—T.p. verso.
    "First published in 1978 by Basic Books . . . New York"—T.p. verso.
    ISBN 1-55815-465-5
    1. Rape—New York (State)—Albany—Case studies. 2. Racism—New York (State)—Albany.   I. Title.
    HV6568.A4G54   1995
    364. 1 ′ 532 ′ 0974743—dc20   95-8587
                                                                                            CIP

To Nini, now my wife,
who lived the story
and prompted the book

Contents

Foreword Robert B. Hawkins, Jr.		ix
Acknowledgments		xi
Introduction to the New Edition		xiii
Prologue		xxxv
1	Sam Beau's Tubes	1
2	Greenville	17
3	To Albany, and Vietnam	27
4	"Rise and Fly" on Clinton Avenue	39
5	The State	47
6	The Street	57
7	Beverly	71
8	The Welfare Trap	87
9	Buddy's Party	99
10	The "Rape"	107
11	Keegan's College	123
12	Clyne's Court	133
13	False Fathers	155
14	Panama Joe	171
15	Washington	193
Postscript		209
About the Author		211

Foreword

For long-time readers of George Gilder's many books and articles, this new edition of *Visible Man* will hold special interest. But for those who know Gilder's work less well, or who are familiar only with his more current writing on technology and society, the book will be a revelation. First published two years before his much better known *Wealth and Poverty* (reissued by ICS Press in 1993), *Visible Man* recounts experiences that impelled Gilder to the social and economic insights that inform both *Wealth and Poverty* and *Recapturing the Spirit of Enterprise* (ICS Press, 1992); and the lessons it teaches are notable for that reason. At its most immediate, however, *Visible Man* is quite simply a good story, with a cast of characters befitting a novel and all the more engrossing for being real. The most real among them is Sam, a highly "visible man," as the author says, "a man of action and news." In the years of this true account, Sam is a handsome, intelligent young man possessing obvious charm and a natural inclination to love and provide for his children. But these attributes cannot keep him out of serious trouble; indeed, he seems to drift into that trouble as casually as he lights a cigarette or joins in a neighborhood card game.

    Visible Man is a departure for ICS Press. The book is a swift-moving narrative with all the color—and language—of the street and embodying an era of urban life that had a blaze of style all its own. Summoned up from the mid-1970s, Gilder's hero and the other citizens who populate these pages appear in their period costume of bell-bottoms, platform boots, snug gaudy shirts, and rakish hats. The larger events of the time intrude, too, as Sam serves briefly with the U.S. Marines in Vietnam. But in many ways, the story is all too timely. It imparts a message that is profoundly serious to its author. Writing this book, surrounded by and immersed in its setting twenty-four hours a day as he did so, helped to confirm Gilder's convictions about the civilizing power of marriage and family and to form his views of the cruelly seductive dependency of the welfare state.

The events in Gilder's compassionately told but tough-minded story, with its wealth of observations and warnings, prefigure the violence wrought in today's inner cities by large cohorts of fatherless and unsocialized young men. Edited and with a substantial new Introduction by the author, in which he relates his narrative to current issues of welfare and the attempts to reform it, this book does more than volumes of impersonal studies to implicate the welfare system as a destructive force in people's lives. Gilder is skeptical of welfare reform—his new Introduction strongly indicts "workfare"—but *Visible Man* makes clear that only welfare reform that keeps fathers in families can have any hope of success. This edition of *Visible Man* delivers an enduring moral that is more tragically clear today than when the book was first written: Welfare subverts marriage and family for those who need them most.

The Institute for Contemporary Studies warmly appreciates the contributions of Discovery Institute and the judgment and guidance of Discovery's president, Bruce Chapman, in the copublication of this volume. Both he and I would like to acknowledge the help of Robert J. Cihak. Dr. Cihak's admiration for the book and his desire to see it available to a new generation of readers have been translated into enthusiastic support and generous aid for this project. Discovery Institute and the Institute for Contemporary Studies are deeply grateful for his assistance.

Robert B. Hawkins, Jr., President
Institute for Contemporary Studies

Acknowledgments

This book is nonfiction. There is no invented dialogue or speculative incident in it. It is based on hundreds of interviews conducted over a two-year period with more than a hundred of the characters, singly and in groups, often reenacting scenes that appear in the book, correcting each other's memories of who pulled the knife when and who said what to whom. Unfortunately, and for reasons which in no way detract from my sense of debt and gratitude toward them, I cannot give their real names, even when they would wish to have them revealed. To preserve the privacy of some, it is necessary to conceal the identities of all (with the exception of public officials). But I give my heartfelt thanks.

I also wish to give special acknowledgment to Gilder Palmer, who has always been far more than a stepfather to me and whose contribution to this book has been indispensable. His powers of observation and insight—based on long experience with troubled youths—helped me interpret many of the scenes and personalities, while his introduction of Sam to the Outward Bound program, which may ultimately provide an answer for him, was of inestimable value. I also would like to thank Bob Rheault and Russell Roderick of Outward Bound for their interest and assistance.

Shelly Jackson did not live to see this book, to which she gave so much, come into being. But she contributed many vital insights and opinions, entered a crucial objection to the original title, and warmed and delighted both my wife, Nini, and me with her gaiety and friendship.

Contributing useful advice and assistance in early stages of the manuscript were Christopher DeMuth, Jane Stanton Hitchcock, Rod and Mellie Gilder, Amy Bartlett, Walter and Cathy Palmer, Mary Davidson, Judy Watson, Susan Arensberg, Carol Southern, Lee and Kate Auspitz, and Susan Kestelyn, who did most.

I want to thank Keith Marks, the splendid young flutist, for introducing me to the wild world of Kelly Street, and Midge Decter for a superb job of cutting and reshaping the manuscript.

Finally, I wish to express my gratitude to my friends at ICS Press, who brought the book back into print, particularly Robert Hawkins and the editor, Tracy Clagett; to Robert Cihak, whose generous backing made the new edition possible; and to Bruce Chapman of Discovery Institute in Seattle, for continuing support and guidance in all my endeavors.

George Gilder
Tyringham, Massachusetts
March 1, 1995

Introduction to the New Edition

"George Gilder, what you need now is dignity," declared my estimable editor Midge Decter when first confronted with the gauntlet of this book, cast down on her desk under the rakish title *Sam Beau*. This title, she said somberly, would have to go. I protested. Hadn't I garnered dignity galore with my honors from both the National Organization for Women and *Time* magazine as Pig of the Year in 1974? Surely such laurels could tide me through any little contretemps over Sam Beau.

Decter was adamant, though. As I recall, she cited Dr. Johnson's prime law of editing: "First, kill all your babies"—cut all your most clever and cherished wordplay and pedantry. In this case it would not be easy. This title was my firstborn. It preceded the book and prompted it. It was my precious Isaac she was asking me to put to the knife. Midge was imperious and important and a gem of an editor, but her voice was more yenta than Yahweh. I demurred. "But there will be protest demonstrations in front of the bookstores," she explained. "Can't beat that for publicity," I mumbled. "They will call you a racist," she said, as if disposing of the subject.

I responded weakly that as a child in the South, my hero had actually been known as Sambo; I was dubbing him a more elegant name, touched with French. But resistance was finally hopeless. As a young man making a living with his pen, I could not readily accept a stigma of racism. I deferred to Decter's better judgment and joined the armies of liberal American whites in treating blacks as if they were children, incapable of accepting or comprehending a normal literary trope. Perhaps in that small way, I contributed to the cocoons of unreality and hypocrisy that surround the lives of blacks in America and lead them to their current sieges of paranoia, in which even such an apparently sane man as Bill Cosby could charge in 1991 that AIDS is a genocidal racist plot.

I should also note that Crown, the publisher willing to go with the title *Sam Beau*, was offering $500 less immediate money than Basic's lordly two-book deal, including *Wealth and Poverty*, for $8,000. Crown did not want *Wealth and Poverty*, regarding it as the less commercial of the two properties. Crown also wished to remove most of the sociology from *Sam Beau* and sell it as a "thriller." So I went for dignity, sociological trappings, and the big bucks, and never looked back. Indeed *Visible Man* did achieve those goals, suffusing me with dignity and sociology and sparing me the indignity of commercial success (unhampered by protesters, the book zoomed out of the stores at a pace of some eight hundred copies within the first year). And it is possible that my Decter-instilled dignity served two years later to foster a respectful reception for *Wealth and Poverty*, informed by the researches for *Visible Man*, and contributed to its sales of some five hundred thousand copies around the world.

But I still prefer the title *Sam Beau*. By it, I had intended to convey the idea that the swashbuckling "bad dude" image of the street was just as corrosive to blacks as the old Sambo image of stepin-fetchit. In the end, though, I went with *Visible Man*, as a tribute to Ralph Ellison's classic and as an assertion that whatever the problems of young black men, invisibility was no longer among them. Moreover, I added a subtitle—*A True Story of Postracist America*—that I imagined was as bold a provocation as the title *Sam Beau*. I was wrong. None of the few and paltry reviews acknowledged the challenge to conventional wisdom that this subtitle conveyed. But it captured the heart of the book's argument.

White racism was not a significant problem of American blacks in 1978, and white racism had nothing to do with the particular problems of my lumpen-hero Mitchell "Sam" Brewer. To the contrary, his problem was the fantasy world of bizarre expectations and entitlements fostered by constant state indulgence and favoritism toward him. These fantasies of entitlement persist, joined with chimeras of discrimination; but if white racism was not much of a problem in 1978, it is manifestly not a problem in 1995.

Among people of influence in America, racism is dead. It died hard, sustained in its throes by several thousand college courses and political analyses to the contrary. It died in the face of testimonies from hundreds of black writers and scholars who interpret all the usual slights and insults, rebuffs and inequities of life as evidence of white bigotry, who descry a racist enmity in the waitress who ignores you, the professor who avoids you, the neighbors who spurn you, the boss who shuns your brilliance while promoting the klutz down the hall, the driver who nearly blasts you off the road while you jog, the woman who changes course to avoid meeting you on a dark Chicago street, the supervisor who gives you a series of petty assignments at your new job or demands that you arrive on time.

With the exception of the fearful woman on the dark street—an inevitable effect of rampant street crime by young black thugs avidly avoided by all races—such unpleasantness happens from time to time to everyone. Look for insults and you will find them. Seek out exclusive parties, clubs, and cliques, and imagine that they are consciously ostracizing you, and you will be able to seethe through life in a perpetual state of grievance and distress that will cause still more people to shun you. Because of limits on time and attention, all social life is discriminatory in one way or another.

Far from being hostile to black achievement, however, American whites celebrate blacks at every opportunity. In the truest test, governed by massive voluntary choices in the marketplace, Americans have made the National Basketball Association, 80 percent black, the most popular sports league, Whitney Houston the most popular and richest American singer, Bill Cosby the most popular and richest comedian, and Oprah Winfrey the most prosperous TV talk show host. American employers, mostly white, have given black women higher earnings, on average, than white women of the same age and credentials. Blacks in America have increased their incomes more over the past thirty years than virtually any other comparable group in the world economy. Blacks in America have far outperformed blacks in any other society with a significant black population.

America has indeed created a job market favorable to black achievement. The single most important finding in *The Bell Curve*, by Richard Herrnstein and Charles Murray, is that after controlling for age, IQ, and gender, the average black full-time worker actually outearns the average white by 1 percent. Let the IQ number stand for real educational attainment (as opposed to degrees in easier subjects and from less rigorous institutions), and it is clear that racial discrimination no longer limits black earnings. A more appropriate standard, though, would include a correction for marital status, which *Visible Man* shows as the most important influence on earnings (white married men today earn some 50 percent more than single men of the same age and credentials). Correcting the Murray figures for marital status, black men would outearn whites by a still larger margin. The fact is that blacks in the United States today earn substantially more than truly comparable whites.

Yet the intelligentsia, black and white, the black middle class, most black newspapers and talk shows, black actors and black quarterbacks, all clutch desperately to their belief in white racism. In *The Rage of a Privileged Class*, Ellis Cose, an ascendant young black journalist, now a *Newsweek* editor, unwittingly reveals a pandemic of delusionary behavior: successful blacks seeing racism in every encounter in their lives. No matter how well they do, Cose claims, they always encounter what he calls the "final door." Of course, there is no final door in society; there are millions of doors, all of them closed much of the time. The search for a final door promises only frustration and pain.

Cose's book offers a vital clue to the problem. The same fantasies that afflicted the denizens of *Visible Man* are now reaching from the white academy into the black middle and upper classes. No less than the street blacks of Albany, the Ivy League blacks of Cose's book display an obtuse incomprehension of capitalism. Cose, for example, believes that "most people end up in jobs for reasons that have little to do with merit." Cose cites a survey of one thousand black bankers in which "virtually 100 percent . . . indicated that the most important criterion for promotion was 'who you know.' . . . Technical competence in their eyes counted for little." Affirmative action and Marxist teaching on the nation's most prestigious campuses have virtually crippled a generation of blacks by giving them a wildly unrealistic view of the market economy, in which somehow people can be paid without producing a profit.

In a competitive capitalist economy, a belief that you get ahead by who you know rather than what you know, or what you can do, virtually defines a loser. Such a belief is surely the mark of a useless employee. Yet nearly all the interviewees in Cose's book show this crippling blindness to the economic facts of life. Cronyism may prevail in politics and bureaucracy and corporate affirmative action tracks. But a company in general must hire and promote the best possible people in all jobs that affect its competitive performance or it will go bankrupt and won't be able to hire anyone.

For the exalted jobs sought by most of Cose's interviewees, most companies are desperately seeking people who can do the work and paying scores of thousands of dollars to headhunting firms for each suitable head. On the basis of performance in this task—the central process of self-definition for every firm—companies either thrive or fail in the marketplace. Finding the best employees is as much of an art as a science. But it is sure that whoever the appropriate choice is, it is not going to be some angry dude who believes that you get the right to make "50 million dollar deals with little more than projections on the back of an envelope" because you have white skin and good connections.

Cose and most of the enraged folk he describes all seem to see the job force as some kind of social cotillion. "They went to all these places [Ivy colleges] and did all these things they are supposed to do . . . and things are supposed to happen." But "nothing happens" either for many white wallflowers with an attitude, or for Ph.D.'s in useless or bogus subjects, such as sexology, social relations, or gender studies. If you have a sense of entitlement and an aversion to enterprise, even a business degree will not suffice. A famous study in the business section of the *New York Times* following the Harvard Business School class of 1956 showed that most of them had stalled in their careers in exactly the same way as Cose's middle-class blacks who trust in credentials and large corporate ladders.

Good things happen to people who make them happen by doing things for others that yield more than they cost. But all too many of the people in Cose's book believe they could soar to the top if they could just get invited to the right parties or the white clubs that most real successes shun.

In an unintentionally hilarious moment in the book, Cose describes the apparently endless frustrations of a black partner in one of the nation's most prestigious law firms. Then, in an apparent afterthought, Cose observes: "For individual blacks, [the partner] sees some protection in 'becoming valuable' by making money for the enterprise," as if anyone gets to keep a job for any other reason at all. When another black executive says that "the only real solution . . . may be for blacks to start more businesses themselves," Cose laments his pessimism. But of course starting a business oneself is the way many whites and Asians achieve success. If you insist on the comfort and security of affirmative action in large corporations, you will also face the slights and frustrations inevitable in bureaucratic politics and the remorseless constraints of a pyramid that gets steeper and smaller as you approach the top.

As I discovered during speeches and appearances related to the original publication of *Visible Man*, there is a further reason that the delusions afflicting the inner city are now spreading beyond it to the middle class. If you tell the truth and deny that racism abounds in America, many blacks dismiss you as a bigot or a fool. Denial of racism today is widely seen as evidence of it. In the face of the fury of the charges of bigotry, whites find it easier to go along than to tell the truth.

Throughout Cose's book, for example, successful blacks report rage at the treatment of Rodney King. Polls show that it galvanized a newly intense feeling of alienation among blacks in America. Yet anyone, regardless of race, who took the police on an eight-mile, hundred-mile-an-hour chase, and then charged at them at the end should probably be grateful if he is not shot—which is the kind of thing that has happened to other people, white as well as black.

Reasonable people learn not to defy or insult police officers who are performing an inevitably messy and treacherous job under tremendous strain. Yet the white media unanimously confirmed the black outrage at the Rodney King incident. By any normal standard the victims in this case were the police who lost their careers after being imprisoned and pilloried for trying to do their job in communities where fully 40 percent of the young men are involved in crime. But virtually no one dared to express this obvious truth. Blacks found their worst fantasies of persecution confirmed by the entire white establishment in America. When the Simi Valley jurors acquitted the police defendants on nearly all counts, the American media rose up and condemned the jury as racist for performing its clear duty.

In effect, all America treated blacks as children who could not be told the truth. The result of this treatment, also accorded to Sam in the events of *Visible Man,* is that many blacks never learn the basic facts of life. The blacks in Cose's book are so eager to find racism everywhere that whites will always find it simpler to go along with them than explicitly to affront this fanatical faith. In the current environment, it is more politic to imply to a black passed over for a job that he was rejected because of his race than to tell him he lacked the technical ability or other qualifications to perform the work. From Harvard Law School deans to ghetto social workers, from the chairman of the *New York Times* to the editors of *Time,* to the steady drumbeat of three broadcast networks, eminent whites are constantly confirming blacks in the crippling comfort of their belief in white racism.

In 1995, I can still paraphrase the conclusion of *Wealth and Poverty:* Many influential Americans of both races seem determined to perpetuate the idea of racism, the rhetoric of it, even as the reality sinks ever deeper into the mists and middens of history. The real Southern sheriff, the strange fruit on Southern trees, the real historic segregation and savagery, North and South, are now emerging in parody as a series of nineties charades: lame notions like "subliminal" racism, UN agitprop like "cultural genocide," judicial figments like "underutilization" of minorities, statistical trumpery like "redlining" and "glass ceilings," even the word "ghetto" itself, so common as to be unavoidable, yet charged with an ideology, vague and out of date, of racial grievance and sequestration.

It is as if there were some strong current in American thought that cherishes the idea of racism, that cannot, indeed, do without it. Many intellectuals, in particular, seem to feel yaws of emptiness and anxiety at the notion of an America, the real America in which we live, in which—for all practical and political purposes, leaving aside the imagery of literature and the phantoms of the couch, Alice Walker's personal demons and the Ford Foundation's dim statistics, and leaving aside the way of all flesh to seek first its like and fear differences—the big threat of racism has collapsed into a bad joke by a Jimmy the Greek or (Cincinnati Reds owner) Marge Schott.

If racism explains next to nothing about black poverty and crime, what does explain it? The chief cause of black poverty is the expansion of welfare state programs based on a compulsive belief in racism as an explanation of the underclass. As dramatized in *Visible Man,* the key problem of the underclass—the crucible of crime, the source of violence, the root of poverty—is the utter failure of socialization of young men through marriage. The problem resides in the nexus of men and marriage. Yet nearly all the attentions, subsidies, training opportunities, and therapies of the welfare state focus on helping women function without marriage. The welfare state attacks the problem of the absence of husbands by rendering husbands entirely superfluous.

Except in a newly acute racial dimension, the problem is not new. In his famous 1965 report on the back family, Daniel Patrick Moynihan quoted Edwin Wright Bakke writing on white poverty: "Consider that the welfare check normally goes to the woman and is often accompanied by female social workers. The man, already suffering from his failure as provider, is further demoralized by becoming dependent on two women, one of them a stranger. He is reduced to an errand boy to and from the welfare office." Citing such conservative sources as J. D. Unwin's *Sex and Culture*, Moynihan concluded that any society that permits such a breakdown is in grave trouble.

In 1986, in his book *Family and Nation*, Moynihan continued the theme: "From the wild Irish slums of the nineteenth-century Eastern seaboard to the riot-torn suburbs of Los Angeles, there is one unmistakable lesson in American history: a community that allows a large number of young men to grow up in broken families, dominated by women, never acquiring any stable relationship to male authority, never acquiring any rational expectations about the future—that community asks for and gets chaos. Crime, violence, unrest, disorder—most particularly the furious, unrestrained lashing out at the whole social structure—that is not only to be expected, it is very near inevitable."

As a politician, however, Moynihan could not confront the anti-feminist implications of his argument, so he subsided into the usual welfare tinkering and "workfare" talk. *Visible Man* describes the harvest of chaos that this approach brings and shows its roots in the demoralization of young men through the eclipse of their civilizing role as providers for women and children through marriage. As Moynihan put it, society is continually beset by "invasions of barbarians," i.e., teenage boys. Unless they are tamed by marriage and the provider role, they tend to become enemies of civilization. The principal lesson of this book is that artificial efforts to prop up female independence are deadly to marriage and family and thus destructive of the social order.

The starting point of any social policy must be its impact on the process by which the "barbarians" are domesticated. In civilized communities, teenage boys in general find structure and purpose, are made into responsible men, through marriage and work. Granted in exchange for productive service and support of families, male authority is the solution to the problem of the underclass, not the problem. Found in the roles of husband and father, male authority is a sublimation through marriage of the natural male aggressiveness and dominance evident in all societies known to anthropology. If this primal force of masculinity does not express itself economically, as in the productive life of civilized societies, it will manifest itself in violence and rapine. For all the claims of matriarchy in the inner city, gangs of teenage boys actually rule, and the mothers cower in their locked apartments in fear of them.

The presentation of such facts of life in the Moynihan report and even more emphatically in *Visible Man* should have prompted a devoted reappraisal of the welfare state and its associated educational system on the socialization of young men. Such an analysis would address such hallowed but anthropologically dubious practices as universal coeducation; compulsive secularization; early sex education and promotion; and female preferences in job training, particularly for once masculine work.

Instead, under the pressure of an imperious feminism, all the public institutions of the society—from government to Hollywood—launched an obsessive and successful effort to increase the earnings of women and to enhance their sexual independence and aggressiveness. Despite the absence of any evidence that black women suffer discrimination, this effort focused on black women, seen as doubly afflicted and doubly suitable for affirmative action on the basis of both their sex and race. In the 1960s, as Moynihan demonstrated with concern, black women were already beginning to surpass black men in the government work force. By the 1980s, black women were earning 106 percent of the incomes of white women of similar age and credentials. Together the earnings and welfare payments received by black women came drastically to exceed the incomes of black men.

This regime prevailed in the highest levels of the economy, where black female college graduates with five years on the job outearned both white women and black men in 1991. And it prevailed in the underclass, where as the *New York Times* reported in 1994, a typical welfare package of benefits yielded a monthly disposable income of $995 compared with employment income of $775 after expenses. Of decisive effect on family formation, the value of female incomes, whether from jobs or from welfare and associated leisure time, far exceeded the short-term value of marriage, and far outpaced the earning power of marriageable young men.

Pushed by dozens of programs and regulations, even nullifying the previous black male advantage in athletic scholarships and in military or police careers, black women came heavily to outnumber black men in colleges and universities, comprising some 60 percent of black students. As a result perfectly predictable at the time—and predicted in *Visible Man* and several of my previous works—the black family as an institution collapsed. In an important study, Charles Murray showed that the families of the white poor—more diffused and thus less statistically salient and less socially visible—suffered a similar catastrophe.

In a 1995 article in *The Public Interest*, carefully scrutinizing the British experience, Murray showed that the British welfare state, without a large minority element, has pushed crime and illegitimacy rates some 40 percent above rates in the United States. But as Murray also showed, the American welfare state focused its ministrations most ardently on the inner city. That was the central campaign and inescapable test of the "war on poverty." Here the effect was most evident. In the arms of the dole, marriage was effectively de-legitimized and out-of-wedlock births legitimized, to the extent that ghetto black illegitimacy rates rose to over 80 percent.

Deprived of any needed family role, robbed of male discipline—and cuckolded by the welfare state—young black men turned to the perennial male equalizers: greater physical strength and aggression, rape and violence. Excluded from their redemptive duties as provider, men turn to their primordial role as predator. As on the streets of Albany in *Visible Man*, their economic relations gyrate between theft and barter. Today, in large American cities, fully 40 percent of young black men between the ages of seventeen and thirty-five are in prison, on probation, or on the lam, and some 40 percent of young black women say they have been forced into unwanted sexual activity. To fear young black males has become a mandate for survival on the streets of many American cities. This unspeakable social tragedy—with all its infuriating reverberations on law-abiding black citizens—is the inevitable harvest of the policies described in *Visible Man*. The tragedy will continue as long as welfare feminism is the regnant ideology of government, ravaging the lives and families of the poor by emasculating and demoralizing their men.

Of all the contentions of feminism only one matters in the inner city: what might be termed matripoly—the denial of a primary and special male role as provider in marriage. The subversion of male providers makes two-parent families nearly impossible, since marriage is based on trading the inexorable maternal superiority of women against the provider role of men. Unless men in general are chief providers, they cannot be husbands and fathers. Unless most of them are husbands and fathers, many will be muggers and rapists. It is as simple as that. Indeed, the statistical relationship between matripoly and crime is so strong that, as Barbara Whitehead observed in the *Atlantic Monthly,* it dominates all other causal factors: all the celebrated links between race and crime and income and crime disappear entirely if you control for family structure in the community.

Today, the same American political order that has entrenched feminism as the one unimpeachable canon of correctness in social policy—with every public institution ordaining affirmative action for females in the workplace—this same political regime is now bent on the agenda of Welfare Reform. The one common purpose of all welfare reform proposals, from Republicans and Democrats alike, is to endow and enforce feminism: to transform the women who comprise virtually all the welfare clientele into active providers for their out-of-wedlock children. That is the function of so-called workfare, whether it is promoted by Republicans or by Democrats, by conservatives or by socialists. By any name, because it directly attacks the male role of provider, it is profoundly inimical to marriage.

There is a great deal of excited conversation today in Washington about "ending welfare as we know it," with erstwhile political opponents rushing to agree on such proposals as returning welfare to the mercies of state governments. In this climate of consensus for reform, President Clinton has even respectfully quoted Charles Murray. Yet for all the streams of sulfurous talk and all the seemingly bold proposals, no one is really changing his mind. Today's welfare revolution embodies all the failed principles of the feckless workfare campaigns and welfare crackdowns of the past. The fact is that serious workfare programs are far worse than the existing welfare system. They represent a potentially huge expansion of the welfare state. If welfarist poli-

ticians are smart—and some of them are—they could use the cover
of tough conservative rhetoric to enact most of their socialist and
feminist dreams.

Informing nearly all current debate and legislation on welfare from both parties are ten key principles:

1. The key welfare problem is single mothers and their illegitimate children.
2. These mothers should work, or train for employment.
3. Government can create employment for them, prepare them
   for jobs, and/or care for their children.
4. Unmarried "deadbeat dads" bear equal responsibility for
   the children and should pay up.
5. The deserving poor—"truly needy"—should receive a level
   of benefits assuring a dignified existence; for them, benefits
   can rise.
6. The undeserving poor should be kicked off the rolls at a
   date certain.
7. The government can tell the difference between the deserving and undeserving poor.
8. Government can support families without requiring
   marriage.
9. Tough welfare reforms have worked in California under then
   Governor Ronald Reagan and and are working in other
   states.
10. Welfare, as we know it, can be ended.

These ten principles are all fallacious. As *Visible Man* shows,
the key problem of the welfare culture is not unemployed women
with illegitimate children. It is the women's skewed and trau-
matic links with men and boys. In a reversal of the usual pattern
in civilized societies, the women have the income and the ties to
government authority and support. The men are economically
and socially subordinate. Favored by the feminist code dominant
at all levels of government, this balance of power virtually pro-
hibits marriage, which is everywhere based on the provider role
of men counterbalancing the sexual and domestic superiority of
women.

Echoing the public opinion polls, the answer of the reformers is to put these women to work. The idea that welfare mothers should work is seductive. After all, 55 percent of all women with young children hold jobs. Why not welfare mothers? The reason why not is simple. They are on welfare in the first place because they would not or could not get jobs that remotely compete with welfare benefits. Too many of them, white or black (and in *Visible Man* they are mostly white), are slovenly, unskilled, and sexually promiscuous. To bring these women into the workforce would require heroic efforts, enriching welfare with daycare, education, and training, and then cutting off benefits and granting government subsidized jobs run by fierce disciplinarians.

The daycare and training components of this scheme expand every year. But the transformation of government make-work into real jobs depends on entrepreneurial supervisors who force their charges to work and fire them when they don't. This won't happen no matter how many times President Clinton quotes Charles Murray; it won't happen if Charles Murray is President.

True, the same public opinion polls that support welfare reform also support creation of these enriched services including daycare and job preparation. But if welfare means a greased track to employment training, free daycare, and a government job, most of the population would join.

The very idea that women with small children should work outside the home is perverse. The welfare state has already deprived these children of fathers. The workfare state proposes to take away the mothers as well.

Workfare would fail even if it worked splendidly, because it focuses on women rather than on men. The welfare state, root and branch, is relentlessly feminist, mandating role-reversal preferences for women on constructions sites, in police cruisers, in Air Force jets, and in athletic scholarships. Workfare programs necessarily concentrate their job incentives, training benefits, and subsidies on women rather than on men because, in general, it is only the mothers who are on welfare. The fathers use the apartments and take the money of a series of welfare mothers, usually without joining the dole themselves. Thus, the recipients of welfare-related work will mainly be women.

But we know from reams of studies and centuries of experience that only fathers can satisfactorily sustain families, reliably discipline teenage boys, and lift a community from poverty. The idea that current welfare mothers can do it while the government raises their children is incredibly naive. No welfare payment can end poverty as measured by an ever rising "poverty line." If it were as easy for government to create jobs and provide daycare as the workfare advocates assume, socialism would have succeeded.

If welfare women and children are not the basic problem, politicians can eagerly bring on the deadbeat dads. A declamation against these monsters has even brought Republican congressmen to their feet cheering for President Clinton. Deadbead dads overcome the key obstacle to welfare reform: its unpopularity with women voters. Here is a welfare crackdown that even Hollywood feminists can applaud. At least outside the pages of *Fortune* magazine, most people disapprove of men who leave their wives as they grow older and run off with a trophy from their business's affirmative action track (as *Fortune* recently explained, they do it for intellectual stimulation).

As a part of welfare reform, the assault on deadbeat dads does not focus on men who divorce their wives and then fail to pay child support. Chiefly fueling the new campaign is the need for revenue for the welfare state. Requiring women to identify the fathers of their "love children" and using DNA to prove paternity, the deadbeat dad crusade is a new way to raise taxes. The focus is less on failure to pay the wife than on failure to pay the government.

Amid general acclaim there now begins a new game of "can you top this" in bashing the deadbeats (they might better be termed DNA dads since many of them have no other tie to the child). The President wants to take away their driver's permits and occupational licenses. Texas Governor George W. Bush wants to lift their hunting licenses as well. Moving to create a generation of American boat people, a group of senators is seeking to seize their passports. A member of Congress wants to expand the powers of the IRS to confiscate their assets. Running for President, Lamar Alexander wants to give them "jail time," presumably so they won't vote. Another presidential hopeful suggests caning, recommending "a trip to Singapore to learn how to administer a civil beating." The Governor of Massachusetts wants to subpoena their DNA, place liens on their houses, and hound them through the bureaucracies of fifty states.

Everyone seems to agree that welfare should be denied to women who refuse to give the names of possible fathers of their children. Everyone seems to support federalizing welfare records, creating a national system of electronic directories containing the names of all new hires, indexed by Social Security numbers, to be crosschecked by computer against lists of child support delinquents (or any other miscreants). In the House, these provisions, minus the IRS empowerment, passed 426 to 5.

Yet these programs defy the facts of life and frontally attack the prerequisites of marriage. Because of the promotion of early sexual activity through television, films, sex education, and the welfare state—all attacking the constraints of chastity and female modesty—the girls of the welfare culture are widely promiscuous from the age of fourteen, whether black or white. Most black youths, in particular, can be linked as DNA dads to some ghetto child or other. Thus the threat of garnishment makes official employment a treacherous arena for inner city men. They can never know when their paychecks will be devastated by a huge lien, representing years of support payments for some unknown child (or even for a known child who has long received payments off the books). Like all welfare crackdowns focusing on desirable activity—honest work, savings, and tax payments—the DNA dad programs will destroy marriages and forcibly drive men out of the official economy into crime and other underground work.

With garnishees substituting for husbands, women lose the last economic reason to marry and domesticate the fathers of their children. Their best strategy is to seduce as many men as possible and then summon the constabulary of the welfare state to collect child support payments from the few who find jobs or win the lottery. After systematically destroying the family, the welfare state offers to replace it with government coercion and DNA tests, requiring that men support women and children without marriage.

Nothing is so fatuous and futile, however, as efforts to force men to support for life a child they "father" out of wedlock. Tying men to children is what marriage is for, and why it evolved. The canons of feminism ordain that the male and female roles in childbearing are equivalent and that men incur as deep an obligation to the resulting children as women do. But in the real world this "moral equivalence" defies the facts of life. Men need be nowhere around when children are born.

The effort to foist "love children" on the technical fathers clashes with "pro-choice" abortion laws that deny men any choice over whether the child is born. It conflicts with the expressed desires of many women to avoid marriage with the men (or "sperm donors") they may bed. It denies the female opportunism and promiscuity that sex education campaigns are avidly promoting. It ignores that many recipients see welfare as a promiscuity entitlement. It denies many of these fathers any economic power to marry the mother or to prevent her from cohabiting with others. When young women command power over income, sex, and children without marriage, why should they marry?

Any policy favoring marriage must begin by grasping the differences between the sexes on which marriage is founded. Male sexual drives are inherently aggressive and promiscuous. Unlike women, men have to prove their masculine powers by performance. Despite the constant projections of insecure men, appraising various women as "good in bed," the fact is that men alone truly face this test of performance. As the sexual proprieties of civilization break down, young women are increasingly explicit and challenging in their appraisal of male sexual adequacy. With high school sex educators now terrifying teenagers with the notion that some 10 percent of them are homosexuals—a condition said to be genetically based and virtually incurable—young men are going to be still more avid to prove their manhood.

All civilization is based on female sexual selectivity and restraint. Men learn love from women who say no and insist on marriage. There is no other way. Although welfare reformers and DNA dad crusaders claim to support the family, they would eliminate all its advantages by giving to any woman who manages to bear the child of a teenager a permanent option on his income, regardless of marriage. While there are many motives for marriage beyond the acquisition of a man's earnings or a woman's children, marriage in general depends on a set of economic incentives that favor these implicit exchanges. However you slice it, marriage suffers from any welfare reform that enhances female employability and income above men's. Thus the current feminist reforms promote the violence and poverty for which marriage is the only workable remedy.

Still, there is the cherished notion, renewed by every upward mobile governor, that workfare reforms have succeeded in the states, beginning with the deadbeat dad of all welfare reforms,

Governor Ronald Reagan's famous California crackdown. Described as "spectacularly successful" in a 1995 editorial in *Human Events*, the California program was based on the key illusion of most welfare reforms: that there are two categories of poor people, deserving and undeserving, the truly needy and the agents of waste, fraud, and abuse. Welfare reform consists in cracking down on the undeserving by changing the rules to exclude them, while even increasing funds for the "truly needy."

Reagan's programs mandated work by the able-bodied, unleashed new police powers against deadbeat dads, and removed from the rolls all recipients who showed up on the computers with excess income or property (in other words, all recipients honest enough once to have declared income, or married a man with earnings in the official economy). Changing the rules of the game in midplay and policing the system more aggressively, Reagan managed to move some four hundred thousand people off welfare and reduce the rate of growth of welfare spending from 25 percent a year to 5 percent.

Indeed, according to *Human Events*, Reagan's reforms were so successful that he could increase payments to the truly needy. He raised their benefits 43 percent and indexed them to inflation. Then he skipped town to run for national office. Following this script today is current California Governor Pete Wilson. The governors of Michigan and Wisconsin are also taking notes after imposing a largely meaningless shuffle of welfare reforms and work programs.

The result was that all during the stagflation of the 1970s, while earned income stagnated, welfare payments and clientele soared in California, perhaps the world's most attractive climate for leisure living. By 1978, California was running behind only Massachusetts in the continental United States in the amount of welfare spending and the number of recipients in proportion to population. Moreover, with 25 percent more cases than economically stagnant New York, California's caseload was growing 40 percent faster in the face of a welfare constabulary enlarged by Reagan to enforce the new rules. Today, with 9 percent of the state's population on AFDC and with one-third of the children born out of wedlock, California faces a climactic crisis of the welfare state.

Crackdowns can reduce the rolls in the short run. But the clientele soon learn the new rules and adapt their lives to them.

Soon enough, after the campaigns against fraud and abuse eliminate all honest clients with any enforceable link to a man with a
legal job, the welfare rolls swell again, full of "ideal" recipients
according to the computers—women with several illegitimate
children of unsure paternity or with unmarried fathers safely
out of the legal economy.

A new generation of reformers now promises to "end welfare as we know it"—to throw these women off the rolls after
two years or five years. They talk tough and people applaud.
Come back five years later, however, and from the streets of mid-
town Manhattan to the beaches of Santa Monica, you are sure to
find a "homeless" and disability crisis. The previous welfare ad-
dicts and their legal aid auxiliaries will merely shift their focus to
other programs. As AFDC slows its growth and becomes increasingly hedged with red tape and hassles, this trend is already
underway. Expanded by some $8 billion under President Clinton,
homeless programs have emerged as a favored source of support for which even the dimmest client can readily figure out
how to qualify.

All the reformers fail to grasp the heart of the problem. In
Wealth and Poverty (ICS Press, 1993), I explained that the key to
all welfare and insurance systems is the principle of moral hazard—the danger that any policy will promote the behaviors or
bring about the disasters that it insures against. This is the limit-
ing point in insurance schemes, and it defines the boundaries of
the welfare state, which itself in essence is an insurance system.

In simple terms, the moral hazard of fire insurance is arson.
When the payoff rises above the value of the building, which
often happens in deteriorating neighborhoods, the result all too
often is spontaneous combustion. When the payoff in leisure time
and income exceeds the value of earnings, disability insurance
encourages the promotion of minor ailments into temporary disabilities, and temporary disabilities into permanent ones. This
process has turned disability into the nation's largest welfare and
early retirement program. Countervailing all the advances in technology allowing the disabled to work, the system reaches out to
new groups, previously rare in the program, such as people under forty and the mentally disabled, each now a quarter of all
beneficiaries.

If people can routinely figure out how to become legally disabled, they can still more easily manage to become legally indi-

gent or truly needy. Regardless of the rules, this problem arises whenever and wherever the worth of welfare payments and related benefits—crucially including leisure time and medical care—rises above the value of earnings. Under these conditions, regardless of reforms and regulations, welfare will be a government machine that fosters illegitimacy and turns dads into deadbeats.

The only welfare reform that makes a difference is a private economy that grows faster than the public dole. This means abandoning the idea of lifting the "truly needy" above the poverty line. Any program that upper-middle-class social scientists deem adequate for the truly needy will outpace the earnings ability of most teenage boys. Welfare benefits must be allowed to decline at the pace of inflation, and marginal tax rates must drop for the rest of the economy. In particular, lower tax rates on capital are at least as important as lower tax rates on labor. Capital gains and other business taxes, for example, crucially affect the incentive to invest in new equipment that increases the return to labor above the value of welfare.

In the U.S. economy, work effort is the most crucial variable, exceeding even intelligence. As Herrnstein and Murray show in *The Bell Curve,* some 70 percent of Americans in the lowest quintile in IQ tests escape poverty. If a man finishes high school and works full time all the year, he has less than a 3 percent chance of ending in poverty. Chiefly motivating this work effort is the desire to support families or to create them—to gain access to women and children. *Visible Man* illustrates that neither marriage nor upward mobility can survive in a government-ruled culture where women routinely outearn men and the lower economic classes in general work less hard than those above them on the income ladder.

A welfare system that retards work effort among the poor will reliably create a violent underclass. Without work or marriage, violence or its threat is the chief way men can pursue women. Nearly all the violence in *Visible Man* erupts in the course of competing for the money and beds of the welfare queens of the inner city. Matripoly thus explains much violent crime as well as male flight from the work force and from family responsibilities. In welfare policy, the rule is *cherchez l'homme.* Make him visible and marriageable and the problem becomes solvable.

The problem of hard-core poverty today lies mainly with violent and disruptive men and boys, not with unemployed or undertrained women. Women already get most of the new jobs created in America today, particularly among the poor. *Among the poor, female domination of work is the problem, not the solution.* By creating more employment and training for women—more advantages over their potential husbands—workfare will only accelerate family decay.

In reality, the vast majority of the hard-core poor, as *Visible Man* shows, do not want to work; they want to "job" the system. As CETA (Comprehensive Employment and Training Act) demonstrated in the 1960s, make-work quickly degenerates into fake work. Far from learning the harsh disciplines necessary for productive labor, recipients learn that you can have a job without really producing value—which is the most crippling illusion both of the poor and of the academic and governmental students of poverty.

So while the prisons fill up and overflow with predatory young men, while our health systems groan under the burdens of new venereal plagues, and while our social system struggles with epidemic illegitimacy, the central cities of our nation move increasingly toward a police state for the young men and a childcare state for the women and children. Quoting Surgeons General and bogus sexologists, the media worry about the dire dangers of sexual repression while teachers wave condoms in classrooms like flags of liberation before boys and girls with hormones ablaze. Meanwhile, the only consistent defenders of real family values—chiefly conservative Catholics, evangelical Protestants, and orthodox Jews—are derided as unrealistic in their appeals for abstinence. As the darkness falls, political liberals and conservatives join together whistling workfare.

It has become evident that secular Americans, conservative and liberal alike, are unable to defend the stern regimen of family values. But it is only through families that we can summon true compassion and understanding. As *Visible Man* reveals, the superficial compassion of government turns out to be a mask for diabolical indifference to the real human beings on Clinton Avenue.

Out-of-wedlock births, now powerfully legitimized by the welfare system, must be de-legitimized again and marriage with children restored to its necessary centrality in our national life. Without a strong religious culture, a secular bureaucracy, with its rationalizing ethos, erodes the very foundations of sexual morality and thus creates the moral chaos it ostensibly combats. Even Margaret Mead recognized that in all cultures family values depend on religious supports and male providers. The effort to inculcate ethical behavior and sustain marriage without religious faith is the great fiasco of the modern age. In order to relieve the pain of the poor our society must come to recognize that their problem is not lack of jobs or lack of money but the moral anarchy originating with the establishment but most sorely victimizing them.

At this point in our history, the solutions are not obvious but they are obligatory. Government training funds, job preferences, and other interventions must be channeled chiefly toward boys and men. Sex education must focus on persuading girls to say no and to insist on marriage, and must teach boys to honor girls. The movement toward single-sex schools for troubled youngsters should be extended, rather than blocked in the courts (a rational judiciary would sack the idea that single-sex schools are acceptable for girls but not for boys). Welfare benefits should be denied to minors with children born out of wedlock; those children with children will have to be accommodated by their own mothers or the babies given up for adoption. With some two million families now seeking to adopt children, the current warehousing of children in foster care should largely give way to the stronger promotion of adoption.

Welfare funds must come in the form of child supports available to both the married and the unmarried, but with substantial premiums for marriage. Tied to the number of children, child allowances, tax exemptions, and earned-income credits can supplement the man as provider rather than displace him as all means-tested welfare programs do. Deadbeat dad crusades should give way to the contrary principle that a woman's claim on a man for support—and a man's access to children—both come exclusively through the institution of marriage.

Visible Man, however, is not a policy tome but a true story that belies most of the assumptions of the regnant policy texts. Unlike them, it focuses on the world of men and shows that change must begin in the relations between them and the blighted female beneficiaries of the welfare state.

The saddest part of this story is that it is now seventeen years old. Sam is a grandfather now whether or not he knows it. And the America that celebrates victimhood has yet to see how its official policies have made the increasingly visible men of Clinton Avenue into victimizers of the society in which they live.

Meanwhile the lessons of *Visible Man* have become increasingly relevant both to whites who imagine that they can sustain a civilization based on liberation from monogamous sex roles and to blacks and whites alike who pursue the *folie à deux* of white racism as the root of all evil. These illusions are addling the minds of millions of Americans and transforming all their good intentions into an insidious spiral of family decline, which threatens far more whites today than blacks. As the white illegitimacy rate moves toward the level reached by blacks at the time of the Moynihan Report—and decisively surpasses it in Britain—*Visible Man* offers a voice from the past that echoes with eerie timeliness in the public debate of today.

Prologue

The events which were to bring me together with Mitchell (Sam) Brewer entered their public phase in Albany, New York, at the Arbor Hill Neighborhood Unit Police Station in the early morning hours of April 3, 1975. A plate glass storefront converted into a police outpost, it glowed fluorescently into a dark strip of Northern Boulevard near Clinton Avenue in what passes in this city for a slum. The station seethes increasingly to life as the night dwindles. After twelve, among these chattering radio terminals, telephones, and video information screens, in this brightly lighted box of bustling police and sullen black young men, transpires most of the remaining drama of the nocturnal city. It is the place to be for news and action.

This book is about a visible man, a man of action and news. What American citizen today is so starkly floodlit, so thronged by reporters and sociologists, so chronicled and photographed, debated and diagnosed, as a young black male, single, fatherless, violent, now in the hands of the police, and beset with a charge of raping a blond?

Much has been said about the hidden or invisible poor: Ralph Ellison's masterpiece of the fifties, *Invisible Man*; Michael Harrington's tract of the sixties, *The Other America*; endless books and articles on the unseen agony of the impoverished and forgotten. But the invisible one today, surely, is not the jobless youth of the streets, or even the welfare mother, but the successful middle-class black with the stable family and the ascendant career. He is rapidly becoming the majority of his race in this country. But as he succeeds, he is explained away; he is young Tom Token say journalists, educators, government officials, and even the leaders of his own "community," and really, if the truth be known, white at heart.

This is the worst racism in America, black or white—the respectable kind—that will only acknowledge blackness if it is holding a gun or applying for food stamps, a racism that claims as somehow "white" the essential values of any modern economy or ordered society. No doubt of it, these successful black men with their jobs and families, their essentially conservative view of the world, are more representative—more significant by far for the future—than my visible man, my swashbuckling, knife-fighting, street-hustling Sam.

But if he is so conspicuous, one might reasonably ask, why then is he so hard to see, so paradoxically difficult to understand? For, the real meaning of the young black criminal, who struts in the spotlights of the media and the university, eludes nearly all who study him and make him so visible. Belittled by pity and charity and sociology, he becomes less a man than a confluence of social pressures. He is said to be crippled by racism, oppressed by a biased system of justice, brutalized by bigoted cops, a victim of "bad" schools and "bad" housing. He becomes a specter of forces in vivid projection, but scarcely a person himself.

Yet a house or a school, even a society, never made a man. It takes a family to do that. The truly significant "social forces" are the ones that strengthen or undermine families—retain or drive away fathers—and these social forces are not understood at all by most of the scholars and apologists of the visible young men of violence. As one moves into the world of the broken ghetto family, moreover, one finds that these young men, its most conspicuous products, are also its major affliction. There is nothing, one discovers, that will so quickly make a neighborhood, a housing project, or a schooling system "bad"—recognized as such by all who are in them—as the presence of a gang of violent and predatory youths.

These young men like to be "bad," possibly, because that way they will be seen and feared; that way they may be acknowledged, in the canons of the new racism, as truly and authentically black and "revolutionary." That way they will be seen as the victims of the hostility they engender, the "bad" conditions they largely create, the "bigoted" forces that are left to fight against them.

In any case, here they are tonight—policemen often frustrated at the slow, fastidious, yet butterfingered law, that will let free most of their prey in the morning. Here they are, the punks, the junkies, the cosseted welfare crooks, the pimps, the hookers, all the haughty street preeners who win more money and sex in a month, some of them, than any halfway honest cop in a year.

Here they all are tonight, assembled at the neighborhood unit station, handsome young white policemen muttering about "niggers" under their breath as they learn of new crimes committed by young blacks in the evening chronicle of city violence. Sam has already made his appearance and been swept away to jail. Now the police are hanging on the words—and hunting them down letter by letter on the Remington electric—of his alleged young blond victim, Marianne Simberg. And although this night I am nowhere to be found in the life of Sam Brewer, he is about to attain, through her account of the evening, a visibility that will bring him into my ken on the sociological beat of the "Sources of Crime in America."

Even beyond her experience with Sam, Marianne, through these last hours, has undergone a harsh ordeal. She has been interrogated by doctors, nurses, police matrons, and even a sleepy representative of the rape crisis center. She has had to explain her predicament to her well-spoken, suburban family. She has had to submit to probes for sperm (positive) and for venereal infections (none). She was examined for bruises (several were found); her pulse raced at 116 but her blood pressure registered a satisfactory 150/80. She had to fill out a portfolio of forms. And now, finally, back in the box on Northern Boulevard, she is at the climax of her statement, being elicited patiently by the questioning and prompting police.

She quotes Sam's bedside words: "I've cut before and I'll cut again. I just got out of Dannemora, two years for knifing somebody. I'm horny as hell." Her refined voice minces among the words as she describes the scene: "He climbed on the bed and began to take off his clothes. . . ." She pauses to glance through the glass partition toward her mother, who is sitting in the outer office; her mother, a polite and well-dressed matron from Colonie, a comfortable suburb, would not want to hear the rest. Marianne lowers her voice: "Then I got a chance to kick up at him and I got him in the chest or stomach. He told me if I did that again that he would kill me.

"He then told me to take off my clothes, and I thought that if I didn't he was going to do something to hurt me, or even worse. I took off my pants and my panties, and told him to back off a little so I could get the rest off. When he did, I got up and took off the robe and threw it over his head and tried to run out. He caught me in the living room by the throat and threw me down on the couch.

"He kept saying to me, 'Do you want to die?' and told me to do what he says and I wouldn't get hurt. He then threw me into the bedroom on the bed, and told me to take the rest of my clothes off. I did and I was now completely naked on the bed. He then took off his pants and underwear, climbed up on the bed, spread my legs apart, and [raped] me. . . .

"All this time I was yelling out for help and crying for him to let me alone. He kept pushing hard and hurting me. He kept asking me, 'Do you like it?' and I kept telling him no. After about ten minutes or more, he climaxed and got off of me, and then told me to get dressed. He then heard noises and someone coming up the stairs. He went out and must have opened the door, because I heard Elizabeth's [her friend's] voice inside. I was still in my panties and I ran out to Elizabeth yelling that he raped me.

"When I got in the dining room, I saw that the police were there also. They told me to go into the bedroom and get my clothes on. While I was in the bedroom, Inspector Voss and Police Officer Bounds came in and asked me what had happened, and I told them that the guy in the front room had just raped me. They asked me to walk to the doorway and point out the person who had raped me. I pointed out the black male in the chair and was told that his name is Mitchell Brewer and that his street name is Sam. The police investigators then took me in their car and we went to Saint Peter's Hospital."

Marianne concluded her account and signed it: Ms. Marianne Simberg, in a neat, orderly hand, and went out to join her mother for the drive back to the suburbs. The newspapers would cover Marianne's story the next day. A month later, however, I learned that there were complications in the case.

In fact, Sam's story was quite different. And it would take me far beyond the squalid exchanges of that dreary Albany night.

VISIBLE MAN

1

Sam Beau's Tubes

Sam's life has looped erratically between his workplace, the Albany South Mall—a looming marmoreal palisade of new government buildings—and his home on Clinton Avenue, a one-mile gauntlet of ornate but now dilapidated townhouses. Between the Mall, high on the city's central hill and Clinton Avenue below, stretches a ravine, containing a few short streets and worn-out wooden houses, amid drab foliage and refuse.

Sam first came to Albany fifteen years ago. He arrived in the company of his mother, and a man with a new 1963 Ford and a desire for construction work. They moved into an apartment in a house on the top of the hill where the Mall now stands. Sam's "stepfather" got a job, and the house was condemned.

Since then the Mall has become Empire State Plaza and, in its glow and growing shadow, Sam has lived much of his life; within its fluorescent rooms and corridors, he worked off and on for two years. It was at the Mall I sought to interview him first.

From the great turnpikes and thruways that approach it on every side, Interstates go, East and West, 787, North and South, and all the whorls of entry ramps, exit loops, bridges, bypasses, and beltways newly unfurling around the city, the Mall's huge bright slabs of marble shine on the horizon like an immense cemetery: luminous, smeared with gold and streaked with blood at sunset; in the daylight, a memorial of ambition and pride, declar-

1

ing that New York under Nelson A. Rockefeller was one of the few American centers of government still unembarrassed to build in the imperial style.

The heights sweep up without horizontal lines; they rise measureless to the eye and loom larger than they are, much larger. For in another sense, in comparison to buildings in other cities, the Mall is not large. In a way, the Plaza is a work of op art. Such is the squander of space, it pullulates daily with less than a quarter of the New York State bureaucracy. A symbol of grandeur and power, it defies efficiency.

I entered one of the buildings through a set of hissing double doors and headed for the elevators. After a swift upward swoosh, a walk down whispering corridors, and a turn through the Parks Department, I came at last to its subdivision, the New York State Division of Historic Preservation. Here I was to meet Sam.

I didn't know exactly what to expect. I knew he was regarded a dangerous man by the courts—a possible sex criminal with a long record of arrests for violence, an average of four or five a year: assault, disorderly conduct, rape, assault with a deadly weapon, resisting arrest, drunk and disorderly assault. He had not been convicted for most of it. Charges were dropped, forgotten, reduced. Plaintiffs failed to appear; or were persuaded, in the hungover mollies of the morning after, to let bygones scar over and reflesh in their own time—out of court, out of mind, out of jail. But it was clear that the police saw Sam—as one said—as "just another nice kid, misunderstood, who commits a major felony every six months."

At any event, he seemed to epitomize my own image of the unmarried ghetto male, whom I had described, statistically, in a book, as the source of much of the violent crime in this country. I wanted to find out what made him tick.

On the other hand, I had the testimony of people I respected at Historic Preservation that Sam was often a good worker—bright, attractive, talented—who could be trusted, without misgivings, with the most expensive equipment in the office—Nikon cameras, xeroxes, typewriters, tape recorders, slide projectors, calculators. "We never thought twice," said his boss.

Nini Brooke, my closest friend in the office, had shown me an 8"x 11" pamphlet which Sam had helped prepare. It described the reconstruction of a sculpted 18th century ceiling at Philipse Manor. This building, once a grand Georgian presence overlooking lawns and pastures sweeping down to the Hudson River across from the Palisades, is now a beleaguered old structure with a parched miniskirt of lawn in the middle of downtown Yonkers.

The most striking feature of the pamphlet was its cover—an ink drawing of the ceiling, laboriously depicting every turn of the intricate tracery: a great cartwheel design, full of detail, fanning out from a central globe, with little angels in the four corners. The cover had been drawn by Mitchell Brewer—Sam. Even if much of it had been traced from photographs, the work showed great care and control and evoked the image of the alleged rapist and thug bent over a drawing board, trying sensitively to reproduce the exact curves and contours in the wings of a cherub.

As for the criminal charges, there was wide recognition at the Division that "Mitchell had an awful home environment" (that was one reason he was taken on a great many trips). He was also believed to have been "deprived of his rights by the police." The rape charge, for example, was said to have been a setup, involving a woman hostile to Sam, orchestrated by the new Albany Rape Crisis Center, founded with the help of the Assistant District Attorney Diane Dubiac, who was prosecuting Sam.

To me, all these conflicts meant an interesting story. Nini Brooke had invited me to come and interview Sam. I arrived at the Division on the morning of July 15, 1975.

Seeing Nini waving from the corner, I wended my way through ganglia of wires toward her desk. She had her phone wedged between ear and shoulder, while she scribbled something in a notebook and motioned for me to sit down. This I did not do, there being no chair; instead I glanced around the large room at the other pretty young women, in up-to-date styles, defending our heritage.

It was a pleasing view, but I could not easily imagine, as part of it, Sam. In fact, as I later came to understand, he was a nearly essential part of it—inevitable as the state flag—even if his presence, in full Clinton Avenue plumage, a shiny purple shirt open to his chest, tight brown pants, platforms, and the bright flare of a floppy blue hat, at times had caused secretaries making deliveries from other departments to retreat suddenly as if they had forgotten something, or had mistaken the room.

Nini turned to me with a sigh that bloomed into a warm smile. She was a brisk, pretty girl with curly brown hair and responsibility for the Division's activities in all the western counties of the state. Her welcoming smile quickly dwindled. "I suppose you're here to find Sam," she said. "Well, if you do, be sure to tell us. We haven't seen him in three days."

"Where does he work?"

"He's been moved to the graphics department," she said. "But he hasn't shown up there since last Friday. The most worrying thing is that he didn't even pick up his check."

"That's all right," I said. "I might just as well talk to some people who knew him here." I was, in fact, somewhat relieved. I did not yet feel ready to confront Sam. I wanted to find out more about him; I didn't want to get off my interview on the wrong foot and stumble to its end without asking the right questions. I did not then realize that I would be talking to Sam for most of the following two years.

I spent the rest of the afternoon getting the address of Sam, his mother, his boss, and his defense attorney and talking about him with others at the Division. He had been promoted to graphics partly because he was black and "the Division needed another black," but mostly because the officials liked him and wanted to help him. They had provided legal advice, bail money, personal loans, special guidance, promotions, regular trips out of Albany; they had introduced him to key city politicians, who had caused courtroom charges to be dropped; and as time passed, they showed nearly limitless understanding for his lateness and absences; and when he returned from jail, they gave assurance of a new job. But, somehow, they all felt that they had failed him in some way—that they somehow were guilty.

I decided to go early the next morning to Clinton Avenue, number 891, the address of Sam's mother. I crossed the Hudson on Route 787 and got off at Clinton Avenue, which runs up a slight incline at right angles to the river, and roughly parallel to State Street across the gully.

The present facade of Clinton Avenue arose from a run of real estate speculation in the late 1860s and 1870s, prompted by a siege of government building on Capitol Hill and industrial development along the Hudson. Within two blocks of the foot of Clinton, amid a clutter of boarding houses, bars, Turkish baths, and hotels, there had sprawled the freight depots of the New York Central; the basin facilities of the Erie Canal; a motley of iron kilns, coal sheds, and lumberyards; an Armour Company pressed-beef plant, a spring mattress works, a brewery, a box company, and two coffin factories. All these are gone today, flattened by thruways, but the Clinton Avenue housing that they evoked remains. The builders used bricks in varied colors, embellished with ornate cornices along the roofs, elaborate lintels over the doors and windows, large stone steps in front with decorated ironwork: dignified homes for upwardly mobile families—bankers, building contractors, businessmen, and professionals—attracted to the growing Albany economy and government.

During this Victorian heyday of the Avenue, there were not one but two viaducts leading over the gully to the State Street office buildings, but when the second broke down in the 1950s, it was not replaced. There now remains little commerce between Clinton and Capitol Hill: chiefly a discouraged traffic among the courts and probation offices on Columbia and Eagle Streets. But except for the usual wear and dilapidation, and the erection of cheap and unbecoming little metal roofs over many of the doorways, Clinton Avenue is visibly much unchanged.

Surviving among the historic houses are several churches, including the venerable Dutch Reformed, the First Church in Albany—indeed, the church of the city's original Dutch settlers. Inside its heavy stone portals at the entrance to the Avenues one may sip communion from the original silver chalices shipped by sail from Holland in 1660, partake of the elegant austerity of the old Protestant liturgy, sit in the very pews once honored weekly by the Theodore Roosevelt family, make offerings for the poor of St. Maarten and West Irian, hear a sermon in the orotund style, touched with Europe, of the Oxford educated rector, the Reverend Bert McCormick, and then get in one's car behind the church, a mere crossroads away from U.S. 787 and the bridges to the suburbs.

One should not assume, however, that the Reverend is only a voice of old Albany, unresponsive to the exciting new currents sweeping through contemporary Christianity in urban America. For example, poverty and crime. For example, muggings on Clinton Avenue.

The First Church in Albany (Dutch Reformed) is moving with the times, in part—opening to the neighborhood—by conducting services in the parking lot behind, using portosound equipment attachable to one's car, for those parishioners who wish to avoid the perilous trek around to the front of the building but who like to worship in the vicinity of a traditional church. The First Church, therefore, now also advertises itself as the First Drive-In Church of Albany.

Regardless of these innovations, however, the First Church has remained essentially unchanged in purpose and appearance for the last one hundred years. The chief current supporters of the church come often from the same families that founded it—the same professional and business classes that have always sustained it. But the familiar facades on up the Avenue rest on an entirely new economic foundation and front for an entirely different social order. The industry that now chiefly upholds Clinton Avenue, pays the not particularly modest rents, the fees of the too seldom summoned carpenters and plumbers—even the fares of the taxis that ply the street in surprising numbers—is not iron, or brickmaking, beer or law or even government contracts; it is welfare. The amount of money that pours in, measured in constant dollars per house, is now many times greater than the original owners could have dreamt. But for some reason it is not enough, and the buildings decay.

But as I passed the First Drive-In Church of Albany this Tuesday morning, I was preoccupied by the matter at hand: finding 891 Clinton Avenue, knocking on the door, and asking for a Mrs. Brewer or a Mitchell Brewer, without being mistaken for a plainclothesman or a collection agent. At 885 Clinton Avenue I pulled to a stop and parked, squeaking my tires against the curb.

I was next to a stoop. A girl with wanly blond hair sat sullenly on the bottom step. She had a sleepy black baby in her lap with a pink plastic pacifier in its mouth. On the step above her were a wet, sat-on newspaper, an empty bottle of Cott orange drink, and a Schlitz can. Leaning against one side of the stoop was an old torn mattress and something in a wet brown paper bag. A young black man with closely cropped hair and heavy black rimmed glasses walked quickly by on the sidewalk in a tight, stiff-shouldered gait the opposite of funky. He wore a jet dark suit with a white handkerchief and a luminous pink tie. I could not read his signals.

The girl did not look up. I did not know how to connect to this scene. I got out of the car anyway and walked up to 891. The door was ajar but I did not enter. I decided to go up to the grocery store on the corner, Joe's Grocery, a neighborhood shop with its name on an off-kilter Coke sign overhanging the street. Inside the accent was on the major brand names—Sara Lee, Kellogg's, Pepsi, Cracker Jacks—bare essentials coated with sweet goo, the source, I suppose, of what I came to know as Clinton Avenue teeth. A large, muscular man behind the counter sold some Winstons to a black customer and asked if he could help me. I bought a copy of the *Times-Union,* Albany's morning newspaper, and walked back down the street to 891. The girl was still on the stoop farther down.

Number 891 was one of the few buildings on Clinton Avenue lacking steps. I walked directly off the sidewalk into a cramped hallway with a vague smell of decay. There were two doors to the right of a dusty wooden staircase. I knocked tentatively on the first of the doors but got no answer. I waited, then knocked again. Still no answer. So I walked to the back and knocked on the second door. It swung lamely open into a room with a mattress on the floor with a pile of dirty sheets on it and a pair of blue coveralls. Next to them were several beer cans with cigarette butts stuffed in the openings or ashes on the top. There was a rotten smell. I became aware that someone was behind me. I whirled to face a large, stooped man, red-eyed, scarred, who stared at me impassively, while I stood there, feeling foolishly frightened, listening to my heart thump.

"See anything you want?" he asked. "Want anything, take it, be my guest."

"No, I'm just . . . looking for someone," I said. He looked at me coldly. "Go ahead, take it . . . or don't you like my stuff, is that it?"

"No, I'm lookin' for Mitchell Brewer."

"I don't care who you lookin' for. You c'in be lookin' for Captain Midnight for all I care, but a man offers you somethin' you take it . . . or you prej'diced or somethin'? Is that it?" He stepped toward me. I looked at his hands. They seemed empty. His face was pocked, and scarred across the cheek and on the forehead, and the scar tissue seemed to have thickened into a ridge of grayish skin, somehow not yet fully healed. His breath was fetid. His eyes seemed rotted, red and brown.

"Get the fuck out of here, you unnerstan'?" he said. . . .

"Oh you don' unnerstan', is that it?" His body completely blocked the way. I stepped tentatively toward him but he did not move. I could not get by him without pushing him aside. I was shaking with fear and with contempt for my fear. An alcoholic old man. But he knew his one real power and reveled in it. I resolved to pull myself together, say something strongly, regain the initiative and get out of there. But he suddenly asked, cutting me off: "What you want Sam for? Sam ain't lived here for two months."

"I want Mitchell Brewer or Mrs. Brewer," I said clearly.

"Mitchell, Sam, don't make no difference to me. Lives across the street at 908. But he ain't there. Ain't *gonna* be there either." The man pushed by me into his room and slammed the door, leaving me in the hall with a new Clinton Avenue address.

"Thank you very much. Thanks," I yelled through the door. "Thanks."

There was no answer. I left.

This encounter left me somehow exhilarated. I had survived and gotten more information. So I crossed to 908, on the corner of Clinton and Concord, diagonally across the street from the grocery and directly across the street from a large, brick Baptist Church. Number 908 had a stoop and an entrance with bells for four apartments. Apparently Sam's prospects, or his mother's, had improved. But none of the bells was listed in the name of Brewer. Rather than guess, I decided to ask at the grocery.

It was my first good idea. I discovered later that the grocery store owner, Joe, could have told me anything I wanted to know, and that Sam had already told him—as well as almost everybody else he knew on the Avenue—that "some dude" was planning to write an article about him. But just then a short, pleasant-looking black man opened the door of 908 and stepped out. He had short hair, a crinkled brown work shirt with a white tee shirt underneath, and despite his apparent late middle age, an engagingly boyish spirit about him, both shy and sly. He seemed friendly and unthreatening after the man in 891.

For some reason, I asked him whether Mrs. Brewer was around. He said, "No, she's at work. What you want her for?"

"I want to interview her for an article," I said stupidly. But the man responded quickly, as if reporters came daily to 908.

"Well you can find her at work. Chase Cleaners," he said.

"What's that?" I took out my pad.

"Chase Cleaners. It's out Broadway. She's there now. 945 Broadway."

"Thank you," I said, turning to go. Then I asked, "What's your name?"

"Oh, I'm Pops," he said.

I went across the street to the grocery to call at one of the phones on the street. A group of four black teenagers walked by, followed a few yards behind by another dubiously blond, ample-bodied white girl, pushing a stroller with a black baby in it. I squinted to read the nearly washed-out lettering that jiggled on her faded pink tee shirt: "Voulez vous coucher avecmoi ce soir?" I smiled. She looked blandly back. I noticed a scar of about three inches along the side of her neck.

I realized that except for the grocer, so far that morning on the Avenue, I had seen exclusively black men and white women. I came to learn this was a frequent pattern in Clinton Avenue society.

I had no trouble getting through to Chase Cleaners, but the woman answering the phone said there was no Mrs. Brewer working there. Did I know her first name? From somewhere I remembered, probably a conversation with Nini, that Sam's mother was named Maybelle. "Maybelle," I said. Then I added, inconsiderately, "She's the mother of the guy involved in that rape case."

"Oh," the secretary answered immediately, "you must mean Mrs. Botson. I'll go get her."

"I guess so," I said. Why, after all, should her name be Brewer after all these years? Three or four minutes passed. I thought I might have lost the connection. Then a high, quiet, almost delicate woman's voice came on the line, with a subtle Southern accent. I asked her if she was Mitchell Brewer's mother. She said yes she was. "Maybelle Botson. Mrs. Maybelle Botson."

I said that a man named Pops at 908 Clinton had told me to call her.

"Yeah, that's my husband," she said.

"Mr. Botson?" I asked. "No," she said.

There was a pause. I decided to let it pass. "I am writing an article on your son," I said, "and I would like to interview you. Could I take you to lunch?"

She said she didn't have enough time at lunch, but I could speak to her after work, at about 6 o'clock at 908 Clinton. She did not seem surprised by my purpose. I was about to hang up, when I thought to ask her if she knew where Sam was.

"He's at Albany Memorial Hospital," she said, "You can see him there."

I was so excited to get this information that I forgot to ask his mother what was wrong with him.

I parked across the street from the hospital in front of a One Hour Cleaners in a shopping center. Albany Memorial was a big gray building, with a new wing still under construction. It stood about a mile up the Hudson from Clinton Avenue at a junction of three roads to the more fashionable suburbs.

The front entrance to the hospital was blocked by scaffolding, so I went around to the back and entered a long tunnel leading to the main body of the building. At the front desk I learned that Mitchell Brewer was in Room 219, in "fair" condition, after a "fair" night's sleep. I wouldn't be able to see him until visiting hours after two, and they could not tell me more until then. I went to have lunch at the Friendly Ice Cream Shop on Western Avenue.

I felt the story was getting out of control and I had not even met the main character. I had been shaken more than I would have liked to admit by my encounter with the man at 891 Clinton. He was old, alcoholic, and unarmed. Yet he had frightened and confounded me. If I cowered before his phantoms, how could I learn to deal cooly with the truly violent world into which my story was leading me? And I had to concede that if the old man had been white, I would probably have just walked quickly by him and out.

That might be a problem for me in writing about Sam: piercing the phantom walls that shield black society from whites—that cause whites to cross the street hastily to avoid an approaching gang of young blacks, and that give some blacks a sense of power, a "bad" space to breathe, a bristling self-turf on crowded sidewalks. I would learn of the cold killer stare. I have met it in young muggers surrounding me, set to hear no human claim, fixed to stand malignantly frozen, behind their icy blades, while I tried to cope, to cool it through, hanging out there in the hopeless chill of their gaze until I shrank and shivered to a beggar's slump, and none of my clothes fit right anymore, and I was ready to bow and lick the street. I gave them my money and ran. I had met the stare too, in that old man—knifeless, mush-muscled, and mud-eyed. He too knew its power; it fixed on his face, click, a grim mask, frog-ugly with drink and bitters, but still a gaze as penetrating and bone-piercing as a midwinter wind off the Hudson, when the taxi drives by because you are black.

Yet I knew my feelings were lurching far out of proportion to the facts of the day: of a warm July morning in 1975 on a pleasantly slovenly city street with a view across the green gully to the high towers of downtown; of a sad old man, hung over, embarrassed by my sharp-eyed intrusion on his life; on the refuse of his morning, on the butts, and beer cans, ashes and soiled sheets, the nonreturnable packaging of his bitter-ended pleasures. If my emotions and his could clash and seethe over such small pickings and whole racial histories rise in the gorge, if I could loom in the garb of a hundred plainclothesmen and welfare fuzz; if he could ride on the remembered menace of a thousand media muggers—statistical chimeras—if we could not meet, and misstep, on a dull morning without summoning a dark trumpery of lurching hates and fears, spectral shapes from a banal and obsolete national nightmare—if we cannot just cool it at last, racism will survive as a folie à deux, denied by all, known everywhere to be irrational, denounced, rejected, disdained, yet passing into our lives with all the impersonal, inscrutable torment and regularity of a collective migraine.

After eating my Friendly Big Beef and Coffee Fribble I returned to the hospital and went up to the second floor. There was a pretty black nurse in charge. I asked where Room 219 was and she motioned down the hall. The room held four beds. Two were occupied: in one was a middle-aged white man, conversing with a well-dressed woman visitor with a society accent; the other bed was concealed by a white curtain. I asked whether this was Mitchell Brewer's room and the man pointed to the drapes.

I hesitated, then stepped over and peeked through a slit in the curtains. I glimpsed a naked black body being sudsed down by a male attendant in a white uniform, with a manner that struck me as effeminate. The body was shiny, jet dark, almost glinting purple under the soap and water, and muscled with heavy definition; the shoulders were broad, the waist thin, the legs sinewy; a young athletic figure, fit for a physical life, a halfback's plays. The eyes were half-closed, the face clean-shaven and handsome. The attendant washed him appreciatively.

This was what struck me: a sense of strength and vitality shining from the nude flesh. I did not quite at first take in the tubes. But they were everywhere, devolving from bottles above his head and running into other bottles hanging beside his bed, tubes running into his nose and from his penis, tubes taped to his wrists, and protruding from a bandaged part of his stomach, tubes which appeared to be keeping the body alive. The attendant looked up at me, and I pulled away.

I left the room and intercepted a nurse walking by, a brown-haired girl with exorbitant horn-rimmed glasses and an air of sincere concern. I asked her what was going on with Mitchell Brewer. She said he was due for exploratory surgery at five. "They don't know just what's wrong," she added, "so they are going to go in and look."

"Is it bad?" I asked.

"We don't know," she responded. "But you should be able to talk to him in a few minutes . . . after they are through with him now."

"He can talk then?" I asked.

"Yes, for a couple of minutes; don't tire him."

The girl walked off down the corridor and I went and sat down in a chair near the front desk. I asked the young black nurse what was the matter with Sam. She said she didn't know and continued at her work. Then she asked me how I knew him.

I said I was a friend of a girl who had met him working for the state. I said I was writing an article about him. "Do you know him?" I asked. She nodded dismissively, and returned to her work.

"Maybe I could ask you some questions about him," I said.

"No, no," she replied, "I can't talk about the patients." Just then I saw the attendant emerge from Sam's room, so I got up and returned to his bed, to his now covered figure, cranked up slightly so I could look into his face.

I introduced myself: "Hi, Sam, I'm George Gilder, the guy who is writing an article on you." I thought he may have nodded. He seemed to be in grave pain and now and again heaved his stomach under the sheets.

"Nini wanted me to tell you there's a check waiting for you at the office," I said. He nodded more clearly.

I asked: "What happened to you?" He moved his mouth slowly, gagging because of the tube in his nose. I tried to reassure him. "It's all right. You don't have to talk. I'll be back."

"I was stabbed," he gasped.

It was obvious I could not interview him, but I added, irrelevantly, or perhaps as encouragement, or self-justification: "I'll come back and interview you after your operation. It will be a good story. Probably *Esquire* magazine." I felt ridiculous. But he nodded to help me out.

"I think I may write a book," I said. It was the first time the idea had occurred to me.

As I walked toward the elevators, I noticed that one was about to descend with the black nurse in it. I ran to catch the doors before they closed, just managing to press the safety device in time.

"You'll get cut in half one of these days," she said.

"Where are you going?" I asked.

"I'm going out to my car and driving home to my husband," she replied.

"I just want to know what you know about Sam," I said as we left the elevators.

"I know all too much about him. Why do you want to write about him anyway? There isn't anything to write. Just another guy who can't stay out of trouble."

"Well I don't think all his trouble is his own fault," I said.

As we walked down the tunnel toward the parking lot, I became increasingly aware what a striking girl she was—bright smile, an engaging ironic touch in her voice, an erect breasty pride in her body.

"What do you think happened to him?" she asked.

"I think he was badly treated," I said.

"You don't think he raped that girl?" She looked at me as if I were a child.

"No, I don't," I said defensively. "I know it was complicated, but I don't think it was really rape."

"You think he's a nice, sweet boy who's been misunderstood," she said, raising her eyebrows.

"I've heard he did good work for the state. A friend of mine likes him a lot," I said.

We walked up to the side of her car, a bright yellow Volkswagen Rabbit. She put the key in the lock, then stood pensively for a moment. She turned toward me and spoke with vehemence.

"He goes for white girls. . . . I don't think he likes being black," she said finally.

"He must have liked you, didn't he?" I asked. I realized that all along I had been preoccupied with her looks—her bronze breasts that swelled and subsided as she walked or spoke, amid a scent of perfume; her large brown eyes, her lustrous lashes, that flashed as she talked—and I could not imagine that these rare powers had escaped the notice of Sam, whom I understood to be an alert young man of normal susceptibilities, at the least.

"He wasn't exactly my type," she said. She conveyed a chasm of class between them and a mild accusation toward me. Would I, she seemed to ask, assume that a similarly situated white girl would go out with a student draftsman with a drinking problem and trouble with the law?

"I don't mean I thought that you might have gone out with him seriously. But did you ever see him in his natural habitat, so to speak? Why are you so hostile toward him anyway?"

She removed the key from the door and leaned back against the car, squinting slightly in the bright light, breathing percepti-bly. She answered with some irritation. "I've seen him. I've seen him drinking. He's violent, mean. He wasn't interested in any-thing but my body. He kinda looks down my dress." I averted my eyes. She noticed and let it pass. "He looks right through me. He's only interested in one thing . . . at least from a black girl. . . . Look, I got to get back," she said, turning toward her car.

"I just want to know why you think he's violent. That's a serious charge," I asked.

She turned back toward me. "I just can tell. I got to be able to tell. He kind of glazes over when he drinks. He insists on ev-erything. He won't leave you alone. There is something danger-ous about him. If she wants to last long, a girl learns to read the signals. I wouldn't have anything to do with him if I was you."

"Well, that's my concern," I said. "What do you think will happen to him?"

"He'll end up laying against some stoop on Clinton Avenue, sucking on a wine bottle in a brown paper bag. . . . That is, if he lives so long."

"You're pretty sure of yourself, aren't you?" I asked.

"I've seen a lot of his type." She hesitated. "But maybe you know better." She smiled brilliantly at me; she was hard to resist.

She got into her car. "Tell me one more thing," I said. "Who stabbed him this time?"

"Oh, didn't he tell you?" she asked. "It was Pops, that guy who lives with his mother."

"Pops?" I repeated.

She nodded and started the car. "Sam probably drove him to it."

"What is your name?" I asked. She just smiled.

"Ciao," she said, waving. She pulled out of the parking space and I watched her drive out of the lot. I returned to my car. I had a lot to learn about Sam.

2

Greenville

For three weeks Sam remained in the hospital and for three weeks his condition was reported as stable. Were there complications? Peritonitis or worse? We did not know. More than once there crept into my mind the fear that I would be robbed of my prospective hero before I had so much as talked with him. Finally, however, Nini called to say he was better, receiving visitors in fact. Bringing his mother to refresh childhood memories, we arrived at the hospital one day at the end of August.

Sam's mother is a stooped, narrow-shouldered woman with a complexion of dark coffee that shines on the cheekbones. She has a lopsided mouth, gilded front teeth, a slightly protruding lower lip and chin, and hair nearly as short as her son's discreet Afro. Her eyes are unrecessed, in the way of Oriental faces, and she has a habit of slinking her arm around the necks of men, when she speaks to them for some coaxing purpose, and the words come in a suffusion of Clinton Avenue smells. On that day at the hospital, as on many other days, a heavy hint of liquor (most likely Calvert Special Blend, I was to learn) suffused her breath. She wore loosely fitting slacks and a white turtleneck blouse, sleeveless, that revealed all across her upper left arm a milky seam of ridged flesh, scar tissue four inches long from a knife or slash of razor. Although she has held her job at Chase Cleaners for five years, she always wants money.

"Gimme some money" or "Gimme tweny dollars" is the way she puts it.

Sam wore a blue striped seersucker wrapper over white hospital pajamas and seemed happy to be healing well. Gone was all the atmosphere of menace and torment that had hovered over his dark naked body in bed three weeks before. The scars on his face seemed swallowed up by the dimples of his smile. One noticed that his hands were soft and smooth with fingernails unexpectedly long and roundly grown for a man famous up and down Clinton Avenue and in the courts and police stations of the city as a feared and fast-fisted street fighter. Even his teeth, though visibly separated in front, lacked the brown caries usual on the Avenue. As he sat, in stiff hospital garb, his face clean-shaven around his neat mustache, he seemed a pleasant and probably successful black employee of New York State; perhaps even an artist or draftsman.

"Gimme some money for cigarettes." The voice came with an imperative rasp, as if accompanied by a weapon. It was, of course, Maybelle. We had just sat down around the formica table in the patients' TV room and we had a limited time to talk. The cigarette machine was on the first floor. I hesitated. She repeated, "I ain't sayin' nothin' less you gimme money for cigarettes."

"Well," I said, "can't we do some questions first and then we'll go out and buy some cigarettes and maybe have a cup of coffee or something?"

She cocked her head to the side, jutting out her lower jaw, in the look of a young teenager making tough beyond her years, and spat out:

"Gimme some money or I ain't talkin'. Gimme money. I want it *now!*"

"Maybelle!" Sam said gruffly. "Shut up."

"I ain't talkin'," she said. Sam looked disgusted.

"Nini, could you please go get her some cigarettes?" I asked.

"The red kind," Maybelle said.

"What?" I asked.

"You stupid or sumthin?" she asked.

"Pall Mall's," Sam said.

When Nini reappeared with cigarettes, the story of Sam and Maybelle was allowed to unfold. Amid cigarette smoke and clashes of mother and son, in accents sometimes inscrutable to me, the past sprang forth and took shape and quite swayed me from any questions I might have posed on Sam's current wounds and bandages.

Let us begin with the names. The only residue of a very brief marriage in Greenville, South Carolina, to a man called "Fats" Botson, Maybelle's last name seems an odd attachment now, but it stuck. This man, like the other key men in Maybelle's life and memory, was not Sam's father.

As far as Sam knows, his own name is Mitchell Brewer. He is so designated on his military identification papers and was so incarcerated at Albany County Jail. He is so identified by his mother, who says he was born in Greenville Memorial Hospital on May 25, 1951. When he applied for a birth certificate in 1976, however, the South Carolina Department of Vital Statistics refused to grant it, saying no such birth was registered on that day. The Department requested five documents at least four years old verifying his name and birth. Lacking such documents or any idea of how to get them, Sam has yet to ascertain exactly how and when the State of South Carolina would certify his coming into the world. It is not a matter of vital concern to him.

Officialdom, however, cares. Birth certificates are the currency of welfare rights, and are being widely counterfeited or falsely obtained. The bureaucracy's defense is the red tape concertina: some fifty-eight forms are now generated by each welfare–Medicaid–food stamps–housing application—about one per dollar dispensed weekly. One result is that increasingly the state reserves its more select "poverty" or "employment" benefits, licenses and registrations, rights and entitlements, to the kind of poor person who can produce on demand five identifying documents at least four years old.

"What's your father's name?" I asked. "Your real father."

Sam hesitated. "Joe Lewis Brewer," he said.

"Nah," his mother interrupted. "That's my name. Brewer was my name. *His* name was Joe Lewis. Period."

"What?" Sam exclaimed. "I'm not named after my father?"

"No," she replied, "you are named after me. My father."

Sam broke into a smile. "No kiddin'," he said. "I learn somethin' new every day." He leaned back in his chair with a look of amazement.

In fact, Sam's situation is normal among the new generation of blacks in American cities. Fully half of the youths interviewed for this book turned out to have been named after their mothers or after the last male ancestor to make his name stick on the mother's side. Among both blacks and whites in America, the matrinomial proportion rises every year, as the social policies of government make it unprofitable for welfare recipients to link their names with men in marriage. The American poor are also matrilocal, since it is the welfare mother who finds and pays for the housing, and matrilineal, since the women tend overwhelmingly to outlive and outsave their men.

In Sam's case, the naming decision was not difficult. On the very eve of his birth, Sam's father left Greenville for a four-year stint in the Air Force. Maybelle was fifteen and her father meant much more to her than her fugitive man. Named in the hospital Mitchell Brewer, Sam still today is known as Mitchell in court and at work and in government files and jails. But everywhere else, he is Sam. It was the name attached to him first by Sam's late Uncle Taft Brewer, either, as is said by some, "because Sam was a *Sam!*, that's all," or as more cynical observers say, "because Uncle Taft forgot the little bastard's name." In any case, it stuck; he *was* a "Sam." In his childhood, the name was enlarged to an exasperated "Sam-bo!" or as I took to writing it in his swashbuckling years on the street, Sam Beau. That is all that is known about his names. There is more to be told about the places.

> *Greenville: "This story begins with the Revolutionary War and the delightful antebellum era . . . "* (Historic Greenville, Greenville Chamber of Commerce, undated).

Well, not quite. But where was Sam anyway, during those early years, the crazy little kid, "fat, short, and jumpy," as his Grandma Millie said, and forever running away, getting into trouble? Not bad trouble, but what you'd expect of a little boy without a father, without a settled home, shuttling among relatives across a sizable city.

"Sambo! Where'd he go?" everyone asked. Out the window again, probably, and onto the street, down behind the old A & P to pick pecans off the little trees; or down in old Frank Earle's pasture in the middle of the city to swim in the creek (though he can hardly paddle and there are whirlpools) or off to see his "girl-friend" Suzie Blake, eight years older and a peach of a stepmother (via one of his lost father's longer flings); or he was out, at age seven, selling watermelons on the street from the back of a truck. "One thing about Sam. He was always right on target for making money. Charged 50¢ a melon," said his Uncle Robbie Lewis, who worked at Greenville Memorial Hospital, "and you couldn't beat 'im out of it." No watermelons on credit, even for uncles. "*Sambo!* Where are you?" called Grandma Millie.

Greenville: "Leading the list of the nation's ten worst cities for Negroes in the fifties, is Greenville, South Carolina. . . ." (Black Almanac, 1955)

Well, the pecans were sweet behind the old A & P and the watermelons juicy in the watermelon truck, and Mr. Earle's creek a sprightly dip in the shadows of the Savings Bank on the downtown's edge. And Maybelle was plump and pretty enough, with rich long black hair, to trouble the pants of Joe Lewis, handsome and young, and to captivate a plasterer, Will Farmer, for trips across the land, from New Jersey to California, while Sam stayed home with sitters, and stepsitters, aunts and stepmothers, even with Mary Mae, Maybelle's crazy happy friend.

Mary Mae put Sam in dresses at six so he wouldn't jump over the windowsill and run away, off into his favorite haunts in the capital of Southern racism; so he wouldn't "mess beside the road and lay it on the cats," or swim in the pool up over his head. "It worked, too," said Mary Mae, "better'n a whuppin'. He wouldn't go nowhere in one of them dresses. I tell you, better'n a whuppin'."

Whippings, yes he got them, too: from Mary Mae, a whipping and a threat of singed hair in the open Franklin stove, he would not forget that; "whuppin's" from big Tom Botson with an ironing cord; and once, even, when he stole a bicycle and lied about it, a special "whuppin' " from Daddy Joe Lewis himself, home on leave. He got whippings with the muffins and cookies and sweet potato pies from Great Aunt Anna Lou and occasionally a whipping from Grandma Millie and from Aunt Earline, and Grandpa John, and young Aunt Holly and step-mother Betty Mae, and girlfriend Suzie Blake—he would've paid to be whipped by her—and Maybelle, and Maybelle's lookalike sister Sally Bee Jones, and more; all got a piece of Sambo's plump behind in those happy years in Greenville, the years Sally Bee remembers, "We was all together and everything was good."

When Sam was seven, it got much better still; for he moved across the city to find a home with the love of his young life, Aunt Ella King, down on Parker Street behind the Saint Paul Baptist Church. They lived in a little bungalow, with green pine clapboards, a porch in back, soft grass, and a sprawling peach tree with low branches Sam could reach and safely climb. From the porch, Sam could see across the yard to the crayon-stained glass of the square white church, hear the voices of the choir wafting "Old Rugged Cross" on the warm evening breezes, or run up to Maggie's general store and get a Doctor Pepper for a dime.

This was Sam's first real home. He could always rely on Ella, rugged, loving Aunt Ella King in the kitchen behind, cooking the collard greens and chitlin's and okra and squash and yams and pork chops that lent hard sinew to Sam's cookie-stuffed pudge, or kneeling at dusk beside the bed while Sam knelt by his cot and they recited together every evening The Lord's Prayer, and prayers for the family and even at times for Sam's errant father. These were the days that Sam remembers most sweetly now.

The signs seemed all good on Parker Street. Soon after moving in, Sam even won a lottery at the supermarket, ten minutes of shopping free. Though the store manager did steer Sam away from the meats and toward the canned goods, the little boy came away with enough of a haul to impress upon himself, for years and despite all contrary experience, that gambling was a way to strike it rich.

Shortly afterwards, Aunt Ella gave Sam a big bicycle, a Roadmaster of orange and silver, with big soft tires, and he could be seen on many a day pumping across the city to visit his Aunt Anna Lou for donuts or his Grandma, or to play with friends on Sullivan Street near his old school. Wherever he rode, however, between the ages of seven and twelve—while his still young mother chased the plastering market across the country with Will Farmer—Sam always knew where to find his home: where Aunt

Ella waited with dinner, and disbelief in all word that he could do wrong. "Sam was her heart," said Aunt Holly. "You say he'd been fightin' and she would tell you 'Sam didn't do *that!* I raised Sam better than that!' "

On Sunday they went to church, where Aunt Ella was an usher and sat three rows from the front, within the very range of spume from the lips of the Reverend Cunningham, as he rode on rising crests of rhetoric, breaking into rhythmic song, biblical chants, whipping his handkerchief from pearled brow to point it loftily toward pearly gates above, until a climax of slammed book and God-curdling bellow brought the congregation to its own feet and testimony of grace: The Holy Ghost was *in* them, they cried out, and Sam said maybe, and sometimes dreamt of his bicycle outside.

Then, one Sunday afternoon in June, when Sam returned from one of his long expeditions across the city, Ella was gone. The Reverend said she was in the hospital and wanted, at her bedside, Sam. She told him all she had was his, including the contents of her savings account. She showed him a little blue book with both their names at the top. She also called her oldest brother, Horton Brewer, a tall, strong man, proudly erect, who ran a successful farm a few miles South of the city.

Horton took Sam for awhile to his farm in the country. It was not Sam's first venture beyond Greenville; Ella had introduced him to the Boy Scouts, and in his ascent to Second Class, he had gone on several expeditions in the woods, sung folk songs around campfires, slept beneath the stars, tied sheetbends at Camporees, and learned the creed.

Horton's farm, however, was different and exciting. In the driveway growled a dog Sam remembers as a huge Great Dane that in fact was a modest German shepherd. There were cows, and pigs, and chickens in the vicinity and broad open fields and a swimmable creek wider and deeper than Frank Earle's.

After a week on the farm, they heard that Ella had died. She was sixty-three. Sam was told that her last words to her brother were: "Hate to leave Sam. But you keep care of him, hear?" Sam returned with his uncle to Greenville to the funeral. It was a major event for the church. According to the custom, Aunt Ella had long before chosen Reverend Cunningham to preach the main eulogy. Aunt Ella's body was brought back to the little green house the night before and brought into the church the next morning as the bells tolled. Carried down the aisle by six young men in dark Sunday suits, sweating in the warm summer air, and between two rows of flower girls in bleached smocks glistening, the coffin finally came to rest in front, where it was opened to view. Sam was in the first row, in full sight of the coffin. On one side of him was his mother, and on the other stood an elderly white couple from a house up the hill and across the street, for whom Ella had worked long years as a maid. There were songs and eulogies, and a long emotional sermon by Reverend Cunningham, and sobs breaking out here and there in the large congregation. But standing in front of the rouged and powdered figure of his Aunt—"she always really laid it on for church"—standing before the open coffin, Sam felt his stomach turn and his mouth warp, but he did not cry.

"I told Uncle Horton I wouldn't cry and I didn't," Sam full-grown remembered. "But I wish I had." He turned away as if to end the interview. "I should have let it out," he said bitterly. "I had to be Mister Big Shot. Always had to be the big man . . . Some man. . . ."

"I din't know then what I know now. If I had known what would happen after, I would have cried, I tell you, if I'd know'd what I was losin' when she died. . . . "

On a moonlit night in a Christmas season fourteen years after the funeral—standing in the very same place where the coffin had emerged into the sun on its way to the cemetery—Sam tried once again to explain. It was his first return to Greenville and much was changed in the textile capital of the South. The colonial bank buildings on the edge of the ravine where Sam had lived with Aunt Ella had been made into mortuaries and medical centers, while the banks themselves now towered far above, an imperial prosperity along new four-lane streets in the spirit of the Mall Sam had left behind in Albany.

But for some reason the little church and the surrounding cluster of wooden one-story houses had been spared in the city's renewal. The houses still stood in the same patterns along Parker Street, and the little store was in the same place where Sam had run for Cokes and Kool Aid or errands for Ella. But, behind the church—in the space below—his little clapboard home had vanished. There remained only a flattened patch of dirt.

In the moonlight, Sam walked over to a small flight of stone steps leading down to where the house had been. "On these steps," he said, "I cut my knee one day. I was runnin' around and I smashed my knee against the edge of the metal railing. It wasn't bad, but it was the first time I had been cut and it bled bad. I ran back to the house"—he looked behind him quickly—"and Aunt Ella was there and she acted like I was dying. She put me on the bed and washed it off and put on bandages; then she called the ambulance and went all the way to the hospital with me to get it sewed up. She stayed and waited and then brought me back."

He hesitated, looking at the small flight of steps in the moonlight. Then he continued.

"That was the first time I ever got cut. I been cut since. Worse. But nobody ever cared about it like Ella." He walked back to the top of the stairs, then turned and looked back. "I wish they din't tore down that house. That was part of me down there," he said, "maybe the best part." He looked toward me fiercely. "Let's get out of here. I don't like this place."

At the hospital that day in Albany, Sam had not remembered so much about Ella. At least he could not discuss her so freely in front of his mother. He had discussed with great enthusiasm, though, the three weeks he spent on Uncle Horton's farm before his mother returned to take him away to Charlotte, North Carolina, with Will. "What's happened to all these relatives of yours?" I asked. "Uncle Horton, your Grandmother, and all."

"I don't know," Sam said. "Gramma had the sugar. I guess a lot of them are dead, or gone from Greenville by now."

"Yes," his mother said, "most of the young ones left Greenville, I heard. They is in Philly or Newark or someplace."

Then the nurse had come by and said he had to return to bed. As he got up, I posed the question I had chiefly come to ask.

"Is it true it was Pops who stabbed you? Your mother's friend?"

"Yeah, it was Pops," he said. "He didn't mean it, though."

"What do you mean, he didn't mean it?" I asked.

"Well. I kind of fell into the knife. I was drinkin' and playin' pool and I got mad, that's all. I didn't press charges or nuthin'."

"He's right," Maybelle said, "Pops didn't mean it. He likes Sam a lot."

3

To Albany,
and Vietnam

And so Sam began his trek toward the North, straggling in what would be the footnotes of an historic migration that was even then, in 1963, eddying—phasing out into newspaper headlines where social trends gasp last and loudest. From Aunt Ella's familiar house with its soft lawn and its peach tree and the choir rehearsing "Old Rugged Cross" in the twilight in the church beyond, he rode the train to Charlotte, a bigger city, with a consolidated school and with a strange and less welcoming home, where the rain clattered on the tin roof and dripped into a pot on the kitchen table and where the garden in back glinted with shards of broken glass.

Like the hundreds of thousands before them, Sam and his mother moved with keen hopes. For Maybelle, there was a new man, by name Will Farmer, who had befriended Sam, and claimed good prospects as a plasterer. They did well enough in the new city so that when they left six months later, it was in a shiny, black 1963 Ford sedan.

Will Farmer was the man who came closest of all Maybelle's friends to becoming a father to Sam. "He was crazy about me, gave me anything I wanted—a bicycle, ice cream, rides in the new car." Sam's warm feelings survived even a "whuppin" Will gave him for playing hooky from the Charlotte school. Alien to

27

Sam were its mixed classes, distant white teachers talking of "civil rights," corridors bustling friendlessly during recess. That anyone noticed, or that Will cared about, his absences surprised him.

When Sam did go to school, he all too often returned afterwards to an empty house. There he would wait on the front steps for a greeting nudge or hug from this man he had known for a few months, and this mother he had seen only a few frenzied weeks during his first twelve years. Sometimes they would not come back until long after dark and he would lie stiffly on his lumpy mattress pretending to be asleep while Will and Maybelle gasped and thumped on the bed across the room. Sam was not unhappy when one day that summer Will heard of heroic plans for the use of plaster in Albany, New York—"Rockefeller's doin' it, man; there's *got* to be money in '*nat!*'"—and the three piled into the new Ford and headed North again.

In Albany, they crowded into a one-room basement apartment at 119 Hamilton Street. The building stood amid a wasteland, shriveling under the gaze of surveyors and contractors for the Mall. Will quickly got a job on the Lincoln Park low-income projects, out of sight below the edge of the Mall tableau, and he left Maybelle and Sam for good in the dark Hamilton Street room. Sam and his mother found themselves alone together for the first extended period of their lives.

A short chubby little boy with a cute smile and a beginning swagger, Sam slept on a cot beside his mother's often empty bed. In her twenty-seven years, Maybelle had seen most of the country already, in the company of men who always somehow got away. Will had served his time and performed his role, bringing them to Albany, and now he, too, was gone. She started going out, "plastering my *own* self," and "fingerpoppin' in the city's South End."

Sam, thirteen, new to Albany, new to the cold, would wander for hours through the snow looking for her from house to house, remembering Will, and Aunt Ella, and the Greenville warmth that he had failed to value before. Sometimes he would give up, go to the Boys' Club on Delaware Avenue, where he would watch them shoot pool or baskets, and sometimes get into a game himself or get an older boy like Sylvester Smith to give him candy or potato chips. Pool was not Sam's forte (though in the future he would attract official notice wielding billiard cues as instruments of second degree assault); and the basketball hoops he could not safely reach with a ladder. Increasingly, however, he could count on finding Maybelle across town at 25 Ten Eyck Street, off Clinton. Toward the end of the year, they moved in, joining, for better or worse, the Clinton Avenue society.

Supplanting Will in Maybelle's life was Pops Smith, a sometimes asphalt layer, who, it was rumored, had been driven from his parents' farm in Georgia by mysterious troubles with the law. Some believed he'd killed a man there. But on Clinton Avenue, Pops was a boon: diligent when he had work, a leavening and calming spirit, balancing as he could the manic-depressive swings on which his neighbors rocked through their days and nights. Sam saw less and less of Will Farmer, and when plastering work began to run out on the Mall, Will departed for Newark, New Jersey, leaving Sam a memory of friendship, an image of fatherhood, and then a feeling of loss, that led him always to think first of Newark when he thought of leaving home.

Shortly after arrival in Albany, Sam entered eighth grade at Hackett Junior High School. Here he quickly learned that to be respected he had to fight. It didn't matter much what happened in the classrooms—that was girls' territory, and lady teachers'. It didn't matter so much if he won the fights; he would take a pummeling, head first, Joe Frazier style, in order to get in a couple of stingers. What mattered was that he stand firm, be accepted by the older boys as someone to contend with, a man with a turf.

The only school activity that excited him was the boys' gym class. Sam became a favorite of the gym teachers, and later in life when he needed character references for applications to judges, it was to gym teachers and coaches that he most often appealed. No other officials, either at Hackett or later at Schuyler High School, remembered this migrant from the South, hunched down in a seat in the back of the class, reading of the exploits of Batman and Robin under the edge of his desk.

At Hackett, he played intramural football and basketball and made three friends he recalls. One, Robert Allen, a special pal, drowned at Lake George, smoking a reefer in a rowboat. Another, Ray Mastie, ran a 9.8 hundred and was set for stardom in two sports when he left school and married. He still lives in the Albany area. The third, Paul Noyes, who told Sam about the Marines, is white and still in Albany. None of them remains in his life. None was called to court.

At Schuyler, Sam's studies further slackened. In Greenville, he had learned to read and write well enough so that when later imprisoned, he could compose literate and interesting letters—a capability beyond not a few college freshmen, not to say English teachers—but Albany high school fare made no significant impression. "The girls were smart," he said, "they studied before the tests." Annually he was promoted, he cannot today recall why. He remembers he had better things to do than study.

One was a soul music band, for which he played occasional drums and sang backup. James Brown or Billy Cobham he was not, however, and when the lead singer made a mild splash, he did not bring Sam along to be spattered with money.

More important to him were sports—football, basketball, and track. As a sophomore, he brought up the rear in a number of races in the quarter and half-mile, and thrown once into a mile, he did a respectable (for a first outing) 5.32. He had good scrambling moves in the basketball court, but at 5'10" he did not score much. Later in the courtroom, his coach would remember him as an honest and attractive boy, no star."

Football Sam liked best, because it best yielded to his yen to hit—to go all out. After years of risking life and limb in games that might be termed sandlot if they were not played on asphalt streets and parking lots, Sam as a junior threw himself into football practice. He was starting as a 133-pound flanker on the Jayvees when one day in the gym he tackled a dummy with such bone-crunching ferocity that he broke his hip.

It was a painful and protracted injury. His hip had to be bolted back together, surgically, with a steel screw. He stayed in the hospital for two weeks, and then spent some months on crutches. In school, he fell hopelessly behind; for football, he was considered irreparable. With girls he felt lame. He sought solace in a dull fling—mostly behind bushes in Washington Park—with a classmate from the South End named Betty Frazier. She wasn't exactly pretty, and he did not much like her, and when they scrunched together for elbowing tussles in the park, they tore and stained each other's clothing. But she was there for him, absorbing him, claiming him, more and more cramping his hints of masculine style. One day they fought and Sam stormed angrily off, cracking a crutch on the sidewalk. A week later, through a grapevine running from her mother to his, he learned that Betty was pregnant. He felt half proud at first, but unready—unqualified—to be a father. He was not, he deeply knew, for all his fight-

ing and football, a man. A man: a person who supports a woman
and child; he knew that—everybody knows that—even if he had
never experienced such a thing. He became deeply depressed,
started seriously drinking.

Unlike virtually all human societies known to anthropolo-
gists, America does not offer virility rites. This society does not
wish to acknowledge that boys have special problems of sexual
passage, caused by their flooding hormones of sexuality and
aggression and by their lack of a specific long-term sex role—
like pregnancy and motherhood in a woman—inscribed in their
blankly bulging male bodies. Replacing the usual series of tests
and rituals is a kind of no-man's-land—a sexually neutral arena
in which you become an adult "human being" by "doing your
own thing." But for most young men like Sam, being tough and
cool, stylish and quick—a success in one's group—means becoming an unemployed punk.

Sam's adolescence was urban, passed fatherless in a family
with only fugitive men, in a school with chiefly female teachers,
in classrooms where girls excelled. But like nearly all boys he felt
a strong need to be tested as a man in the company of men. It is
one of the most pervasive human impulses. When it is frustrated,
the result is often violence. Boys form gangs, with secret codes
and rites of admission, performing feats that are prohibitively
masculine, tests of strength and speed, audacity and aggression,
done competitively with other young men—and if girls move
onto the turf, the boys raise the ante, change the rules, or move
out. From rock bands to basketball teams to street gangs, the
virility game galvanizes most male achievement, shapes most
young men's lives.

Without such opportunities, boys all too often resort to the
lowest terms of masculinity: sexual violence. Or in wild driving,
alcoholism, promiscuity, drugs, they beat their heads and bodies
against the transparent, impassible thresholds of manhood. But
for many young men, there remains one way out, partly out: the
military, or more specifically, the Marines.

Even if "the Marines build men" is no longer the specific
slogan, it remains the subliminal message. Sam had heard how
women swoon before the Marine uniform. He laughed, as many
do, and as many also do, half-believed. He saw friends go and
return sleek and tough and talking big; nightly, on television, he
saw the war. It was something real and undeniably male.

Sam dropped out of school, threw away his crutches, and went to the Marine Corps recruiters. Somehow they overlooked his birth certificate problem, his continuing limp, and the screw in his hip. He could go in a month, they said. Immediately his spirits lifted. The word passed quickly down Clinton Avenue. Sam had signed up for the Marines. The young boys looked at him with new respect. Some of his friends disparaged it. "Warn't nuthin' but the man tellin' you what to do, pushin' you around." One kid would stick out his stomach and goose step whenever Sam came by, "Hup, two, three, hup, two, three." But they were talking about him in a different way. He could tell. Then he met Linda.

A light-skinned girl with a bright smile, he had seen her around before, but always from a distance, and with other guys. She wore pretty dresses in pastel yellows and greens that matched the ribbons in her hair, and light soft sweaters that opened in the front and fell loosely, swinging with the rhythm of her walk on warm days. Her younger brother, who knew Sam, introduced him to her at a basketball game. "This is Sam; he goin' to the Marines." Sam stayed and talked, then he took her to his home. There was no one in, and they sat and drank beer at the table. "Yeah I'll be goin' to Vietnam, I guess," he said. "I sure hope to see ya . . . ," he paused, "when I git back." They spent the next two weeks together, then decided to get married before he left.

Somehow it didn't happen. Sam claims it was her mother who delayed everything until it was too late. When he was about to leave, they went out one last time, promised to write one another, and Sam promised to send rings. Then it was time for him to go; it was the middle of February 1969.

Soon he was on the plane headed South, toward Parris Island. It stopped often to pick up other young men who blustered about what they would do to any drill instructor who so much as laid a hand on them, who strutted and swore like every group before them—until humbled suddenly by meeting a few real Marines in an airport lounge. Callow, long-haired, just months before, these Parris Island veterans were returning from leave as crewcut oracles, tanned and fit just ten weeks beyond their wide-eyed, thronging clients, ten weeks that made all the difference.

The recent graduates rose to the occasion. They spoke of alligators and water moccasins in the swamps on the landward side, of sharks, visible in the ocean from the causeway, and of helicoptors hovering regularly over the marshes, searching out the handfuls of recruits who every week were willing to take their chances with the mud, the quicksands and the snakes, rather than face the snarling drill instructors. There were stories of how the D.I.s "rearrange" as the manual puts it, "the recruits' clothing." "They take you into the showers and slap you first in the face to straighten you up, then slug you in the gut to double you over— it sometimes takes twenty minutes afore they git it right." Sam shook his head. "No way I can hold off while a man beats on me." Like almost all the others, he would.

The plane landed at Beaufort, South Carolina, and all those going to Parris Island were herded into military buses for an hour ride to the island. Sam joined a commotion of recruits— "maggots" as they would, for the next week, be called—forming a motley lineup on a chilly corner of the huge black parade grounds.

Later the winter sun would rise and dispel the chill, even bring a daily sweat to Sam below, forever marching to and fro on the asphalt, laboring under a loaded seabag, doing the manual of arms with his gun, running in place, pushing, pulling, sitting up, struggling in the dirt under loose telephone poles in the log drill, battering and being battered with fake, sponge-wrapped rifles in the bayonet drill, growling from deep in the throat with every thrust, or yelling, "Kill! Kill! Kill!" while the D.I.s stood erect and aloof to the side with their pressed green trousers and spit-shined shoes and Smokey the Bear hats and mostly Southern accents— alternately bellowing and hissing commands.

In Marine training, everything good is male and collective, everything bad is female and individual. The worst thing said about anyone in training is that they "squat to piss." For the first weeks, anyone not a maggot is a "cunt." For eighteen hours a day there is not a moment of liberty; even the bathroom calls are made in groups and last a few seconds only. "First squad into the head," the D.I. yells. Then as each recruit struggles to get down his pants, or rebutton them without catching himself, "First squad out of the head," "second squad into the head" is bellowed. Sam did not crap for his first ten days in training and wrote a letter to his mother asking her to get him out of there and to a quiet bathroom. Like many recruits, he even seriously considered trying for P.O.U.—Psychiatric Observation Unit—the only way off the

Island without risking attack by the sharks and water moccasins, which the drill instructors described with relish as the only alternatives to themselves. But the fact was that you nearly had to *be* crazy in some way in order to act crazy enough to get out; and the D.I. would beat you so much when you acted up that it was easier just to last it out. Then soon enough the group went to the rifle range, where the training gets more serious and practical and the harassment less intense. There was time to write reassuring letters to his mother and fervent ones to Linda Voss, who, to his delight, had started writing him. One letter informed him she was pregnant.

Sam was not an exceptional shot; he managed a marksman's medal only. He qualified, though, and did not have to stay back, like the sad recruits who scored less than 180 on the five ranges.

What most surprised Sam was that after awhile he got almost to like Parris Island, got to respect the drill instructor, and got to feel a real warmth toward his fellow recruits. When, at last, on "graduation day," they all put on their summer dress uniforms, "tropicals," with their visored hats and Marine corps emblems, and marched for inspection by the general of the base, with a band to the side, in front of the Iwo Jima Monument, Sam felt exultant in a way he had never before experienced. He felt he could go to Vietnam and surmount anything; he was invulnerable, invincible, and there flickered in his mind the image of . . . Batman.

Later he was sent to San Diego. One day he found himself on a street lined with jewelry stores on both sides, with salesmen who left their shops to give a spiel to any Marine who slowed to let his gaze fall on one of the window displays. Sam went in and emerged with two rings, one with a diamond and one plain gold, that he mailed to Linda back in Albany. They cost $255. They were to be a Christmas present. Shortly afterwards Linda called Sam at Pendleton to tell him she had lost the baby.

Sam spent six months in San Diego, four as a marksmanship instructor, before receiving orders to go to Vietnam. He was to be part of an M.P. guard battalion at Da Nang. But before embarcation, he was given a thirty-day leave to go back to Albany.

He spent most of his time with Linda and they committed themselves to get married on his return from Vietnam. Meanwhile, however, Betty Frazier had her child, a girl whom she named Michelle. "Michelle Brewer" said Sam. But Betty would no longer acknowledge Sam as father and refused to let him see the baby. Though he did not press the point, he secretly hoped to see her when she grew older.

As the plane landed in Da Nang about ten days later Sam knew from the flashes of light across the dark sky, and the bombs actually visible in the air, that he was at war. The group trampled across the wet pavement and assembled in a receiving station, where he awaited the reading of his name. He was surprised first to hear the name of a friend from Schuyler High in Albany; they met briefly and without particular enthusiasm, just as they would meet again, three years later, on the crowded yards of the Albany County Jail.

The next day Sam's strongest impression of Da Nang was the stink—defecation in the streets, whores in the mud, poverty. The M.P. compound was fenced in by big whorls of barbed wire, of the sort called concertina, that he had learned to cross on mock landings on beaches near Camp Pendleton. Beyond the wire were twelve large sandbag bunkers, and one hundred fifty yards farther out in the underbrush were a number of listening posts. Sam, by then a lance corporal (one grade above PFC), was named leader of four marines assigned to one of the listening posts.

The commanding officer assembled the battalion and said that a few days earlier a group of Vietcong had snuck into camp past a similar listening post and cut the throats of sixteen members of the platoon called Proud Rifles. If that happened again, rumor had it, there would be court martials. Sam was impressed with the importance of his job.

His stay in Da Nang quickly assumed a pattern of sleep, rifle cleaning, gambling, beer, and duty. For the first time in his life, he actually found himself winning money at cards and was able to send some $500 home, divided between his mother and Linda. During the first several months, there was only one bad incident. One Saturday night a heavyset corporal from Georgia— well known in the platoon for bigotry and belligerence—piled up several cartons of beer in cans on a table in the common room and told everybody to come and get it. Sam came over, and the corporal sneered at him: "You don't count," he said. Sam said "Shove it, mofucker." The man said, "Let's go out and fight." That was a bad mistake. They went outside and Sam broke the man's jaw and nose with his first swings.

The next day Sam was called before his commanding officer. He expected a court martial. But the man began with merely a severe reprimand; then he fell silent. Sam waited to be dismissed. The Captain looked at him solemnly. "One more thing, Lance," he said. Sam trembled. This was it, he thought. "Your platoon leader has recommended you for NCO school, so you'll be leaving us for a couple weeks. Don't let us down. You understand that?"

"Yes sir," Sam said, straightening up.

"Dismissed," said the Captain.

Sam was one of the only two men, among the thirty eligible, who were recommended for promotion. Others in the platoon looked at him with new respect and several came to congratulate him. He felt he had finally found his calling; he would be a Marine. He considered re-enlisting, "re-upping," for two more years.

He enjoyed NCO school and thought he was doing well. But at the end he had to take a written test. It did not simply cover the materials taught at the school; it also included questions of mathematics and logic.

Sam flunked. It was another link in Sam's long chain of contacts with the schoolmarm meritocracy, standing at every access to the ladder up, insisting: They shall not pass if they cannot parse, rearrange the squares and triangles, put the words and numbers in the designated rows, stay silently in the square assigned, speak clearly when called. Later, Sam was to say that the test was the worst experience of his life—one invisible cut, following all the schoolroom cuts, from which the secret blood of a man drains out. He hadn't expected it from the Marines.

The next night Sam was back on patrol at the listening post. Depressed and preoccupied, he tried to avoid the eyes and the useless sympathy of his men. It was all he could manage just to do his job. His assignment was to lead his fire team on a reconnaissance patrol out beyond the listening post, out through the tall serrated elephant grass—nearly sharp enough to shave with—that for most of the war had served so well the Vietcong. The footing was treacherous and the murk ahead could contain any kind of abrupt terror. Suddenly, Sam found himself reeling into a pit, a trap, he assumed, that now would impale him on one of the fishhooked bamboo spikes, the punji sticks used by the Cong, or explode him into a blood-mooned void. But he merely tumbled on down in a crash—then silence.

It turned out to have been a hole, six or seven feet deep, dug to hide one of our own tanks. Sam, however, was more than embarrassed: there was a painful throbbing in his hip. At first, he was disgusted; then it occurred to him that his little hip throb might mean freedom—might get him out of the stinking city, the harrowing war. Even though the pain had ceased by the next day, he limped into sick call, and the story of the steel pin in his hip secured him passage on a Medevac plane, with a hundred other casualties, going back via Guam, to the United States.

He was sent to a hospital in Brooklyn, where he repeated the story. To his surprise, the X rays revealed that the little steel screw in his hip had broken in two. The doctor did not believe that new surgery was justified, so he recommended Sam for a medical discharge, honorable conditions. Soon enough Sam would be back in Albany. The date was July 11, 1970.

Sam's period in Vietnam, this time of combat pay and peril, turned out to be the only year of his post-academic life that he escaped unscathed and unscarred, physically unblemished; the only year he never lay, his candle guttering in blood on some beer-can-cluttered sidewalk, after a siege of hand-to-hand fighting; fist against razor or switchblade, carving knife against cleaver, brandished chair against broken bottle or billiard cue—the impromptu panoply of the saloon and the street.

In Vietnam, Sam had been safe. Only the U.S. Marine Corps saw fit to wound him, though invisibly, there. The wound, however, was deeper than he, or the Corps, could know.

I remember the first time I saw Sam in his apartment. It was a lifeless, graceless oblong, with an unmade bed in the corner, a bare dangling bulb, a couple of torn chairs, a beer can used as ashtray, and a television set. The first thing Sam did on entering was to turn on the tube. It was always the first thing, the most reliable ghetto reflex, found even among major jazz musicians during their practices, or while they are interviewed. If Marshall McLuhan has voiced any notion that does not risk finally to deplete the ozone layer, it is his idea of the vestal television, the TV hearth. It must be lit before we sit down.

Sam settled in one of the torn chairs and started to speak. But first he was caught by the image on the screen. It was a young black man, dressed in disheveled denim, shuffling down a street that could have been Clinton Avenue, probing successively into the metal garbage cans. A rich gospel voice surged above, "God save the children," the woman sang, "from hopelessness and despair. Gotta get an ed . . . joo . . . cay . . . shun . . . or the jobs won't be there . . . God save the children. . . ." The man on the screen kicked one of the garbage cans and its top clattered down the alley. Then a suave voice burbled: "In this complex technological society, you have to get an education to qualify for a good job. Don't throw away your future. Don't drop out. Stay in school and get your high school diploma. Your future is too important to waste."

Sam shifted his weight awkwardly in the chair. "My hip is starting to ache"' he said.

4

"Rise and Fly" on Clinton Avenue

On the bus up from New York City, Sam's thoughts focused on Linda Voss. She had written him six or seven letters, but none recently, and only one since their child was lost, though he had continued to send her money, and write of an early wedding after his return. The death of the child, their child, much disturbed him; it was an omen.

Linda's pregnancy had lifted his spirits and weakened his ties to his earlier child. Now Linda's miscarriage—or was it an abortion, a deliberate deletion of his sexual presence in her body?—once again pressed his anxieties toward Michelle, now one year old, and being withdrawn from his reach.

He rode the bus North apprehensively. He worried about both his daughter and his love, and he saw them, in a way, as alternatives. If he could have Linda, he would not feel deep pressure to reach Michelle. But if Linda was gone or taken, he would want to see his girl; he would demand his rights.

Perhaps in vague tribute to the mythical magic of the Marine uniform, he wore his tropicals. They made him look more crisp and prepared than he actually felt, as his bus finally pulled into sight of the scaffolded towers of the Mall and spiraled down the ramps toward the terminal below. Sam got out and waited for his seabag, a canvas cylinder which held everything he owned, or wished to retrieve, from the Marines. It weighed about one hundred pounds, sixty-five less than he did. There was no one at the station to meet him.

He threw the bag on his shoulder and went out to get a cab. He gave the driver the address of Linda Voss, at the corner of First and Ten Eyck Streets. Approaching her house, he worried what to say. Should he mention the child? No, he would be natural. By pretending that nothing had changed, perhaps he could recover the feelings of the year before.

As the taxi pulled up, Sam saw Linda sitting on the stoop. She was with another Marine, Scooter. From Scooter's lap, she greeted Sam as if he had been living next door, and had just gone out for cigarettes. She seemed changed to him. Her eyes looked dully out from a new darkness within. She had lost more than her child. She told Sam she would stay with Scooter.

"Where are my rings?" he asked.

"When you didn't come back, I pawned your rings," she answered. Sam didn't have anything to say. He felt powerless with her. She could wound him tracelessly, and he could not retaliate, without deepening the wound with a lesion to his dignity. Sam turned to Scooter, almost ready to fight. But the day, the trip, the heat, the seabag had weighed him down. He needed a drink. "What happened with you and Martha Mae?" he demanded.

Scooter laughed. "Oh, I left her weeks ago. I don't hardly see her no more." It was a memorable moment, a memorable laugh. Sam remembered the laugh because he could not feel humorous, and therefore it was he who was in part the object. Scooter could laugh; he was relaxed and in command. The laugh certified Sam's loss as it told of Martha Mae's.

(Sam was to recall the laugh again, three weeks later, when he heard that Martha Mae had stabbed Scooter four times in the chest and killed him, something the Vietcong had failed to do in a year. Martha Mae is a "very nice" woman, Sam says, "but you got to watch her when she gets mad." The case went to trial and she was acquitted on grounds of self-defense.)

At this point in his life, returning from the male circuits of Da Nang, Sam, as it happens, was determined to have a wife and children. But it wasn't working. He waved in disgust toward Linda and Scooter. "See you around, Sam," Scooter said.

"Yeah, see you," said Sam. He hurled his seabag onto his shoulder, and walked off toward his only home, his mother's apartment around the corner at 59 Ten Eyck. He found her, too, on a stoop—with Pops. She hugged Sam happily when he arrived.

"Hey, Sam, what's wrong wit' you?" she asked as they went inside. "Your hip paining you?"

"No my hip's all right." He told her about Linda.

"Oh, don't worry about her. There's lots of girls I can inaduce you to. Ain't there Pops? . . . Pearl, he should see Pearl. She's cute. . . ." Sam did not respond. "Lookit that man's uniform, you a lady killer," Maybelle continued, "ain't you, Sam? An' you worryin' about girls? She-it!"

Sam laughed and sat down at the table with his mother and Pops. They opened three cans of beer.

"Hey, Maybelle," he asked, suddenly serious, "Have you seen Betty around with Michelle?"

"Sam, you better forget about that woman. She ain't gonna be *no good* to you," she said.

"That girl's my daughter," Sam said.

"Look, Sam, you gotta git one thing straight. Ain't no girl your daughter 'less the woman say it your daughter, and there ain't no way you gonna make her say it—no way you gonna *want* to make her say it. An' that's the truth."

"She's right, Sam," Pops said.

"How you gonna support a kid any *no* how?" His mother asked. "You go get yo'self a job afore you start looking for children."

Sam moved in that afternoon, but he did not spend much time at the house. Soon after, he attracted the attention of Phil Russell, a slim, soft-spoken and articulate black man, about twelve years older, who, like Pops, was in the blacktopping business, applying asphalt to roads and parking lots. Coming out of the Marines, Sam struck Phil as a quick and intelligent kid, with a kind of smoulder within that lent him a rich warmth, or mixed with alcohol, sometimes smoked his eyes and his mind with a sullen air of menace. Although he didn't exactly seek out fights, Sam walked down Ten Eyck as if he were claiming it for his country, and within the china shop of the macho street, his very swagger was an act of aggression. Russell worried that Sam would provoke or affront one of the real killers in the neighborhood: Lewis Carlson, a vengeful loudmouth just out of Attica after eighteen years for murder ("did him no kind of good," says Sam) or Clivis Rawls, a young tough who would readily knife you in the back or throw lye in your face, if you got in his way. Sam usually restricted himself to blunter instruments or more impromptu ones—a chair, a stick, or, on one occasion, a dog's choke chain, "very effective" when whipped up into someone's face. Phil, himself, avoided fights. A slight, careful man, he deterred attack by keeping a large arsenal of firearms, famous on the street. It worked.

Sam, however, went on his brazen way, rarely carrying a weapon of any sort but telling anyone who would listen, "If you cross me and you can't fight, you're in a world of trouble." One day, Rawls laughed at this, and Sam picked him up above his head and hurled him back down onto the pavement.

"You shouldn't have done that," said Phil.

"Now he got to worry about me!" Sam replied.

Sam's mother was right about Betty. She had another man and she didn't want Sam around, and Sam didn't really want to be around her. Sam continued to live with his mother and subsist on his discharge pay—a few hundred dollars that were quickly draining away in his attempt to gamble them into thousands.

Toward the end of August, the three moved to 97½ Concord Avenue, just half a block down from Clinton, four or five addresses beyond Joe's Grocery and toward the river. It had once been a middle-class residential street, and from that early prominence there remained three shriveled trees, and across the street, on the corner of Clinton, a large brick Gothic church. Now this stretch of Concord was a daytime social area for that section of upper Clinton Avenue and Arbor Hill.

One hot day of late summer 1970, the street salon was in full swing. In the windows of 97 ½, Sam had set up two speakers and Wilson Pickett harangued about the Midnight Hour into the afternoon sunlight. Below, around the stoop, six or seven women were talking, apparently oblivious to the music but feeling its rhythm, not fighting it. Every now and then, one would peel off from the conversation and do some bumps and grinds on the sidewalk, then catch a word or phrase of interest and plunge back in with an intense spiel.

A little down the sidewalk, in front of 95, where there was more space, the men were gathered around a card table. Everyone was drinking beer or Canadian Club whiskey, or both, out of glasses and plastic cups, and by three o'clock, there was an active surf of beery conversation, occasionally leaping up into a frothy fury of argument, then ebbing as the subject changed or new cards were dealt. Though the sounds were familiar in the neighborhood—the usual blusters and loud noises of street life—any whites coming from the other end of the street would cross and pass by on the other side. Every now and then the police would drive by and tell the group to keep it down or to lower the volume on the record player. The police did not seem much concerned; it was just something to say, registering their presence. When they left, Sam turned the music back up.

Around the card table were Sam and Phil Russell, playing against two friends. The game was bid whist, a form of bridge that in its Clinton Avenue version brings the players frequently to their feet to declaim about their hands and bid the destruction of their opponents. The rule was "rise and fly," which meant that the losers had to give way, each game, to two others. Watching the show was a lanky black man about 6' 3", wearing a bulbous, white-flecked Afro—with a feathered black-and-white checked Robin Hood hat propped foolishly in the middle of it—who drank and blew hard about the game in a high whine: "You guys can't do nuthin' with them cards. You guys full of shit, you know it. Anybody play like that upstate, he be *gone* by now!" Next to him hulked a dark-clad, somber-faced man who was not enjoying the commentary and who punctured it regularly with: "You full of shit, Lewis," or "You crazy Lewis."

Also watching, but less attentively, was Lee Cobbs, a former Green Beret and Judo black belt, who had befriended Sam after his return from Vietnam.

The man with the Afro, "High and mouthy" said Sam, was Lewis Carlson. The man next to him, who seemed to be flexing his muscles all over, from his round cheeks to his massive arms, as he seethed at Lewis's act, was Jasper A. James. The tensions were rising, but Lewis just went on, oblivious perhaps, or provoking. He seemed driven to cause trouble, itching to get the others to focus on him.

On the stoop, meanwhile, the women were arguing about the South. "White folks is worse, down there, I tell you," Maybelle was saying. "They don't give you nuthin', no welfare, nuttin'. In Greenville, fifty men, they lynched a dude, hung him right up on a rope, an' the judge like to give 'em the key to the city. The Sout', shit."

"White folks are the same anywhere," said Bernice, a pretty light-faced woman in a yellow halter. "But Atlanta is nicer than that. It's warm an' you can work."

"This ain't warm enough for you?" said Maybelle. "Shit. The winter here keeps you 'wake. You just sleepin' down South. That's why you like it."

At that point, Lewis Carlson suddenly turned away from the game and looked up the street toward Clinton. Approaching was his woman, Denise Rich, on the arm of John Raveling, a recent arrival in Albany, with a bleached and creased denim suit that looked out of place on Clinton Avenue. Denise was a close friend of Maybelle's and, according to Phil Russell, was a "healthy and spunky" woman. Her spunk in the past had brought her large scars on her face and neck. She came down Concord that day looking juicy and feeling "evil." Her John felt ready for anything that could be intimidated by the shiny new pearl-handled revolver that he kept in the pocket of his Levi jacket and fondled, for reassurance, with one hand as he fondled Denise with the other. All the while Wilson Pickett was singing, wheedling, insisting that "everybody *dance*" in the "Land of a Thousand Dances."

Lewis's voice, which was already pitched at a penetrating whine, clashing with Pickett's jaunty rhythm, began squeaking like chalk across the minds of Sam and Jasper. Both had noticed Lewis, for some months, as a new presence on Clinton, to be accepted as Denise's man. But both now were concluding that he was insufferable. Phil Russell, aware that a fight was likely, was looking nervously toward Lee Cobbs. Meanwhile, Lewis chimed stridently on.

"Denise, you ain't worth shit and your John ain't worth the smell of yo shit. Hell, he ain't worth the piss of a dog, you ugly bitch."

John was not up to this. But he told Lewis to shut up. At this point Jasper suddenly broke his clenched silence with a roar.

"Get the hell out from in front of my house, boat of you."

Lewis replied, "Stay out of this," and pushed Jasper tentatively aside.

All afternoon Jasper had been waiting for this shove; all afternoon Lewis's loud insistent voice had been scraping on his eardrums; all afternoon Jasper's muscles had been grinding almost madly together, rubbed by Lewis's high gravelly tones; all afternoon his stomach had been churning with the acids of violence, the rage to kill that rises from the sense of impotence and humiliation caused by another man invading your space, consuming your very air, the very breathing room of your balance and sanity, tweeking the very soft and throbbing tissue of your mind as a man, pinching, kneading' probing until you feel a near sexual wound, inflicted by a mere pelting of words not even directed exactly toward you.

Jasper swung once, hit squarely, and saw his prey buckle in the knees and reel slowly to the ground as the blood poured crimson from his nose and across his dark face and his Robin Hood hat followed its feather into the gutter of Concord Avenue. But it was all much too quick. Jasper had hardly begun to discharge the painfully compressed gasses, the whiskey-drenched reaches of his hatred; the others did not have time to react. Sam, his back to the action, did not even see it.

Jasper kicked Lewis in the stomach as he fell, hurtling him harder onto the asphalt and propelling Lewis's beetling Afro off his head and lamely onto the street. So that's why he was called Wiggy. It looked for a moment to Sam, in the bloody blur of head and hair, as if Lewis's skull had been split in half and part of it had rolled away onto the pavement. Near unconcious on his back, however, Lewis could be seen strangely recomposed as a bald, elderly Negro with a gray Roy Wilkins fringe around his shiny pate. Screaming hysterically, Denise ran forward to pick up the wig which she had bought her man. Then she leapt at John and reached into his pocket for his pistol. She got it half out but John held onto the handle. Sam yelled to watch out for the gun. But Jasper was oblivious, stomping now on Lewis's soft unprotected face. The day, it became suddenly clear, was veering now toward raw horror.

Galvanized, Phil and Lee Cobbs ran to stop Jasper, Sam tried to pull Lewis away from his blows, and John struggled to pull the gun from Denise's grasp. "Shoot him," she screamed, "Kill that crazy nigger. Shoot him." It was a moment when death hung at every turn: one errant kick to Lewis's temple, one errant finger on the trigger of the gun, or one sudden knife pulled out and plunged by one of the fighters, and the police would converge from everywhere and several of the men would be carted away, until one way or another in the shambled carnage, the law could entrench its own categories, cut out its own sharp claims of witness and guilt, among these mingled veins of Clinton Avenue life.

But these things did not happen that day. Seconds later, the gun had been wrenched from Denise and pocketed, Jasper had been subdued, and Sam was laboring with Lewis's battered body toward Maybelle's apartment. There he laid Lewis gently on a couch, and Maybelle ministered to his face with bandages and liniments, and Sam called an ambulance. Lewis's first words as he regained consciousness, spitting blood through broken teeth, were a safely impossible plea to return him to the street where he could "get that mother." Then he gagged on the blood and fell back into a stupor. All this, from the time of Jasper's first blow, until Maybelle's first poultice, took less than two minutes. No police came by, no charges were pressed, no crime statistics compiled. Medicaid would cover all.

Before Lewis left for the hospital, Denise tried to reattach his wig but she was only partly successful. He arrived at the emergency room with the wig hooked on one ear, making his head look even more hideously lumpy than Jasper had left it in his fury.

The fifteen minutes of attention from Maybelle gave Lewis his introduction to the house at 97½ Concord Avenue. When he returned from the hospital, he moved in to the top floor apartment. Rewigged, his battered face was seen, and restored, his rasping voice heard daily in the little apartment that Sam shared with Pops and Maybelle. But on all of Clinton Avenue, let alone in that one cramped and creaking building, there turned out to be not nearly enough space for both Sam and the man whose life he may have saved from Jasper that day on the street. Saving Lewis's life, as it turned out, was very nearly to cost Sam his own.

5

The State

Several months earlier, Mark Lawton, the director of the New York State Historic Trust, was driving toward Albany at 4:30 A.M. in the snow. He had been at a long meeting in Little Falls, New York, with citizens fighting to save the Greek revival shell of a defunct bank, and on the trip home had had to pull to the side for a few winks. He was awakened by a sharp rap on the window from a state trooper and went on in the pre-dawn December darkness. Then he saw a hitchhiker standing beside the road in a blur of snow.

Like many ex-Marines who remember the long thumb-borne dashes North from Camp Lejeune for fevered liberties in Washington or Philly, Lawton had made it a practice to give rides. He pulled to a stop by the Central Avenue Motel, and a scarred black face framed itself in the car window. "Get in," Lawton said, opening the door. Afterwards Lawton was to explain, "Anybody on the street at 5 A.M. is too fagged out to do anything bad." But the fact was that he was a man who picked up hitchhikers and that was that. And since giving rides to strangers is, among other things, a continual trial of one's prejudices, it is no ordinary bureaucrat—trapped in the paper towers, forms and files of official reality, fearful of the shadowy, three dimensional world beyond—who would automatically pull to a stop at 5 A.M. in the snow to pick up a black man whose face he could hardly see.

47

"Where are you going?" he asked his rider. Lawton noticed he was wearing a dark leather coat, and his shoulders were fringed with snowflakes. He hunched forward in the seat looking straight ahead and rubbing his hands together. He had taken off his hat, leaving a strip of flattened hair around his head where the hat-band had been.

"Downtown. To Clinton Avenue," he said.

"You're in luck," Lawton answered. "I'm going all the way to the end of Central. But I can cut across. . . . I'm Mark Lawton, what's yours?" he asked.

"Mitchell Brewer," he said. Lawton noticed Sam glance at some Christmas packages he had in the back seat. "Presents for the kids," he said.

"I got a kid," Sam said. "It's a girl, though. I don't know what to give her."

They drove a few moments in silence, then Lawton changed the subject from presents. "Where you coming from?"

"I've been out partying," he said, "with some buddies in Schenectady. I had somethin' good goin' too." he smiled. "But I got to get back home, get ready to ship out."

"You in the service?" Lawton asked with interest.

"Yeah," Sam said. "The Marines. They're about to ship me out to Vietnam. . . . But if this snow keeps up I don't know if I'm gonna make it right away."

"I guess the Cong can wait," Lawton said.

"I guess so," Sam said without enthusiasm. "I hope my C.O. can."

"Sure, you're all right in this weather," Lawton said.

"I'm broke too," Sam said. "I don't even have a ticket."

"What you going to do?"

"Oh, I can borrow money from the recruiter," he said. "They take it out of your pay later."

They drove silently for awhile.

"I was in the Marines," Lawton finally said.

"What you make?" Sam asked.

Mark hesitated.

"What rank?"

"Oh, Sergeant," Lawton said.

"I'm only a Lance," Sam said.

Before he dropped Sam off at his house, Lawton suggested that he look him up at the state offices when he got out of the

Marines. Sam forgot the suggestion. But less than one year later he was out of the service, and after several violent and shiftless months on Clinton Avenue, he decided to get a job. It was October 1970. The state Employment Office sent him to Parks. Soon he found himself, with several other young men, working in the Parks Department printing room, under an affable Irishman with a big red nose, named John Reilly. Mark Lawton, unknown to Sam, was three stories above him.

Although many of his workers were black, Reilly had not been able to keep up with the ever-changing manners of racial relations in America, but he had surely tried. Though to this day he refers to his charges as "boys," he earnestly fumbles with words like "unprivileged" and "minorities." When I asked him—in pursuit of my story about Sam—how his men got hired, he turned to them and said, "How is it you boys was hired anyway? What is that program—unprivileged people, minorities, actions, I don't know." "The Urban League," suggested one tall, well-kempt man in his mid-twenties. "No. It had unprivileged in the title. I know that much."

Reilly turned to me, "My boys, I treat 'em good. . . . They treat me good. . . . Ain't that right?" He addressed the group, then added, "Except Billy over there. He ain't worth nothin'." He walked over and put his arm around Billy Grant's back; Billy perceptibly cringed. "Nah, I'm just kiddin'. Billy's a good boy, a real good boy, ain't ya Billy?" Billy Grant had been introduced to the printing room by Sam in 1971 and had stayed ever since, taking Reilly's "boy" talk in good spirits. He smiled with only some slight unease.

It was this Reilly who in 1970 took to Sam right away. They regularly lunched together, or went to the Lark Tavern for a few beers after work.

"I was like a father to him," Reilly says now, and when Sam is asked about his former boss, those words still sometimes come to his mind, "He was like a father to me."

On Fridays after work, the two would go off together in Reilly's car for a few hours hopping bars through the Catskills. They would stop in a roadside tavern, have a couple of beers, and then move on. Reilly would complain about two white workers in the printing room who he thought were out for his job or about the women in his life, his wife who had divorced him a few years before, a young secretary who could not resist him, all the other women in high heels and dense perfume who thronged his fantasies as they did the Xerox machine, which, being in the printing room, allowed him to imagine himself the Casanova of the Parks Department.

On their trips together, Sam would listen to Reilly and nod admiringly, or commiserate, or tell tales of his toughness or his exploits in the Marines. The relationship was real to both. Reilly still talks about it, a connection to a lost youth and manliness in the swashbuckling world of the street; and Sam in trouble looked to Reilly first for help, as if he, the printing room czar and Xerox Casanova, could impress judges or raise money for bail. An odd couple, these two, a divorced man, garrulous and lonely, uncomfortably fast growing old, and a young, volatile black man, unmarried and with few stable friends in the world: each finding something in the other, a common human ground of unacknowledged loneliness and need, disguised in beery braggadocio in a series of bars where no one knew who they were, where they always made their getaway before they could be exposed. The life of single men: rotating spurious big wheels, without traction, getting nowhere except older and alcoholic.

Sam was also having women problems that they could discuss. Linda Voss was gone and Michelle was growing older in the South End with Betty Frazier. Sam did not like Betty but he wanted his child, and Maybelle told him she would care for it. Betty was not interested in this proposal. Instead she demanded less of Sam's bright ideas and more of his money. It was an impasse. Sam thought he might break it, with the help of his powerful friends at work, but he did not mention this hope to Betty.

In fact, Sam had made a connection with a genuinely important official. One day while delivering documents, he noticed a familiar face: Mark Lawton's. Sam introduced himself and Lawton immediately expressed delight at seeing Sam in the Parks Department. An orphan who had dropped out of high school to enter the Marines and had worked his way to the top levels of the state bureaucracy at a young age, Lawton always responded affectionately to Sam. He asked where Sam worked and resolved to bring him, as soon as possible, into a better job at the Historic Trust.

In July, Sam was moved upstairs and assigned to the staff of Jack Waite, chief of the Architectural Bureau, which was in charge of the restoration and maintenance of decaying historic buildings in the state. Sam had mentioned to Mark Lawton some drawing classes taken in high school, so he was made an assistant draftsman.

Jack Waite early discerned that Sam's presence on his staff was a blessing not unmixed with lateness and unexplained absences, or still more disconcerting, absences flatly justified on the telephone by pleading a hangover—or sometimes, a jailing. This was a period when the police were clearing the streets every night of people suffering, or enjoying, the legal or physical state— since rescinded by the Supreme Court as "excessively vague"— termed "public intoxication." These dragnets along Clinton Avenue, now and then (some fifteen times in four years) came up with a somewhat bedraggled Sam, whose fits of "excessive vagueness" sometimes leading to his reappearance days later in stitches and heavy bandages, became well known—and a staple of office gossip for years after—at the Division of Historic Preservation.

Mark Lawton's interest, however, meant that Sam was to be indulged, and it soon became clear that he was not without drafting talent. In order to bring it out, Jack Waite arrived at the strategy of overnight travel. Waite's valid hypothesis was that, in a Holiday Inn in Syracuse or Yonkers, Sam could escape his Clinton Avenue troubles.

It was altogether a motley crew in that office: Waite, in charge, a tall, dark-haired man with a boyish smile and a little cigar between his teeth, now privately employed in one of the leading preservationist firms in the state; Clayton Pauley, a paint specialist, about 5' tall and nearly as wide, all muscle, with a chemistry degree from R.P.I.; Steve Ballard, twenty-seven looking seventeen, an experienced draftsman whose truest interests and passions were left behind weekly at the Lebanon Valley Stockcar Speedway; Doris Manley, a shrewd and skeptical draftsman in her forties who liked to arrive at the office on her Harley Davidson, for which she was never quite licensed beyond her learner's permit; Fred Cawley, an architectural graduate of Rhode Island School of Design on his way to a master's in Historic Preservation at Columbia, whose occasional tours with the state were fraught with jokes about the frayed elbows and threadbare seats of his wardrobe, all Brooks Brothers; and John Shank, a thirty-five-year-old architect with a ginger beard and professional appearance, now working for the distinguished firm of Ben Thompson Associates in Boston. It was Shank who chiefly assumed the task of teaching architectural drafting to Sam.

In such a group, Sam tended to stand out and, in fact, during the months of his service, his progress preoccupied the entire office. As he became more interested, he would occasionally stay late, riveted to his drafting board; his devotion to the Philipse Manor project is still remembered in the office as fanatical. The only man skeptical of Sam's new activity, regarding it as a dangerous snare, was John Reilly. "He falls apart when he's out of my hands," was the word from the printing room, "you wait and see."

One November day on Clinton Avenue, Sam, if he could not be said to have fallen apart, dismantled the jaw of a white man named Bruce DiGrigoli, who threatened him with dire punishment if he continued to talk with Angie Costello. Also involved in the fracas was one Rocco, a TV repairman and friend of Sam's. DiGrigoli called the police and both Rocco and Sam were jailed. Sam stayed penned for seventeen days, but luckily Rocco was released on bail and persuaded Bruce to drop charges. Unless the police enter a complaint themselves, this normally ends the matter. Sam's time in jail, however, created a more than usually noticeable break in his work schedule. Called into the case by Lew Rubinstein, the National Register Supervisor, was old "Uncle Sam" Aronowitz, Albany's most venerable and prestigious liberal lawyer, closely tied both with Mayor Corning and the civil rights community. Aronowitz was induced to make discreet calls which were believed to have expedited Sam's release.

Sam returned to the state Personnel Office to reclaim his job. But a secretary loftily told him to leave. Sam left in a rage and never came back to work, despite Mark Lawton's repeated assurance of welcome, dispatched by messenger to Clinton Avenue, together with word that Sam's career with the State might eventually earn him around $20,000 a year.

Back on the street and unemployed, Sam preoccupied himself with drinking and feuding and playing cards and trying to gain custody of his little girl. A particular nuisance was Lewis "Wiggy" Carlson, who was still living with Denise in the apartment above Maybelle's on Concord Avenue, where he had stayed since the stomping by Jasper. When Sam had a job and a woman, he could barely endure Lewis's presence. But during this period, he found it unbearable. Carlson jibed at Sam in a whiny voice and harassed Maybelle, who complained to Sam in a whiny voice.

It was just a matter of time, Sam thought, before he would have to fight Lewis.

He also was increasingly determined to get custody of Michelle. Sam had not yet fully comprehended the Catch-22 of American manhood. Although a man might need women and children most when he is moneyless and dejected, it is precisely such a man, at those times, who is barred from all durable access to family life. Sam was seeking from women and children the very sense of manhood and affirmation that he would have to have already if he was to get them. The chief way men like Sam can get women is on short term, without children and future, and paid for often in sex and blood.

Maybelle, too, apparently miscalculated. She was eager to have Michelle, possibly because she would qualify her again as a welfare mother, but she overestimated Sam's ability to get the child. Sam had mentioned powerful state connections; but it was doubtful that Lawton or Aronowitz, or even Governor Rockefeller for that matter, could have persuaded Judge Tepedino to take a little girl away from her mother and award custody to an unemployed man with a record of some six arrests in the past three years for violent offenses. However Sam may have struck his state associates, he perhaps did not spring first to mind as a potential nurturer of a little girl.

Sam's disdain for the state offices, meanwhile, was not so strong as to keep him away from the Parks Department's annual Christmas bash. It began for him downstairs in the printing room at what Mark Lawton called the "rump session of the party." After much beer, there erupted that evening one of those fights which afterwards looms ever larger in the symbolic memories of all those who are touched by it.

To Reilly it was "The Time I Saved Mark Lawton's Life from Mitchell Brewer Beserk in the Printing Room." To Mark Lawton, it was "The Day I Saved John Reilly from Brewer's Lethal Fists and Thus Saved Sam from a New Jail Sentence" ("since we would have had to do *something* if he killed Reilly"). To Dave Evans, mild-mannered, prematurely graying, it was "Hardly Any Fight at All," just some mild shoving, but it reminded him of "The Day I Knocked Brewer over Some Crates in the Printing Room to Show Him I Couldn't Be Pushed Around": "I'm an ex-Marine too."

To Sam, it was a completely uneventful party, though he does remember one time flipping Evans over some boxes when he questioned Sam's skill in judo. In the continuing oral history of the Parks Department, however, it was a terrific fracas, involving cops with sirens on Central Avenue converging on the scene, an auto stolen by Sam and crashed into a police car, "Uncle Sam" Aronowitz brought in for legal advice, blood on the printing room floor and by the Xerox machine, terror among the secretaries. . . .

In any case, there were no arrests and the evening mellowed out later at the Wigand Post of the American Legion, where Sam and Mark Lawton grew sentimental about their respective little children, "You got to come and see Michelle," Sam said. "She is so cute you can't believe it."

"Yeah, I know. Billy's the same age, cute as hell too," Mark replied.

"I always used to think I wanted boys," Sam said, "and I still do. But Michelle kind of changed my mind."

"They're all good when they're good," Lawton commented.

"You gotta come see Michelle." Sam had drunk a great deal that evening and was sliding into that mood of stuck persistence that is so charming a trait in his mother. But Mark Lawton had not quite noticed.

"Yes, I'd really like to see her sometime."

"Tonight," said Sam. "You gotta see her tonight."

"No, not now, Sam, it must be almost eleven," he said.

"That's alright. Betty will be up. She'd like to meet you," Sam said. "Let's go."

Lawton couldn't think of any reason to say no. So they stumbled out to Lawton's car and with Sam giving directions, Mark found himself driving deep into the South End of Albany. They parked down a dingy street which Mark had never seen before, at least after six, then proceeded to a stoop cluttered with newspapers and empty beer cans, and into a dark hallway that smelled vaguely of urine. Loud voices broke out above them from upstairs apartments. They climbed the stairs. "You sure we should do this?" Mark asked.

"She's my daughter, ain't she?" Sam asked. There was something about Sam's tone that disturbed Mark. Reaching the upstairs hallway, they maneuvered around a half-burned mattress and a broken TV set. Mark was ready by this point to turn and go back. He was feeling very small and white to be in a black tenement at 11 P.M. In his near drunken state, Sam was not reassuring. "But I didn't realize anything was really wrong," Lawton said later, "until Sam knocked down the door."

They found themselves in a sizable apartment of the sort available to a welfare mother in Albany with only one child. It was better than Maybelle's. Seated around it on worn furniture watching TV were Betty Frazier and three large men.

"What the shit you doin', bustin' in like that?" Betty asked startled. "Git your ass the Hell out!"

"This is Mark Lawton," Sam said' "He's an officer from the State. We came to get Michelle."

"The Hell you say," Betty replied. The three black men had stood up. They looked angry. Mark was withdrawing step by step, "hunching up my collar to look like a cop." He thought a fight was on the way. "Keep your back to the wall," he told Sam.

"I want to see Michelle," Sam said. "She's my daughter an' I kin' see 'er if I want."

"You can't see her less you support her," Betty yelled. "Get the fuck out now. I don't care if he's Governor Rockefeller," she sneered in Mark's direction. He shrugged as if disassociating himself from Sam's claims.

At that point, one of the men snapped open a knife. Sam looked around the room. He saw a bottle on his right. Mark said urgently, "Let's get out of here, Sam. We can follow this up later."

"I'm countin' to five," said the man with the knife. "Put away the knife," Sam said, "this ain't got nothin' to do wit' you. It's between me 'n Betty here."

Just then, a little girl appeared from the doorway behind her mother, waddled out into the middle of the room, and cast her lustrous brown eyes around the tense faces. Sam had not exaggerated her prettiness. Her features were all perfectly shaped and her complexion was smooth and brown.

"Michelle, come here!" Sam ordered gruffly.

The little girl looked at him in fright, her mouth soured into a pout, and she burst into tears. She ran over into her mother's arms. "Fuck it," Sam said. "We'll come back tomorrow," he said to Mark. They left.

and sell it in nickel bags ($5 apiece), outside Dinty's bar. Sam used to like to sniff it, until it made him itch and his nose burn. Some woman had told him it was a signal. When your nose burns, stop. Other guys on Clinton Avenue would o.d. that year and die. But Sam was smarter and tougher, so he thought; he could take it or leave it or sell it, as he wished.

After a month or so, however, the police began cracking down on his new white hope. His pusher friend was nearly arrested. There was talk of a Rockefeller program of life sentences for drug offenders. Sam's nose was burning more than usual. It was a combination of things. But Sam suddenly decided that heroin was unhealthy and never picked it up again. There was even, therefore, a fair possibility that Sam could survive the year out of jail.

Nonetheless, one cold winter evening in January, he found himself sprinting shirtless down First Street with a meat cleaver in his hand, chasing a man with a feather curl wig. If he could catch Lewis, Sam said to himself, he would cut his head off with the meat cleaver. It was certainly sharp enough, and under normal circumstances, catching Lewis would not have been a problem because Sam was faster and stronger. But that night, Sam was in new platform shoes and First Street was coated with ice, so every time Sam got in reach of Lewis and began to swing the cleaver, he would throw himself off balance and slip. He kept missing Lewis's neck and cutting First Street instead. By this time, too, they had covered about two-thirds of the block and were headed toward the corner of Northern Boulevard by the neighborhood unit police station. Outside were parked several yellow police cars. Pretty soon, if things continued as they were, with Sam repeatedly catching up, lifting the cleaver, throwing himself off balance on the ice, and missing Lewis wildly, pretty soon it would attract the attention of the police. They might even interpret Sam's perfectly plausible self-defense as a felonious assault— or worse, if he managed to decapitate Lewis in their laps. It was hard to tell what the police would do. But Lewis was counting on them because he was too old for this kind of strenuous activity on a cold night. If Sam didn't get him, Lewis thought, he might have a heart attack. Lewis, in fact, was clearly slowing down and Sam's cleaver was getting closer each time. As it was going—as they approached the station at the corner—Sam seemed about to present to the Albany police a murder with the kind of witnesses that judges prefer.

Sam, however, was also losing heart for the chase. For one thing, Sam was not in as good shape as he should have been. He had been smoking a couple of packs a day at least. His wind was weak. For another thing, there was a huge gash running from the bottom of his shoulder across his chest to his stomach and it was leaving a red track on the ice all the way down First Street, with a big red smear each place he had fallen. His entire body seemed to throb, as if his heart had swollen to engulf his whole chest, and reach toward his head. And all the running made his heart beat faster even when his feet slipped. All the exercise meant he was losing a lot of blood. The outcome was still uncertain.

The feud had begun shortly after Wiggy had moved upstairs. "Whaddya do," Sam had asked Phil Russell, "when you have a crazy killer move in upstairs?" Phil thought it was a good question. Sam had quickly discovered that he could not tolerate Lewis. He couldn't bear his voice. He didn't like the way he fondled Maybelle. He didn't like the way he hit Maybelle. For his part, Lewis didn't like the way Sam swaggered around the block as if he owned it, treating Lewis as if he was too old and feeble to be a threat. Lewis had said he would kill Sam; he had killed before, spent eighteen years "upstate"; he deserved respect. Instead, Sam kept calling him Wiggy. It wasn't fair.

But all this hostility might not have led to bloodshed if they did not live so close together and if Lewis's woman, Denise, was not such a good friend of Maybelle's that they were always in one another's apartments. Maybelle often babysat for Denise and Lewis just thought he could walk in whenever he felt like it. The situation was not helped by the fact that neither Sam nor Lewis worked; neither had a car. Both were around all of every day. And like the thousands of other, "unrelated individual" black men in Albany—some of them not even listed in the census— both men subsisted on women.

Sam, to some extent, and in the last resort, still relied on his mother for food and lodging. But increasingly he had learned to use other women, who would feed him, put him up for a night or so, even a month or so, in exchange for sex or in response to pressure: the subtle, implicit, somehow seductive threat of violence in the moneyless, sex-driven man. Sam's ability to find these women and exploit them gave him some confidence in his virility. It was an exciting game, the pursuit and catch, and when he pulled them in, writhing in his arms, at first as slippery and sinuous as a fish, then soft and absorbent and submissive, briefly all his, he could forget the briefness of the flesh, his childlike dependencies, his fear that he would never get a firm hold on life, his gnawing knowledge that there were but twenty years and a feather curl wig between himself and Lewis.

As for Lewis, he, even more than Sam, was bereft of family and work. In an earlier impasse, he had even killed his wife—a final confession of male fecklessness—and left his best years in prison. Emerging into a new city, without friends or connections, he lived on the edge and had to struggle even to keep a meager footing of self-respect. Denise, in her most touching act, had bought him a wig to cover his premature baldness. But his pathetic loneliness and emptiness remained, to be covered only by a wild bluster of virility that fatally conflicted on Concord Avenue with Sam's own imperious claims. Their lives were hopelessly snarled and it seemed there was no way they could cut themselves loose and free without using a knife.

It was a week earlier that the feud had reached a head. Sam had recently made a thoroughly charming discovery. There were white girls in Albany—not just the losers and lesbians that frequented Dinty's, not necessarily the whores and teasers he could find at other bars in the city—there were foxy, voluptuous white girls in town who wanted black men, preferred them, were hungry for them, would do things for them that few black girls would consider. One was Phil Russell's girl, Sandra Collins. She was a spectacular looker, with big breasts that jiggled high above a thin waist and with a sultry feline way of moving. She was enough to permanently banish any memories of a Betty Frazier. But she was Phil's. She had a friend, though, named Angie Costello, once a friend of DiGrigoli. Angie was less shapely and sumptuous than Sandra but warmer and more womanly, with a sweet smile and large soft brown eyes that seemed to Sam an escape from the world. These white girls, it appeared at first, did not demand money. Angie seemed to accept Sam at face value—and not to see through him, as black girls so often seemed to do, to the fears and failures below. Before her, above all, he had to save face. But

Lewis the week before had actually begun fondling Angie in Sam's very presence.

"You think you can have everything for yourself," Lewis had said to Sam.

"Maybe not," said Sam, "but I sure can take you."

They were playing cards together at Phil Russell's: Sam and Phil against Seymour Belton and Lewis. Sandra was leaning against the sideboard behind Phil, with her arms straight in back of her, pushing her shoulders up and forward, doing wonders, Sam thought, for the sideboard. Angie Costello was standing between Sam and Lewis. They were playing bid whist, "rise and fly," which meant that night that when one of the teams lost, the two losing men would get up and the girls would play. There was no money being bet. But bid whist is a complicated game, with a system of bidding, trumps, and trick taking rather like bridge, and it commanded most of Sam's attention. Phil, however, noticed that Lewis was reaching out and fondling Angie's leg and behind. Angie kept edging away toward Sam. Phil finally caught Sam's eye and nodded toward Lewis. Sam looked over and saw Lewis withdrawing his hand.

"Keep your paws off my old lady," Sam said.

"What the fuck you talkin' about?" whined Lewis.

"You just watch it, Wiggy, I'm tellin' you," Sam said. Lewis leapt to his feet. Phil said, "If there is gonna be any fightin', it better be in the street."

Lewis said, "All right," and left the table, angrily spilling some cards. Sam did not follow him. "Let's finish the game," he said. "I can handle him later." Angie sat down and they dealt another hand. Sam stayed seated in front of the door, with Phil opposite in front of the sideboard. Phil surreptitiously pulled out a drawer halfway, so he could get a knife quickly if Lewis came back.

A few minutes later Lewis did come back, bursting into the room, with a large wooden-handled butcher knife in his belt. Sam elaborately ignored him and continued to play. Lewis pulled out the knife and for a second Phil thought he was about to stab Sam in the back. Phil reached into the drawer beside Sandra and grabbed a boning knife, a razor-sharp dagger used in meat packing plants for cutting meat away from the bone. Phil had wielded it professionally in his earlier career as a butcher. He got up, brandishing the knife, and ordered Lewis to drop his.

"I know how to use this," Phil said, "I used it on pork chops for five years."

Lewis shook with anger. "Fuck you and Sam too," he said, but he did not stab Sam's back as he had seemed about to do. Holding the boning knife out in front of him, Phil strode around the table toward Lewis. It was Phil's house. He had the territorial rights. But Lewis had the adrenal rage. If Phil showed a moment's doubt, he might be lost. "Get the hell out of my house," he roared. Lewis stood his ground for a moment, glancing at his knife and at Phil's. Then he stormed out, slamming the door.

Seconds later, he returned. The knife was back in his belt. He apologized to Phil for disrupting the game.

"I want you," he said pointing at Sam, "you punk faggot." Sam looked across at Phil. "What would you do?" Sam asked. "Do I kill the bastard or what?"

Phil said, "You go outside and fight like men, with your bare hands." He turned to Lewis.

"Give me that knife," Phil said, "or I'll call the cops on you right now . . . we'll see who they'll believe." It was an extraordinarily rare threat between men on Clinton Avenue. Lewis hesitated, then once again succumbed to Phil's authority. They walked quickly down to the street.

Lewis must have realized that without a knife he could not cope with Sam, for all the way down the steps, Lewis kept saying, as if to convince himself, "I'm gonna whip your ass." They walked down the stoop to the sidewalk. "I'm gonna whip your ass," Lewis said. "I warn you, motherfucker, I'm an expert in karate."

Sam had been tense, wondering what Lewis would do. But at that he could scarcely suppress a smirk.

Lewis assumed what he thought to be a ferocious karate pose; it was a boxer's stance, knees bent, head cocked, except his hands were stiffly open. Sam reached out quickly and tugged at the wig, pulling it awry. Seymour, Phil, and the girls laughed nervously. Then Sam suddenly picked up Lewis and hurled him down on the street. Lewis was briefly breathless on his back. Then he said, "You tripped me . . . wait till I get up." The group laughed openly. Sam reached down and pulled the wig all the way off.

Lewis rose, looked in rage at Sam, then walked over to pick it up. There was no fight in him as he limped away. "You shouldn't have any more trouble with him," Phil had said.

A week later, though, Sam could not resist calling him Wiggy when he met him in the street coming out of Joe's Grocery. Sam was on his way to his friend P.K.'s apartment on Concord, where he planned to change into good clothes for the evening. He hoped to look up Angie Costello. Sam had doffed his old clothes, put on some pressed brown slacks and new platform shoes, and was spraying deodorant, when Lewis burst in the door with an eight-inch switchblade. He slashed Sam viciously across his chest and ran out down the stoop toward First Street. Sam brought up his hands instinctively as if to stanch the bleeding but managed only to drench them. He dashed into the kitchen and emerged with the cleaver. The chase was on.

Down the street they ran, Sam slipping and sliding on the ice, Lewis gasping for breath and for life, down the dark street by the boarded-up, eyeless buildings, toward the lights of Northern Boulevard, Sam's blood oozing out, Sam's blood on the handle gooing his grip, Sam's absurd shoes nearly tractionless on the frozen street, Sam on his knees with the cleaver sliding away on the ice like a skate and safely under a car. "A crowd of people and cops appeared suddenly out of nowhere," Sam remembers. Two policemen began to pick him roughly up, then were so startled by the blood they nearly dropped him. Don Gavigan, Sam's favorite Albany cop, sprinted around the corner, his gun high, after Lewis. "Stop or I'll blow your head off," he yelled. Lewis stopped.

"Gimme that knife," he ordered.

Lewis dropped the knife. It was over. Gavigan brought him back toward Sam and breathlessly thrust Lewis into the hands of two other policemen, who pinned him on a police car. Seeing that Sam was watching, Lewis muttered, "Get off me or I'll knock you guys out."

"Sure you will, Wiggy," said one of the police.

Don showed the knife to Sam.

"Is this the knife that cut you?" he asked.

"Yes," Sam said.

"Will you press charges against this man?" asked the policeman. Sam, in the past, had given the impression that his very last words, gasped breathlessly from a pool of blood, as his life oozed away down a Clinton Avenue gutter, would be a nearly inaudible but bravely uttered: "Don't press charges." But this time, he said quickly, "Yes, I'll press charges . . . when are you going to stop the blood?"

At that point, Denise emerged from the crowd. Even she had had enough, "I want him locked up," she told the police. "But can I have my wig back?"

Sam did not hear the answer. Whatever it was, it was submerged in the siren of the ambulance. It streaked through the night down Northern Boulevard and skidded to a stop, just three feet from a police car. Sam was put on a stretcher and rushed to Memorial Hospital, where they injected him with Novocain. He fell asleep on the operating table as they sewed him up. It took forty-one stitches, and it was a week before they released him. When he got out, Lewis was in prison. Three weeks later Lewis pleaded guilty to first degree assault and was sentenced by Judge Keegan to six months in Albany County Jail.

When he got out, he had one further fight with Sam and was again badly battered. He tried to move back in with Denise, but she rejected him, refusing even to give him back a suitcase he claimed was his. It was finally enough. With his belongings in a brown paper bag, he boarded a bus for Brooklyn. What he found there, where he stayed, what he did during his last few months is not known. Six months later, though, he was shot dead on the street.

"I guess they don't use knives in Brooklyn," Sam said. But it was over at last: a solution had been found to the problem of the crazy killer who moved in upstairs.

Sam had other problems, however. Having left his job and committed himself to the street, having foregone drugs and other profitable felonies, he had to find a way to make a living. He could live with his mother for awhile. But she didn't earn much at Chase Cleaner's—perhaps $65 a week take-home—and she already was supporting Pops some of the time. Besides, she got on Sam's nerves. A man could live with his mother only so much without feeling like a boy.

Sam also might himself apply for welfare. But the money available to an able-bodied single man was not worth the hassle and humiliation it could take to get it. For some $47 every two

weeks, a man would be required to sign for various work programs, forty-three hours a month of self-abasement—patronized
by social workers and poverty officials—emptying clean ashtrays,
sweeping floors with a group of crones, decrepit, beaten: Lewis
Carlsons, all of them, without the wig or willingness to fight.
Sam didn't need money as much as that. He had quit the State in
order to escape this kind of "Mickey Mouse." On "work relief," it
would be worse.

Sam's situation was not unusual on Clinton Avenue. It is
difficult to judge exactly the number of street males. Young black
men tend to elude that net of the census; in Albany hundreds
simply disappear from the figures at about age fifteen. But even
among the black men listed as unrelated individuals or out of the
labor force—a segment far greater in the Clinton area tracts of the
survey than elsewhere in the city—only about a quarter accept
public assistance, though their mean reported income is under
$1,000 a year.

Men without money, ironically, tend to be men who will not
accept a dole. Because they lack wives, and worthy jobs, they are
acutely sensitive to the symbols of manliness. A true man does
not go down to Howard Street and have his failures probed by a
social worker in order to qualify for $94 a month, with regular
sieges of stepin-fetchit. The word would get out, Sam knew, and
it was better to skirt starvation than suffer the jibes of one's friends.
Welfare officials discovered this unwillingness of young street
men to accept the dole when a program was started at the jail to
qualify inmates for welfare, so they would not return moneyless
to the street. Only a few older convicts showed any interest and
the plan was dropped.

But as Sam and all the others knew, there are many ways of
getting money without interviews and humiliation. Many of these
ways are criminal. Sam had very rarely resorted to them. His
way, the favored way of making it on Clinton Avenue, the route
to Howard Street money without paying for it in flesh and spirit—
a vertebra, a nerve, a sinew a week—until you are too soft and
boneless to get a woman or to be a man, his way was the welfare
mother. There were about 300 such women in the Clinton Avenue area, 600 in Albany. Half of them were black. They had an
average of over three children apiece, which means that they had
monthly incomes, tax free, of $258, plus a net value of $140 a

month in food stamps. Their medical care was free. In addition, they got $187 a month to pay for a heated apartment: this amount would get them at least three rooms nearly anywhere in the city. To one of the "unrelated individuals" of Clinton Avenue, those figures meant wealth beyond the dreams of a working man.

It is not clear from the census figures exactly how many black men like Sam were in pursuit of these women. The census indicates about 750 "primary men" out of the work force. It is enough, in any case, to make the competition fierce and exciting, particularly if one restricts oneself to black women. It is a contest in which the winners get warm lodgings, good food, and a woman in bed, and the losers are on the street or in the bars, scraping by, and looking for a chance to move up. Emotions run high, as one might expect, and violence is rife.

Of course, these statistics offer only an outline of the possibilities. Swelling the numbers of available women are the working girls. Few of them, though, will put up for long with an unemployed man, unless his charms are rare indeed. Sam was charming. But so far he had failed to land a woman with money who was not on welfare. It is the welfare mothers; they are the ticket. If you are a working man, you can leave your job; if you are a man of the street, you can come into money and comfort. So it seemed to Sam in early 1972.

After seeing Sandra with Phil, and after his time with Angie Costello, Sam no longer thought he should restrict himself to blacks. Angie would have been fine for him if he still had a job. But she didn't have children or want them. What Sam needed, when he returned to the street from Memorial Hospital, was one of those 300 or so white women on welfare. A black woman would do. But to a black man without a job and in need of conspicuous winnings to keep up appearances on the street, there would be nothing quite like a blond.

If it had been spring in Albany, he would have ambled up toward Washington Park at dusk, when most of the whites hasten to their apartments, and hundreds of blacks move up from Clinton Avenue with six-packs and transistor radios, to pass the evening in easy society and soul music on the Olmsted lawns. The white girls who remain find themselves rather rapidly surrounded by black men. Some like it; some leave. It is Washington Park on a summer evening: the arena.

When Sam recovered from his wounds, however, Washington Park was deep in snow and the arena had moved indoors, to the bars of the city. Closest to him was Dinty's. But if one wanted white girls, the choice there was slim, and all too often lesbian. For some reason, lesbians had begun to gather on Clinton Avenue, and in 1972, there were some fifteen or twenty in the vicinity. Several frequented Dinty's. Down the Avenue a few blocks was Demings. Also a neighborhood bar, it too attracted lesbian women. But there were also hookers and a few possibly available whites. More inviting were The Woodshed on the corner of Ten Eyck and Livingston, Happy Hour on Madison, The Tower Hall Tavern, and farther away, The Foxhole in Troy. Each of these assembled a funky crowd every Friday and Saturday night. There would always be a few whores, black or white and often pretty, who would do a good business in half-hour stints at nearby hotels. There would be a few black women, and slightly more whites, and only an occasional and furtive young white man, often a client of one of the hookers, or an older man left over from the weekday clientele from the neighborhood. It was the black men and white women who tended to dominate this scene, and Sam in 1972 was in the midst of the fray.

Before hitting the bars on a Friday night, many of the street men bolstered their confidence with weapons. Under their jackets, stuffed into their belts, taped to their legs, or merely plopped in their pockets, were a panoply of guns, knives, hammers, screwdrivers, choke chains, and razors. One Clinton Avenue stud, in his thirties, invariably carried a quarter-pound hammer, no nails. Another bore a golf club, with a leather thong, no white balls. Also favored were sawed-off pool cues, notched around the handle to hold a leather strap. There were knives galore: butcher knives, pocket knives, steak knives, and roofing knives. Lewis Carlson often wielded a roofing knife: a curved blade, eight inches long, with a hook at the end, for ripping up asphalt shingles. And there were guns of every sort and caliber. All these weapons, except the pocket knives with blades less than three inches long, were illegal, as Sam was to discover whenever he was arrested for public intoxication. He soon decided his fists were enough, sometimes augmented with a choke chain. But most of the men armed themselves more heavily before their weekend excursions. Several of the bars were crowded with men and weapons rubbing together, and against the women, from five until closing.

Yet these weapons were only rarely used, even in fights. At Dinty's Tavern, two or so fights erupted every week, often between men who were heavily armed; fists were flung, dire threats issued. But in general, the balance of deterrence held firm; deadly weapons remained hidden or clattered to the floor unused. The panoply of blades and clubs reposed as symbolic reinforcement for the man who wouldn't take shit from nobody, who would fight at the drop of a threat or a slur, but who most of the time would keep his steel to himself.

Complicating the situation at The Foxhole and the other most popular weekend haunts were the scores of prostitutes, black and white. To get to the back room of The Foxhole, with the jukebox and pool table, one would have to pass through a gauntlet of breasts and nipples, swelling loose in thin halters. Many of the women were young welfare mothers, looking for freelance cash that would not be reported to Howard Street.

Perhaps half of the younger recipients, caught in the welfare trap, aware that family life was prohibited them, resorted to such supplementary income. But some of the girls were of a different class altogether: students from the colleges nearby in Troy, from both state and private institutions, seeking excitement, while earning, as they said, "athletic scholarships." It was a free and easy scene, with few pimps involved. The women were often willing to connect for longer periods with men who pleased them.

But the crucial fact was that the women controlled the play. They were free and independent. They did not need the men. The men, one way or another, had to pay or perform. So they drank beer and felt in their pockets for the reassurance of weaponry. They swaggered in both movement and speech. The ones who had been paid at work often succumbed for a twenty minute trick; the others angled for cheaper action or sought out the women who were not then for sale. As Sam was to discover it was a tough game, and he followed some of the toughest girls of all.

A few years later, Sam was to go to the movies to see the new version of King Kong. As he saw it, the film offers a blunt racial tableau. Kong had been appeased in the past by offerings of six or more black women tied to stakes outside the stockade. After gobbling them up, the ape would plunge back into the jungle, satisfied. But when he finds, proffered in like way outside the walls, a Hollywood honey blond, Kong is perplexed. Rather than eat her, first he plays with her, then he seems to fall for her in some crude and wordless simian form of love; finally he is led to his doom, while she lies in tears watching his magnificent struggle and mock-tragic demise bestride the twin towers of the World Trade Center.

Sam, like nearly everyone else in America, was rooting for Kong. With Jessica Lange cowering in Kong's huge black hand, Sam supplied a nearly ecstatic commentary. "Get her Kong baby; you want her pussy don't you Kong? But you're too fuckin' big. Ain't that a bitch. Ain't that a bitch. But you get her anyhow. You can figure somethin' out, can't you Kong? All right!"

As he left the theater, Sam clapped his hands. "Shit, I know what happened to Kong," he said, "King Kong, he was used to black women all tied up and shit. Had 'em every day. He'd eat 'em right down. But he never seen a white woman before. He thinks it ain't *cooked* yet. Thinks he'll watch it, play with it awhile. And the first thing you know the bastard's in love. They'll do it to you them blonds. But you better not catch 'em. Them womens ain't cooked."

7

Beverly

When Jasper had been drinking, he especially liked to drive. When he was drinking, his 1968 Buick Riviera could actually give him "that GM comfort difference you can feel." Ninety dollars down and $30 a month to DeNooyers would get the thing on the road. But nine Knickerbocker "naturals" would make it fly. Beer-borne, Jasper forgot the dirt and dents, as he wrestled the wheel to keep the car on course and out of the plate glass windows in the drive-in Bankers Trust, The Hamburger Heaven, the Italian Patisserie, The Happy Carwash, the Dutch Boy paint store, The Eckankar Soul Travel Center, and other impromptu parking slots along the Avenue.

But despite all, that day early in 1973, Jasper on Central Avenue was mad and frustrated. The chances are good that he had missed prepublication notice of Susan Brownmiller's theories on rape; rape, though, was a subject to his interest, if not understanding.

With a man like Jasper, it is sometimes hard to distinguish rape from his other blandishments. I was to meet him, by coincidence, at the very moment Sam spoke about him during an interview in Dinty's Tavern. Sam was, it seemed to me, describing King Kong. Jasper was big and he was black and he was *bad,* to such an extent that even Sam did not abound in stories of great victories over him. Jasper had accosted Sam with a twenty-two rifle one day, and Phil Russell intervened with a higher caliber piece, and negotiated détente. Sam and Jasper had met in inconclusive tussles now and again. But in general, they kept their wary distance, which is to say, on Clinton, they were nearly friends.

As Sam described him, I listened with a light touch of skepticism (he might be *bad,* but not *that* bad), when a huge fist plummeted down on the table between us, hurtling a beer bottle foaming to the floor, and I found myself looking up, up into the grizzly scarscaped face—no doubt about it, bad—and gorilla brawn body, dressed in grim black, of a hulking dark troll—maybe even superbad—who bellowed down at Sam, "Sam, ya ugly motherfuckin', scarface bastard, get outta my way." I desperately pulled back my chair, muttering prayers and curses, and ogling for exits. But Sam only gazed up at him coolly and replied: "Jasper, my scars ain't no uglier 'an yours." Jasper sat down at the next table, as I recall, and glowered over a beer. I began reassembling my papers for an interview elsewhere—"Maybe it would be easier to concentrate back at your place, Sam?"and as soon as bare dignity allowed us, we departed.

Jasper has that kind of effect on people. If women do not exactly fall at his feet—or he does not knock them down in general enthusiasm—they tend to stay away, or to do what he says, for in his chivalric moments, he is apt to miss the point of subtle demurrers. He just wouldn't notice. So it was that day in the spring of 1973, on Central Avenue, when Jasper spied, beside the road, a comely blur—the glyph of his desire—a girl, a woman, a girl-woman, honey of hair and rosy of complexion, the girl known on the streets of Albany, where she made her most enduring home, as Beverly "Baby Doll" Burden. She raised an elegant thumb.

Four years later, I was to see Baby Doll Burden's elegant thumb raised in front of Albany police court on Morton Avenue where she had used it to point to her Aunt Mabel. Her Aunt Mabel, two days earlier, had thrust into her hands a broken Pepsi bottle which Beverly had shoved into the face and fending wrists of a black girl named Punkin, causing a gash of thirteen stitches in her forehead. It was Bev's first assault.

Seeing me that morning on the courthouse steps, Beverly had bounced up and down clapping her hands exactly like a little girl.

"Hey, George," she had trilled, "why don't you come to see me anymore?"

Beaming at me with her bright fleshy smile (short only one-and-a-third incisors for full toothsomeness), and her sparkling brown eyes, needlessly shaded with mascara, her hips near bursting the seams of fluorescent pink slacks—a cartoon Okie princess of sex and innocence—she turned discreetly to spit out a piece of spent gum, and focused radiantly forward, toward me.

I was put into a delicate position. I liked Bev. She was one of God's most perplexingly enticing gifts to men. At seventeen, she had had two children, and seen and undergone more violence, in better spirits, than most of us watch in a year of TV prime. Now this ebullient creature, under charge of first degree assault, was leaning toward me on this paved courthouse patio, arms wide for an embrace, which I evaded; then lips close—for a kiss?—no, a whisper: "I need some money, George—it's for the kids."

"Sorry, Bev, no money." My problem was that also on the patio, apart from Aunt Mabel, was Beverly's father, with his wife and stepdaughter, Bev's half sister (all one person). And Punkin, with a large white bandage on her forehead. It was Punkin's reactions that concerned me.

Not that I needed to worry. Not that there were any hard feelings, as it turned out. Punkin did not press charges, all's being fair, apparently, in the heat of drink. Instead, she sat in the front row in the courtroom together with Beverly's family and friends and dandled Bev's little daughter Daisy on her lap.

"See Mommy through the glass," she said to the little girl. The woman pointed at Bev, standing on the other side of a transparent partition, chewing gum as she listened to the judge. Then Punkin noticed Daisy's slightly disheveled hair. "Hey, Daisy, you need to have yo' hair done; I'm gonna ask yo' momma if I can fix yo' hair when we git home."

That was the way it went all morning in front of the bulletproof glass among the No Smoking signs in Albany's sometimes smoke-filled police court. Meanwhile, the steps outside, where Beverly had greeted me, effervesced with a spirit of family reunion, fashion display, and carnival. Beverly, the defendant, managed to star both indoors and out.

Just as, three years earlier, she had been starring, in her inimitable way, thumb out, on the roadside next to Central Avenue, when Jasper drove by. Jasper careened to a stop and opened the door to his car. Beverly looked timidly in. She had qualms. One of Beverly's problems, though, is that qualms melt in her mouth. She got into the Buick next to Jasper.

As we have seen at Dinty's, Jasper is nothing if not direct. He began the conversation. "I've been wanting to fuck you for a long time," he said.

"Well, I'm going to Rensselaer," she replied with some fervor, "so let me out here."

"That's all right," Jasper answered, always accommodating, "I'll fuck you in Rensselaer."

"I'm jail bait, I warn you. I'm thirteen," she said, exaggerating her youth by nearly two years.

"She-it," Jasper replied, "it won't be the first time, will it?"

"You keep your hands off me," she cried, "I'll tell Sam."

"Hey, you gotta sense of humor, don't ya?" That was the way it went that day on Central Avenue and across the bridge over the Hudson, and that was the way it continued in the back seat, in the park in Rensselaer. Perhaps Beverly was raped by Jasper, though she could not think of any very communicative way to resist, and Jasper would have been startled to hear from Susan Brownmiller that he had committed an unspeakable crime, and indeed Beverly would have been perplexed by the notion that his abuse of her body might have unutterably altered her mind. For Beverly the event was hardly a fate worse than walking to Rensselaer.

As for Susan Brownmiller's revelation that rape is less an act of lust than of power, Bev would have gone along with that. But all sex is in one sense the assertion of male power over women; in fact, the male erection in part depends on a male feeling of dominance and control. If this power is not implicit—or signaled by the submitting woman—it may flare out in violence. The man may have to be violent, then, in order to lust. Vicious and deeply impotent men may always use violence, or the imagery of it, to arouse their lust. Some men, as Beverly had reason to know, could feel most lustfully dominant in sexually attacking their own, or others', children.

Beverly had first crossed that bridge over the Hudson alone five years earlier, in 1968, on her way to Rensselaer on foot at the age of nine, when the bridge was iron trestles. On that occasion, also, she was preoccupied with a rape.

She was living in Albany with her family in one half of a two-family house on Livingston Avenue. She was fitfully attending the local elementary school, P.S. 24, predominantly black. Beverly and her family were predominantly, if ambivalently, racist. Her father was a rangy middle-aged man of 6′ 2″ and 225 pounds, with a craggy face, a perpetual cowboy hat, and the general demeanor of a country music star in the soulful ex-convict line. He worked at St. Peter's Hospital as a security guard. Her mother was short and dark and an object of enthusiasm among the male patrons of a bar in Nassau where she worked. By the time I met her, in 1976, her looks had gone. She had had thirteen children, of whom Beverly was fourth or fifth. Four of the younger ones, including a pair of twins named Ray and Sally, were by black fathers; and three of the eldest, all white, were in jail—one in Utah (four-year sentence) and two in New York State. Three of the thirteen are now dead. One black baby died in a crib accident. One teenage girl, allegedly lovely, died of hepatitis and cirrhosis of the liver. The oldest of the girls committed suicide in her thirties.

It is very difficult to tell the story of Bev's upbringing—of her family—without breaking into the kind of spontaneous uncomfortable laughter that attends the contemplation of disasters too gruesome for the mind to accept seriously.

Bev's very arrival was the occasion of tension in her mother's household, since her husband, a man named Monroe, was not the father. Bev, in fact, was the third such child presented with some qualms to Mr. Monroe and received by him without paternal pride. Two of the children were put up for adoption. Bev, too, might have been given away, but weeks after her arrival, Mr. Monroe, perhaps getting the hint at last, died of a heart attack. Carl Burden left his seat at the bar and moved in. Soon after, he took the family to Rensselaer. Since we cannot know how Bev's two siblings put up for adoption have fared, we cannot easily guess how much better she would have done outside the Burden household. She has survived, and in a way, prospered. Most of her known brothers and sisters were less fortunate.

Her half-sister Jane married Mr. Burden's brother, Bev's Uncle Bill, a plumber and roofer, known to be proud and dependable, and moved to a farm outside Albany. Jane was subject to fits, in which she would sometimes swallow her tongue, and other times commit assault. The doctors had prescribed tranquilizers. They had been married four years when Bill suffered a heart attack and stroke that forced him off the farm and into an apartment, onto the welfare rolls and into a depression. One day before Thanksgiving they locked themselves in, stuffed the doorbell with toilet paper, took the phone off the hook, and turned on the gas. They left behind them only some forks and spoons, and a turkey in the refrigerator.

Another of Bev's siblings, Shirley, an attractive half-sister, is currently married to Beverly's father and has borne him a son, who is at once Beverly's brother and nephew. A previous sister-niece died in her crib. The relationship between Mr. Burden and his Monroe stepdaughter began when she was thirteen and Beverly seven, but Beverly did not become aware of it for two years.

As Beverly describes the scene, one day she returned from school and found the door to Shirley's bedroom hanging askew on a hinge, kicked in. On the bed was Shirley, her legs held up high by Mr. Burden, as he huffed and puffed over her nude body. Shirley was enjoying it, according to Bev.

Bev left the room and waited until her mother returned. She told her mother what she had seen. Her mother called her a liar. So Beverly took her in to look. As Mr. Burden turned red and started yanking on his clothes, Mrs. Burden launched an attack on Shirley, "What are you doin', bitch?"

After that, Bev's mother told Shirley to move in with Mr. Burden, marry him, for all she cared. Beverly thinks that one reason was protection: Mr. Burden would not dare to hit his former wife if she could testify that he had been cohabiting with his stepdaughter. Shirley, for all her youth and good looks, Bev says, makes her father miserable now. In public, however, they make a reasonably presentable couple, an ornament to Clinton Avenue society and its accessory courthouses.

The discovery of her father with Shirley revolted Beverly. Hours later she ran away from home for the first time. She decided to go back to Rensselaer, where she had lived the happiest

years of her childhood. She walked along the road all the way to
the Rensselaer bridge, a mile and a half away, went out onto its
quarter-mile span, and crossed it most of the way to Rensselaer.
The weather was cold and windy. Ahead of her was a home long
abandoned. Behind was a wasteland of raw dirt and massed rock
from the Mall demolitions. What warmth in that rubble? Cars
whipped by. She had not brought enough clothes. Grit blew in
her face, her eyes. She could not go farther. She started back toward Albany. But she could not bring herself to return home.
So she started back on the bridge again toward Rensselaer. There
on the bridge she stayed, walking to and fro, for perhaps a half
hour, near frenzied with fear and cold and confusion—a nine-
year-old girl driven from her home but unready to run.
Finally the state troopers picked her up and returned her to
her father, who beat her long and hard on her rear with a large
leather belt.

As much as she disliked her home, however, she preferred
it to P.S. 24. There she found herself in a perpetual war with the
little black boys whom she had learned to hate, even while her
mother was sleeping with black men. It was a typical case of school
integration in a big American city: the only whites in attendance
at P.S. 24 were the offspring of parents who didn't even care
enough—or were too poor—to save their children from the blacks
they had taught them to hate. On some days, Mr. Burden would
walk Bev to school, and was stoned himself. It just went to show,
he would lecture Bev, that blacks were no damn good. "Stay away
from them," he said, delivering her to her classes. She attended
as little as she could, but never in all her life managed to follow
his advice.

Outside of school, Bev remembers her next two years in
images that for us evoke amazement—to her, just the way things
were. She remembers being locked out back of her house, with
her retarded brother, "Dingbat," without food for thirty hours or
more, until he began eating raw meat from the garbage. She remembers her mother's pregnancy with a child Mr. Burden assumed was his until it turned out to be black. She recalls, as her
own body began to ripen, her father ripping off her clothes, with
her head half under a pillow. Later he saw her befriending a black
acquaintance of her mother's. He railed at both mother and daughter as "nigger lovers."

Beverly's mother, no less than her father, had told her to shun blacks. She believes that her mother turned to black men because they were the only ones around after Mr. Burden moved in with Shirley. By all reports, her main black friend, a man named Eddie Smith, stood out, wherever he went, chiefly for his spectacular nose, which had grown back dangling and twisted after a knife fight. The birth of the twins, according to Beverly, required an emergency operation that almost killed her mother. Beverly remembers them as ugly babies, "all wrinkled and shriveled up."

Ray and Sally, however, grew into strikingly beautiful children, with golden bronze skin and innocent summery smiles. The mother, who loved Beverly, but "never any man," apparently loved these children. Shining out amid the chaos of the family, they are a source of pride and hope for both Mrs. Burden and Beverly—a strange and unexpected grace.

After her father's attack on her, Bev again ran away from home. Although her mother always treated her well, Beverly could not feel safe under the same roof with her father who was still living in the same house, though no longer in the same rooms. At age eleven, Bev broke successfully from her parents.

At first she moved in with a fourteen-year-old friend in Albany named Jo Anne Dolinsky, and from there she moved to the street. But after two weeks of scraping by—taking food and lodging, accepting pills, pot, and "blue boys," sexual passes and other attentions from strangers—Bev was found, feeling important, by a children's worker named Gail Gorke from the Albany Social Services Agency. At age eleven, Beverly had finally made it from the charge of her real father and mother into the hands of the nation's institutional parentage, the Department of Health, Education and Welfare, with which she would be embroiled, as child or mother, for the next six years and more.

Bev was assigned to a large state institution in Utica. Following the gauntlet of Burdens and the teenaged company on the Albany streets, however, she could not easily adjust to the downbeat regimen of the state home. "I thought I was Miss Big Shit," she says now. One winter day, after a few months, she decided to run away again—to attract attention, perhaps to be expelled.

She was not expelled. Instead they began giving her tranquilizers—"nerve pills," she called them—which succeeded in quieting her down for a few months and allowed the state to consider, as a solution for Bev, the device of foster homes. Thus, over the next year, Bev was to move rebelliously from one undeserving couple to another—five in all—until finally the social services agency gave up on this approach and dispatched her to the improbably named Highland School for Boys, a heavy-duty home for delinquents.

Here the staff did a good job in impressing her with their concern, with their belief that "I had good in me." She passed the psychiatric tests, piled the blocks in the correct patterns, and at last began to behave. "For six months," she said, "I was a good girl." But what she remembers most fondly at Highland were the letters she received from her mother; she was deeply moved—a rare experience for "Miss Big Shit"—when her mother sent her fourteen-carat gold earrings for her thirteenth birthday.

Finally, at age thirteen and a half, she persuaded her mother to sign for her and get her out. By this time, Mrs. Burden had remarried, to a Mormon named Bob Wilson, who took her for long stretches to Silma, Utah, two hundred miles from Las Vegas. Bev ended up living in Albany with friends of her famly named Paul and Ann, whom she persuaded to take her in.

Ann, Bev described as a "weirdo," with a good figure that she liked to display in a body suit in supermarkets. Paul turned out to be very protective toward Bev, his Baby Doll. He worried about her; he wouldn't let her go out; he wouldn't let her out of his sight. As Beverly describes it, he wouldn't let her out of his hands. He fondled her. When he raped her, she called her parole officer, a Mr. William Harrell, and Paul was locked up for six months. He threatened to kill her, Bev remembers, but soon enough after his release from prison he began taking his business elsewhere. He is currently serving a long sentence for the statutory rape of a nine-year-old.

After all this supervision from Paul, Beverly moved into freer circles on the streets of Albany, where she emerged in her Baby Doll guise. Staying with a seventeen-year-old friend named Mary Ann Swan, Bev met several girls who were to set the pattern of her life for the next six years. Through them, she was introduced to the charms and excitements of Clinton Avenue.

Bev found herself on a sharp social upgrade. Like attractive street girls all across the country, whose bodies at twelve began outrunning and overrunning their minds, she combined beauty and vulnerability in a way irresistible to men. Soon enough she might learn her power and place, become market-savvy, wise to the scent of loser rot through a haze of Brut and Lavoris. But at first—with these street urchins every man could feel needed, dominant, sexual; felt he had a chance. The girl could not yet parse the sad rigid classes of sexual power.

Like a lottery winner who could not understand money, Bev was thronged by wishful counselors who wanted to tell her where to invest her parvenue riches. Aspiring male providers abounded. To clarify her thinking, older men and boys plied her with pills, and pot, and booze; they drove her in their cars, took her to rock shows. "Miss Big Shit" had come into her own at last.

Within Bev's new circle was a girl of like experience named Sandra Collins. A quiet child from the suburbs, lief to curl up with sentimental books about horses, Sandra at twelve was startled from her reading by receipt of a body, at once lithe and sumptuous, that led grown men with jobs and wives and families to the helpless contemplation of felonies. Like Bev's, Sandra's childhood climaxed with an attack by her father, a large, muscular blond-haired man who drove a garbage truck in Delmar, a suburb of Albany.

The Collins family lived in a small hilly village in the township of Canaan. At the bottom of one of the hills runs the New York Central Railroad, now Conrail. At the top stands a steepled white church and two rows of simple houses, all white. From this chaste and tranquil place, Sandra had been dispatched at three, on the divorce of her parents, to live with an aunt in New York.

Growing up, she had been pleased to move back to Canaan to stay with her father again. They lived together in an apartment over the "Family Style Restaurant"—"home-cooked good food." It was over this restaurant that he crept that night to take his daughter's body.

She moved out and into Albany near where Beverly was living with Mary Ann. Soon after, Sandra met Sam's old friend Phil Russell, then married with children. Over thirty years old, he loaded her down with gifts and other attentions—diamond rings, expensive dresses, trips to Lake George and Saratoga. It was during this period that Sandra and Bev began seeing one another, and met Angie Costello, a friendly girl with a lovely sweet smile, who had her eye on a twenty-one-year-old ex-Marine, handsome and tough, named Sam Brewer.

But Beverly's fateful encounter with the love of her life was not to occur for at least two months. She and Sandra first made the mistake of "going shopping" at the big Westgate Mall Shopping Center on Central Avenue. Although reduced by lack of money to items beyond the immediate gaze of guards, they managed to find gifts for each of their friends, and many of their siblings, as well as supplies for themselves. Into their large paper bags and copious undergarments went stockings, dresses, blouses, and shirts, bottles of cosmetics, combs and brushes, bathing suits. But, in the end, after successful sprees in J. C. Penney's and W. T. Grant's, generosity, in Grand Way, gave way to greed. There, in front of a two-way mirror, they tried to stock up on enough footwear, of sufficiently varied sizes, to outfit several friends on Clinton Avenue. They made it back to their congested car before they were caught by a solemn policeman who asked Bev to explain why she had a pair of shoes sticking out her rear. Bev tried to explain. But she and Sandra kept breaking into hysterical giggles, laughing and crying at once. Finally, she said that she had just gotten carried away by the quality of the merchandise. So once again Bev found herself back in an institution, this time with Sandra. Its name was Hospitality House in Albany.

Once again, Beverly submitted to a variety of psychiatric attentions of the sort that first were flattering and later tedious. After a few days she started to plan her escape. After a couple of weeks she ran away. To her surprise, the state seemed to have lost interest in her. No attempt was made to get her back. Sandra, on the other hand, spent eight months, and during this period, under a siege of earnest social servants, she began losing interest in Phil Russell. Things were never the same between them after she returned.

Back on the street, Beverly connected to a seventeen-year-old black boy named Leroy with a job in construction. His chief appeals, Beverly says, were money and clothes.

One spring morning at about noon, however, she was sitting with Leroy on a stoop, when Sam Brewer came around the corner with Angie. It was a bad moment for both Angie and Leroy. By the middle of the afternoon, Sam and Bev were together, embracing in the back seat of Phil Russell's russet Oldsmobile with the black vinyl roof, while Phil's nephew Billy Grant drove them out to a secluded place in the woods near Ravena. By five, Sam had asked Bev to be "his old lady." Bev had demurred because she had heard of Sam's problems with drink. But by 5:30 or so, she had removed her white blouse and soon after, her black skirt. They made love in the car, while Billy took a walk.

Beverly now is ambivalent about those early days. Sam was better than Leroy, that was for sure, but he was also black, and Beverly doubted she could love any black. She says that in the beginning she didn't even find Sam particularly handsome, and his ability to attract women mystified her. For three months after their first encounter, they saw one another from time to time. But Sam was seeing other women—Pearl, now and again, and even Angie—and he was drinking—beer, wine, Thunderbird—and many a morning found him red-eyed and sullen, with a deep stench of bad booze. Beverly liked him, but she could do without him.

Then an event occurred that changed everything. Beverly became pregnant, and only Sam could be the father. She found him on a stoop on Clinton and confronted him. He reacted vehemently. "Who me? Shit." He jumped to his feet. "Woman, you gotta be kiddin'. Get outtah here." Beverly burst into tears and ran away down the street and around the corner to Concord. She ran up to Sam's apartment.

Her condition frightened her. She had seen her mother dragged through the years, on a chain of exhausting pregnancies, from a comely youth to a wizened and cronelike middle age. She had seen her mother's once round breasts wither to dry flaps of flesh. She had heard of her mother's pain, near death, with the twins, the black twins, who had arrived so small and shriveled, after wreaking such baleful vengeance in the womb. Was it the blackness that caused the pain, the punishment?

She felt her own body growing—not merely the child, Sam's child, but the fats of her hips and haunches, her thighs. Would she ever be pretty again, ever again command the power she felt on the street, the power to bring men bearing gifts to her feet, their eyes melting like soulful spaniel eyes, their bodies hardening fiercely for her softness? Without Sam, the pregnancy would be intolerable; without Sam the child would be unbearable—a symbol of her new ugliness, new impotence, the severing of her life from the sustaining world of men; her entombment in the poisoned and tormented circle of her mother's entrapment and decay.

Only Sam, she thought, could save her. She must persuade Sam to be the father of her child, the body in which their two bodies, their two bloods, were forever fused. If they were together, in love, then the child might become an incarnation of love and renewal, a link to a new order of life. Love—it came to mean something to her then; it came to affirm a future, to assure her—and how at fourteen years of age she needed assurance of this strange fact—that adulthood need not inflict isolation and cruel decay; that at fourteen, her monthly blood, now pent and swelling in her, would not poison her and make her old, but might wash her and wring her clean, restore her youth and love in connection with a man and a child.

Love-blood, that came and changed her two years before, that repelled her and enticed her father, that befouled her and empowered her to enfeeble men. That ultimately brought her Sam, when she scarcely cared, and now cost her Sam, when she rawly despaired of life.

She called her friend Gloria to Sam's apartment, among the clutter of clothes and broken TV. When Gloria came, Bev took a razor and silently sliced into her own left arm, on the inside just below the elbow. The blood poured. Together they stopped it. Then Beverly told Gloria to go to Sam and tell him what she had done.

"What happened?" he yelled. "You crazy bitch."

At that point, Beverly raised the razor and cut herself twice more, two more three-inch slices in her left forearm. Sam ran up to her and grabbed her right arm, started to twist it.

"You're gonna break it, Sam," she cried.

"Damn right, I'll break it; I'll break it in half 'less you drop that razor." She dropped it and fell back on the bed and the blood just poured, welled up and drenched the bandage, sluiced down her arm and settled in her pain-cupped hand. And Sam ran. He was gone. Beverly cried out and swooned.

Then she felt him by her again, saw him standing with a whiskey bottle and a roll of toilet paper.

"What are you doing? I don't want a drink," she screamed, "stop the blood!" He poured alcohol on the wounds to clean them out, swabbing up the blood with the paper; and he noticed under the sliced skin, the "white meat" of her arm. Then he tied his shirt around the wound and her shirt around her upper arm. Finally the bleeding stopped. But Sam was so mad he could hardly speak; he wanted to beat her, beat some sense into her, beat some notion of limits into her swollen body.

But Beverly spoke: "I love you, Sam," she said, "that's why I did it. I had to find some way to get to you, tell you I love you; make you stay. . ."

"She-it," Sam began to speak, then halted.

"Some way to make you know the child is yours," she said.

Sam was silent. "I know Beverly, I know," he finally said. "I'll stay wit' ya. I won't go."

Sam stayed. He kept her in the apartment and for awhile returned every evening after work. Sometimes he would drink, and Beverly would rail at him; and for some reason, he would take it. He began watching her closely and proudly, and at Dinty's, he would brag about his impending child. He said it would be a fighter, tough like him. It would come back and knock the shit out of the guys that laughed at Sam then. He became possessive and wouldn't let Bev out of his sight on the street. He supported her.

Nonetheless, Bev was only fourteen, and truant. Sam was twenty-one, an ex-Marine, a black. Legally, the relationship was statutory rape. Beverly's pregnancy, moreover, had become an unmistakable confession of lascivious carriage. She was brought before Albany's family court, where Judge Tepedino ordered her to the Hudson School for Girls for prenatal care. If she misbehaved, he said, ran away or anything, the baby would be taken away.

Hudson is about fifty-five miles Southeast of Albany. There was no easy way for Sam to get there, and he did not try. With Bev absent, he began to see other women and drink. Now and again, fights erupted. Bev waited. No word for a month. A sense of isolation and ugliness again beset her, a sense of entrapment and rejection. Finally, she could bear it no longer. Without money, without even a clear idea of where she was, she ran away.

At first, she planned to hitchhike. But no one stopped before she reached the town of Hudson itself. There, in a Stewart's Ice Cream Parlor she saw, sitting over sundaes, a black man with a white girl. She went in and sat next to them. Their presence comforted her. But she did not speak to them until she saw they were close to finishing. Then she blurted out her story. They gave her $15 and took her by taxi to the train.

Its arrival seconds after she reached the station gave her the feeling her trip was blessed and would turn out well. But once on board anxieties flocked to her mind: the loss of the baby to the court, the loss of Sam to someone else, the loss of her looks, her youth, her life, all the impending pain and punishment. But she kept on. In Albany, she took a cab to her friend Annie's house; then they went off together in search of Sam.

They found him quickly, at Dinty's, not yet drunk, "doin' nothin'," surprised to see her, but pleased. They stayed together for three days. Then Bev went down with her mother to see a friend working at a garage that serviced police cars. There a policeman saw Bev and reported her to family court. Once again she appeared before the judge and was sent back to Hudson in a state car between two social workers. Before she left, Sam promised to come and sign for the child.

Once again, Sam failed to call or write or visit. But a day after the child was born, Sam was told to go to Hudson by a tubby red-headed black man with a reputation on Clinton Avenue as a psychic. Sam went. It was a girl and they called it Melissa. "The pain," Bev says, "was terrible. I wish the man could have the babies. I didn't want ever to have a baby again." After her ordeal, however, she wanted to keep Lissa—to love her and feed her from her swollen breasts, to complete in peace the circle begun in pain. But she got sick in the hospital and had to stay an extra week while the child went home with Bev's mother.

When she left the hospital, Bev returned to Sam. The week, however, had cost her a certain sense of intimacy with her child. The hormones of mothering had subsided, and she no longer felt such pressure to breast-feed Lissa. Family court investigators began to take an interest in the fluids with which Lissa was fed in the guise of formulas and in the places Beverly stayed in the absence of a stable home. Some days she was at Sam's on Concord

Avenue, others they spent at a rooming house on Clinton Avenue. At times, the child was left with Beverly's younger brother, Roger. Then one day, Beverly decided to hitchhike to Rensselaer to seek help from her mother. Shortly after raising her thumb on Central Avenue, she got a ride.

Beverly ended up riding with Jasper to Rensselaer, in his beat up yellow Buick Riviera, with the queen-size back seat. After the rape, she stayed with her mother for a week, and though she never told Sam about her encounter with Jasper, it was not the same between them when she came back.

The rape had completed the circle. The twisted circle into which she had plunged: the long months of pregnancy, followed by the week-long loss of the child; the nervous suspended time with Sam, while, as she describes it, the reality of motherhood dimmed, lost its physical force, and the love for Sam waned, curled into an extended, scarcely any longer asked, series of dull questions. Then Jasper broke in, ripped her new blue coat, injected his poisons, soiled her sexual flesh, once churned clean with child. Bev returned to Albany again with a cynical eye, a usable body, soured to Sam, prone even to the street and new men. Sam complained, but went out with other women. Beverly called him a "dirty nigger." Sam hit her. Something about that exchange satisfied them both and they settled into a routine of bitter fighting and rough sexual reconciliations, followed by long sieges at different bars.

At this point, about a month after the birth, an agent of the court persuaded Beverly to give the child to St. Catherine's Home for Orphans and other needy children (PINS or CHINS they are called—Persons or Children In Need of Supervision); she was to receive training in motherhood. But she returned to the street.

8

The Welfare Trap

Bev's weaknesses as a mother were understandable. She was fourteen years old. Perhaps at age fourteen a girl brought up as Beverly was lacks the maturity to raise a small child. Yet in many societies around the world, fourteen-year-old mothers are common. Beverly's chief problem was not her biological age, nor even her psychological condition. Her problem was government policy. Girls under age sixteen are not eligible for funds as mothers under ADC or AFDC (Aid for Families with Dependent Children). Therefore, if they want to keep their children, they must rely on men with jobs—normally young men, with mediocre jobs; in Bev's case, Sam on unemployment, promising to go to work at $3 an hour for a few months when it ran out. As was clear to most women on Clinton, a man with a job anywhere near the minimum wage cannot begin to compete with welfare in providing for children. A year's income at the minimum wage, in fact, was worth about $1,500 less after taxes than welfare, food stamps, and Medicaid for a mother and child.

At the time Melissa was born, Sam's unemployment checks were about to run out. The belief, pervasive in Washington, that there are hundreds of thousands of ghetto men miserably jobless brings rueful smiles, at least to the faces of men on Clinton Avenue. Washington has already created many alternatives more inviting than work. For example, to most people paid unemployment is obviously preferable to many jobs in America. Even Sam's working friends only rarely sought jobs before their unemployment expired. If you asked one of these men during a fallow stretch if he would like a job, he would say yes, he was "lookin'"— and you could find the men "lookin'," in beer cans and bars, around card tables, along the street; men "looked" at leisure.

Some of them had seasonal work in construction and expected to be rehired in April. Others chiefly depended on their girlfriend or on part-time work, paid in cash. A job was a last resort, for which one appealed if one's woman, having lost hers, or messed up her welfare, demanded it. One took a job for a few months for a specific purchase or emergency. Or one took a job if it was coach of the Knicks, or an indoor sinecure. But almost no one on Clinton saw his job as a career that he pursued faithfully in the hope of raises and promotions. A job was a "gig" or a "slave" that one pursued in the hope of "unemployment" benefits.

Being under sixteen, however, Bev needed a man who could support her while Lissa was a baby. Sam temporized for awhile and then, in April, joined Phil Russell at a blacktopping company. Sam's role was to push a wheelbarrow full of asphalt. It seemed to him very much like work. For one thing, it roughned his hands. "My hands were in terrible shape," he said three years later, "you can still see the calluses." He scrutinized his smooth palms. I could see nothing. Then he pointed to small ridges below his fingers. "I see," I said. It was not the sort of work he would ever do as long as he had a woman on ADC.

In October, blacktopping and other construction jobs expire, and Bev persuaded Sam to get new work. His friend Red told him of a job for $2.50 an hour, at Concord Lumber Company, out Central Avenue off Everett Road. Sam took it. For a year, he operated a fork lift (illegally, for he lacked a license), unloaded freight cars, and delivered lumber and lumber products—doors, windows, and other wooden building materials—to Albany addresses by truck, using a series of temporary driver's permits. Sam never did the paperwork needed for a regular license. He lacked the patience to make an appointment a week or more ahead of time, so he would take a bus to Schenectady intermittently to renew his learner's permit.

At Concord Lumber in 1973, Sam earned approximately $100 a week before taxes, $87 after. Fifteen dollars went to support his child, Michelle. This left $62 to bring back to Beverly. Toward the end of the year, his take-home pay rose to $118 ($3.50 an hour). But his child support payments jumped to $25, leaving him $93, on those rare occasions he bothered to pay the new amount to Betty Frazier.

In Betty's belated court actions to enforce child support, Sam had encountered one of the most perverse aspects of welfare crackdowns. In justifying these suits, the newspapers normally evoke images of wealthy stockbrokers abandoning their wives and children and forcing them onto the welfare rolls. The more usual reality is a young man, never married, who scarcely knows the welfare-ticket children whom some woman is assigning to him, sometimes by guesswork, on a welfare questionnaire, children who were conceived by their mothers in many cases in an atmosphere of economic safety created by ADC. They are really ADC's babies. As welfare rolls exploded under the welfare-rights and poverty programs of the 1960s, the illegitimacy rate for first or welfare-ticket births to teenage blacks rose to nearly 60 percent.

Most of the time the welfare system pays little attention to the names of the absent fathers of children supported and in part induced by welfare. The applicant lists the fathers if she knows them (Betty Frazier now has four to list, a different one for each of her children), but only rarely does the government actually investigate.

But this time they investigated Sam, found him to be guilty of receiving a legal wage, hailed him into family court, and made him pay the $15 a week. As long as Sam held a job in Albany, he had to fork over the amount or more for each eligible child.

In the early months of Melissa's life, Sam was getting only the $62 a week from Concord Lumber to bring home to Bev. This amount was inadequate to buy food and rent, beer and television, for three people in Albany in 1973. It might have been enough, ironically, if it had been absolutely all there was. Most people, all over the world, live on far less when they have to. By cooperating with other families in similar straits, sharing housing, baby-sitting, and food, Sam and Bev could have lived sparingly until Sam got his raise. But as it was, they took a more conventional Clinton Avenue approach: they cut drastically the most dispensable part of their budget, housing, replaced half the food with beer and kung fu movies, and let first the orphanage, then occasionally a grandmother or aunt, take the child, while they waited for a better future on welfare.

During 1973, they spent some of their time with Sam's mother, some with friends of Sam along Clinton, some with Phil Russell and Sandra in a basement at 97 Concord, and some at $5 a night in a small rooming house, farther down Clinton toward the Hudson. They could afford to live from day to day, because soon enough at age sixteen, Beverly would come into money. Becoming an officially "poor" adult with children, she would qualify at last as a welfare mother, eligible for ADC—money that would not be fired in a slack economy, or otherwise burned up before it reached her; money that would not be taxed, or stop at Dinty's on the way home, or be siphoned off for the welfare-ticket kids of old girlfriends.

Of course, Bev could not get these benefits unless Sam left his job and pretended to leave her apartment. So, of course, soon enough, he would. Why work at a job that would not increase at all the money available to his children—that merely would displace ADC and make some DA look artificially tough?

The worst thing he could do, for both of them, would be to commit himself to a mediocre career and marry Beverly. Then Bev would lose most of her welfare, and by her legal tie to Sam complicate greatly her future status with ADC. Once on ADC, a woman quickly learns above all not to complicate her status; that means more paperwork and more chances to be kicked off during those inevitable periods when the politicians decide to "crack down" and "tighten up" in their inevitably capricious and unpredictable way.

Almost no proposed welfare "reform" would help much. HEW makes a great effort, paying high fees to many consultants and computer operators trying to rig up welfare in a way that preserves "work incentives." These efforts, as Bev well knew, were futile because welfare itself is only one of many programs that penalize work. Among Bev's losses, if she married a man with a job, would be food stamps ($1,044 net, at a rate of $20 a week for $42 worth of food); Medicaid, which would be worth at least $2,000 a year to a young, accident-prone family with Clinton Avenue connections; legal aid, and any other poverty rewards Congress would pass under President Carter.

In addition, as part of the work force, Sam and Bev would have to compete for housing with all the welfare mothers who are authorized to pay between $179 (family of three) and $187 (family of four or more) a month for rent. In Albany, that means three or four furnished rooms. (Moreover, with their transient, furtive, volatile men in the house—that is, men who get their money by extorting it from women—welfare families tend to reduce the attractiveness of surrounding apartments. A third of the houses on Clinton Avenue had been abandoned by 1977, after landlords had decided they weren't worth fixing in a welfare neighborhood.)

In 1973, however, Bev was too young to have the welfare option. This was the only year after Sam met Bev, therefore, that he spent working daily. Toward the end, in fact, he even increased his hourly wage by a full dollar. Beverly acknowledged that she needed his money then.

"I din't like it, but he was boss." Whether or not she enjoyed his bossing, she also says that "those were the best times for Sam and me." They were the best times despite the lack of any place they could call their own, despite the frequent pressures of a difficult child in diapers, despite an income and benefit level far below what welfare would bring them later.

Their free housing arrangements, sponged from parents and friends, did save them rent. They were left a substantial amount of spending money after Sam got his raise and stopped paying Betty. But Sam thought it was time that he and Bev rented their own place. They moved into cramped quarters at 871 Clinton, two rooms for $125 a month. There they lived during the suspenseful days as Beverly's sixteenth birthday approached. Both of them looked forward eagerly to the day.

For Sam, it would mean moving into a large apartment, off Clinton Avenue, and it would mean a kind of liberation. He would no longer have to take so much "shit" at work, no longer have to cringe before his boss when he was late, or get up early in the morning after a long night at Dinty's. He would not necessarily leave his job, he thought, but he would damn well do it on his own terms.

To Bev, welfare also meant a bigger apartment in a better part of town. But as her birthday approached, she began to see ADC in other ways too. She also began to entertain the idea of liberation. If she had money, she would go out with other guys, as Sam, she suspected, was already sometimes philandering. In time, she thought, she might be able to get rid of Sam altogether. Welfare, she hoped, could give her a new life.

Then, on July 26th, the day before her birthday, Sam went off to work and did not come back. Early that evening, she heard he had been arrested and jailed for failure to make child support payments to Betty. Sam in jail was for Beverly a final blow and a welcome opportunity. She resolved that when she went on welfare she would leave him.

Normally a late sleeper, who sheepishly tells friends not to call on her before noon, on July 27, 1974, Beverly awoke early, scrubbed clean, and dressed in her best clothes. She left Melissa with a neighbor, and went off to pick up Sandra and Gloria for the expedition to 28 Howard Street, the County Office of Social Services. They arrived in the lurid yellow waiting room, low-ceilinged, fluorescent-lighted, at nine o'clock sharp and lined up to get an application form.

Almost half the applicants were men, mostly middle-aged and seemingly hung over, many uncombed and unshaven, in several layers of soiled clothes, seeking entry into the work relief category. This form of welfare for the childless, which at best pays less than half ADC's amounts, requires its recipients to work about forty hours a month, usually sweeping floors or emptying ashtrays, whether they need it or not, at one of the city's social service or community action centers. Sam tried it once and immediately decided that he was better off as an unlisted welfare recipient: one of the hundreds of thousands of men who feed off the welfare system without joining it—by feeding off welfare mothers without marrying them. It was a dangerous life because without money the currency of the streets is ingenuity, violence, and sex.

The mothers eventually get bored with the sex and frightened by the violence of moneyless men, and try to kick them out. A man on the way out has to find another woman quickly, elbow another man aside, that very night if possible, to get food and lodging. On Clinton Avenue, these transitory, musical apartments often run with blood when the music and money stop. But to Sam anything seemed better than the humiliation of standing in a line with the expectant women and wearied beaten men at 28 Howard Street, in order to win the privilege of emptying clean ashtrays at PAD (the Parents Against Drugs center).

As an uncounted free rider on welfare, Sam was independent. Except for an occasional dash to the closet or window with an armful of clothes, he was exempt from crackdowns and investigations, free from the need to lie endlessly to social workers about outside income, free from all the little emasculations that the system chooses to inflict on its male recipients whenever public indignation at welfare rises.

The indignation is at "cheats" and "frauds," but the crackdowns are normally against new applicants in emergencies—defeated men without work or a woman, or women newly arrived from the South—or persons linked by marriage to a wage-earner, whether present or not. The crackdowns rarely affect men like Sam who exploit welfare mothers already fully qualified.

Surrounded by friends, that morning Beverly, in her frilly white blouse, with a peek-a-boo decolletage and her pink slacks luminous under the fluorescent tubes, was experiencing none of the humiliation of welfare. In the line of glum applicants, she even managed to smile at the red "be cheerful" cards and yellow "smile" faces on the wall. Then she saw her old favorite foster parent, Steve Rabelli, a pleasantly sleek security guard with a thin black mustache, who worked at the welfare office. She jumped up, squealed, clapped her hands, put out and cast down her half-smoked Winston, and ran up to him. It took all his official dignity to escape a wet kiss. He did greet her warmly, though, making her feel still more at home, while two disheveled men, one white, one black, dropped to their knees to retrieve her cigarette. An unshaven white man, with a shock of dark slept-on hair, came up with the butt and lighted it triumphantly.

After she filled out the forms with one of the receiving clerks downstairs and had her picture taken for an I.D. card, she was sent to the Child Services and Housing departments upstairs. In Child Services, she met more of her friends from the old days, when *she* was the recipient child. They wanted to know all about Melissa and beamed warmly when Bev bubbled on about the baby's smile, her first upright steps, her light caramel complexion, her twenty-five pretty pounds. "Sam's a good father, too. All I could ask," she added, oblivious to her contrary statements downstairs. Then she went to the housing unit where she was given a form for a landlord to fill out and a list of the phone numbers of twenty-three landlords who were known to welcome tenants on public assistance.

Altogether the process took about three hours, until noon, when the three girls left to get a lunch of fish and chips at a fast food restaurant in a nearby savings bank building. Beverly had listed Sam as Melissa's absent father, of unknown whereabouts. She told her friends, over a pile of french fries and catsup, that she didn't expect to stay with him much longer. She mentioned that she might even go visit her mother in Utah, where jobs, she had heard, were plentiful for young women and where she could leave Lissa with her mother. "And it's only a hundred miles from Las Vegas," Bev said, "Oo la la!"

That afternoon, after a session in family court at which Michelle's child support payment was raised to $25 a week, Sam returned to 871 Clinton Avenue to await Bev's return from welfare. He sat in a big battered armchair in front of the $30 Salvation Army TV, and sullenly watched the afternoon's succession of game shows, soaps, and personality interviews flicker by in a blurred gray. Then Beverly came back.

"Hey, I thought you were in jail," she greeted him.

"Nah," he said. "You get on welfare all right?"

"Yep," she said. "No trouble."

"That's good," he said, "cause I'm thinkin' of not goin' to Concord tomorrow."

"I think you should keep going, Sam, you should keep workin'." She sounded concerned.

"Yeah . . . but they've been givin' me a lot of shit. I might be able to get something better anyway."

"Well, you should do something," Bev said earnestly, in a way that alerted him to trouble.

"Why you so hot on me workin' anyway, if you're on welfare?" Sam spoke with a note of apprehension.

"I been thinkin' of maybe movin' out," she said.

"Yeah, we should get out of here now," Sam replied. "Welfare will pay for it—give us moving expenses, won't they?"

"Maybe . . . but I'd like to be alone with Lissa for awhile," she said.

Sam stood up angrily. "What you mean *alone* with Lissa for awhile? The hell you say."

"Just maybe 'til the welfare man comes by," she said quickly.

"You just let me worry 'bout those mothers," he said.

"Well, I just want to be alone," she said. "You got plenty of money."

Sam reached out abruptly and slapped her hard in the face. Bev suddenly realized he was in a rage.

"Damn you, bitch," he said. "You get some money and you just think you can move out. Who the hell is it? Tell me who the fuck it is."

"Ain't nobody. I just want to get away, that's all. Get away from you yellin' and hittin' me. . . ."

"I'll give you somethin' to talk about 'less you tell me who it is." He grabbed her by the throat and Bev realized that she was in danger. It happened that suddenly. It was the only time she could remember Sam getting so violent without being drunk. "Tell me," he yelled furiously, shaking her against the chair, "tell me." She opened her mouth in the rictus of a soundless scream. Then he tossed her down on the bed and kicked a beer can across the room.

Finally Bev said, "I didn't mean nothin'. Honest. I din't mean I don't love you, Sam. I love you Sam. Ain't nobody else. I love you." She burst into loud sobs.

"Where you move to, I move," he said firmly, settling the matter. Then he lay down beside her, looking dully at the ceiling. After a minute, she reached out a hand toward him, and they clung to one another, shaking quietly for a long time.

A few days later, they moved together to 98 Columbia Street, a handsome gray stone building on a steep hill next to the County Courthouse. It was a large, airy three-room apartment owned, coincidentally, by a lawyer Beverly had met in family court. The apartment cost $165 a month and though Sam was irked at having to crowd into the closet with all his obvious belongings whenever the landlord or welfare investigator knocked on the door, he and Bev now had more money between them than ever before. In any case, if he stayed in the back room and kept the television on at all times to conceal voices, he felt safe enough. Perhaps the

TV reflex begins in the common predicament of the welfare father.

After about three weeks at Columbia Street, Sam lost his job at the lumber company. It was not because of anything he did, though his work and attendance had become more fitful as time passed. Concord simply went out of business due to a recession in housing. The Mall was nearing completion, mortgage interest rates were soaring, and the national economy entered a serious slump, in which housing starts plummeted. Construction unions, their pay scales jacked up by the Davis-Bacon Act, preferred long sieges of unemployment to any decline in their wages. It was a time when you had to be rich to afford a new house, and new "middle income" housing projects were charging $400 a month for three-room apartments. Sam found himself back at Columbia Street watching television in the afternoons.

"I was there all the time," Sam remembers, "but I wasn't the man of the house anymore." He started drinking more and spent long hours at Dinty's. Beverly went out by herself or with Sandra. One day Sam found Bev on Clinton Avenue at Deming's Tavern, arguing with a large plump black woman named Buddy Goodhue, recently moved up to Albany from Newburgh, New York.

Buddy was a lesbian, out of the closet with banners flying, and on the street, hawking her wares among the more down-trodden of the Avenue's white women. She worked at the Elite Cleaners on Clinton, but rumors were rife that she also offered her followers to men for money. One of her regular companions was Marianne Simberg, a petite white girl with short blond hair and a bruised and beaten look, who sullenly accepted Buddy's often mumbled orders. "Get me a beer . . . go sit at that other table . . . don't go until I tell you to." But Marianne was not present that day at Deming's.

Sam told Buddy to get her "filthy faggot hands" off Beverly. Buddy slugged him, pushing him backwards against the juke-box. The bartender ran around the bar to break it up. He dragged Buddy to the door, while she screamed curses at Sam. He turned toward Beverly and saw her laughing, but he wasn't sure whether it was at Buddy or at him.

Now and again, Beverly would be gone when Sam returned from drinking. Sometimes he would forget his key and have to break in. A few of these entrances severely damaged the back window. Though Sam taped it up well enough to prevent the wind from blowing in, it was an invitation to burglars and Beverly was afraid the landlord would be angry. He had already complained about the dirt and mess, the stench of diapers and untended garbage, the broken furniture damaged in the fights that were erupting more frequently between them. Both were drinking more and staying out with other people late into the night, while Lissa was left with neighbors or with Beverly's younger brother, Roger, sometimes known as "Dingbat."

Nonetheless, even though Sam was not earning any money—except for an odd job on the side—they did well financially on Columbia Street. Beverly's welfare check was $165 on the first and the sixteenth of every month, which meant that one whole payment went for rent. But $20 would get her $42 worth of food stamps which could be used virtually as cash, at most stores. They spent only $20 a week on food. That left them about $120 a month for clothes, utensils, and entertainment. They often went to the movies with Phil and Sandra during this period, rarely missing a kung fu or karate film, a genre that Beverly enjoyed about as much as Sam.

In all this spending, Beverly was in control. "She paid the rent so I had to do what she said," Sam says. Though she fed him and bought him clothes—socks and underwear—she rarely gave him more than $5 at a time. She felt he would spend it on beer and gambling and she knew that Sam with several dollars worth of beer in him, after a series of losing rolls of the dice, was a dangerous and unpleasant person to have around. One day she found him at Dinty's, having lost about $20 of his own money, drunk and surly, and persisting in the game on borrowed quarters, and she grabbed him by the arm to try to take him home. "You ugly dumb nigger," she said, causing the group around him to laugh uproariously. He pulled his arm away, jerking her towards him, and hit at her with his right. He didn't mean to hit her hard, he swears now, and she agrees. But the momentum of her head against his fist broke her jaw and two front teeth. "And I always had pretty teeth," she says now through her jagged incisors. Although she didn't press charges and Sam felt doubly humiliated and apologetic, she decided then and there to leave him.

Bev's mother had said she was really set up well with Bob in Utah. So, two weeks later, Bev left for the West, investing $90 from her $165 check in a bus ticket. With Lissa sleeping on the floor between the seats in back in a heavy overcoat, and Bev herself warmed by hopes for success in the Sunbelt, she rode for three days and nights—from Cleveland to Chicago, through Nebraska to Salt Lake City, and finally to Silma, Utah, a small town in the desert well over a hundred miles from Las Vegas.

She found her mother and Bob living for $18 a week in a cramped motel room, with no air conditioning and a fitful shower, across the street from a junkyard called Ernie's where Bob worked dismantling automobiles. Bev noticed that Bob seemed cruder than usual and her mother had lost her looks completely. They spent much time trying to borrow money from Beverly. There was no work and far less welfare. Before two weeks passed, Bev packed up again and headed back toward the East and Sam, another dream dissolved, another way out closed. She got back in time to pick up her next welfare check, but the landlord had chained off the apartment and Sam was gone. People on Clinton Avenue told her he had been drinking and gambling heavily on borrowed money and was living with his mother. Bev was very pleased, despite her still tender jaw, to hear that he missed her badly.

9

Buddy's Party

Without Bev, without an apartment, without a job, and with winter coming on, Sam found himself thrown back onto the stoops and into the streets. It was the worst season. He spent it begging for beer money from Benny Williams and Phil and eating a meal a day with his mother. Unable to land a new welfare woman, he finally chose to make another stab at work with the state. An indoor job would be nice for December.

Mark Lawton, now Deputy Commissioner of Parks and Recreation, accepted him quickly as a trainee in the graphics department. Here he worked making state I.D. cards, tracing maps and other visual aids for Parks Department pamphlets, doing paste-ups and other preparations for the printers. He was paid $470 a month take-home, an amount, with Blue Cross, comparable to the combined value of Beverly's welfare, food stamps, and Medicaid allotments.

Almost immediately after Sam got his new job, Beverly returned from Utah. Finding the apartment chained up, she was forced to move; no surprise, since she had paid her landlord for only three of her six months of tenure, having been told by someone that cockroaches exempted one from rent. She chose a place on Madison Avenue in the historic district next to Washington Park. It was as pleasant an area as one can find near downtown Albany. Her apartment opened into a sizable kitchen, large enough to accommodate two chairs and a table, led backwards into two bedrooms, and offered a sunny, if uninspiring view of back lots behind. Bringing another television set from the Salvation Army, Sam moved in soon after.

Sam quickly sensed, however, that things had changed. He did not know why. Perhaps it was the broken jaw and the trip West. Perhaps it was, as he would later have reason to suspect, that Sandra had introduced Bev to the treats of tricking. According to some reports, Bev and Sandra, on their weekend jaunts to The Woodshed or The Foxhole, would pass their evenings doing favors for men. Bev was said to enjoy the money and excitement of it. It entailed no humiliating submission to a pimp; it gave her new independence from Sam and a rich new sense of power over men.

Whatever was going on during these excursions, it did not help her with Sam. They argued bitterly and often. One time when Sam refused to come in from the stoop when Bev wanted to talk to him, she took his old Marine photograph album, full of pictures of himself and friends in California, and burned it.

"You sure know how to hurt a guy," he said. Then in April one evening, he heard a rumor that Bev was a hooker. He didn't know whether to believe it or not and he didn't mention it to Bev that night. He sat sullenly in front of the television set, rarely speaking except to threaten Lissa with the belt when she got in the way of the screen. Bev would then yell at him, and he would ignore her. He merely resolved that the next day, Friday, pay day, he would make sure she didn't go out alone again with Sandra.

When he got back from his office, he found Beverly dressed in her tight slacks and halter.

"Where you think you're goin'?" he asked. "You think it's summer or what?"

"Out dancin' with Sandra, it gets hot," she said.

"It get hot, do it?" he said with heavy irony. "Well you just stay home and cool it tonight."

"What the hell. You go out alletime. Why can't I?" Bev asked. Her face grimaced like a little girl's.

"I don't want you going out to those bars with Sandra, and that's the end of that," Sam said.

"You don't give me orders, Sam," Bev replied. "If you don't like it, you can get the hell out of here. . . . I don't need you. I pay the rent. I kin get better baby-sitters somewhere else."

"Say that agin," Sam said, rising from his chair. "You think I'm some kind of baby-sitter?"

"You ain't stoppin' me from goin' out, I'll tell you that. Here you are makin' all that money an' I never see a cent of it hardly, an' you have the gall to tell me I can't go out at night." Bev's voice cracked with anger. "Well, you get the hell out of here. I don't want to go wit' you no more."

"All right, I will," Sam said, "You go an' whore around as much as you please."

"Who you callin' a whore?" Bev screamed. "You filthy nigger." Melissa started to cry and Sam stepped forward as if to hit Bev.

"Yeah, hit me, you filthy nigger coward. Hit the baby. Why don't you hit the baby? She's more your size," Bev said. Sam pushed her angrily aside and, pulling on his coat, stormed toward the door. "Don't come back, either," Beverly cried out as he reached the door. He turned around, came back, brushing angrily by her, and flung open the closet. He grabbed an old suitcase and began stuffing it with clothes. "You goin' ain't you?" she said in a different tone, as if she already regretted her words. "You give me some money for the baby?"

"I'll send some by," he said, rushing for the entrance. He stopped to put on his big, hard black hat.

"You look silly in that hat," she said.

"Fuck you," Sam growled back, slamming the door. He ran down the stairs. He had $145 in his pocket. Maybe he wouldn't come back after all and join some foul queue between her legs. Maybe he dare not come back, because if he found some man with her, he would. . . .

"All's fair in love," I bantered once to Sam about Bev's other lovers. But as Sam walked out onto the street toward the Mall, he was ready to hit, to crush, to inflict a pain to balance his own. Walking down Madison Avenue, by the park and its array of bare, lighted trees, past the elegant historic houses, past the heavy stone medical office buildings, with brass-plated doctor's names on the portals, and potted plants in the large glowing windows, toward the corner of Lark Street ahead, Sam's jealousy rose to a high boiling oil of sexual rage, that now and again frothed or spilled in his gut, burning him with a sudden need to act, to hit. He wanted to make the world cringe at last and give way, the stones crumble, the jaw break, the glass shatter, the muscles tear, the thighs open, the bones crack. . . .

He would watch the ooze of blood from the green wounds of vengeance; his own inflicted out on others, in a chain of unhealing hurts in an always bleeding, jealous, and unrequited life. There were some things in Sam's world, that a man, whatever the cost, whatever the pain, did not tolerate. A humiliated man is sexually dead, useless. To humiliate a man is to threaten his life: his ability to connect with women who are the source of life. On Clinton Avenue, he will react, if he has a residue of self-respect, with the exiled man's last resort: violence.

But there was nothing for him to hit. Sam glanced out toward the street at the cars; calm drivers behind shatterproof glass, swirling by, in big sleek cars, in unending chains, disgorged from the parking lots of the Mall, headed for the suburbs.

"Shit," he yelled. "Shit." Then suddenly he stepped off the curb in a resolute daze, without at all looking, yet knowing the light was red against him. Not looking, uncannily he sensed every car as it hurtled toward him, shrieked to a halt, shuddering, swerving, the drivers bawling obscenities, mud slapping up against his pants, car-wind whipping by his out thrust face, he stepped firmly, swinging out with every stride his full suitcase, blindly sure, just missed by a delivery van. The driver snarled at him, "asshole," as he walked, carelessly, in the hands of a higher care, as he blithely evoked in others a rage to balance his own rage—"asshole" . . . "nigger" . . . "want to get killed?"—he felt at last a smile of calm and an access of power. No, he didn't after all, want to get killed. He could not be killed or stopped. He stepped up onto the opposite curb. He could have been run over, but he lived. There was a force of favor somewhere. Fuck Bev. He was strong. He had been given fresh life, in a new night to live. He was at the door of the Lark Tavern. He must have been going to the Lark Tavern. He stepped in feeling warmly better. He sat down at the bar and ordered a can of Bud. It flowed cool down his throat, a balm.

Instinctively, he looked up and down the row for Reilly, with whom he had so often drunk on Friday nights in the past, sometimes at the Lark. Instead he saw a girl from the office, a black girl, who looked away from him nervously. He walked over behind her. He liked her, looked too long down the top of her dress before remembering to speak.

"Whatcha' doin' tonight?" he asked.

"I'm very busy," she said curtly, turning to speak to the man next to her, who seemed surprised.

"Fuck her," Sam said to himself, "she thinks she's better 'n black. She thinks she kinda shines. Fuck her." Sam laughed and tipped up his glass, finishing it, enough for the Lark, and stumbled out the door, feeling the money in his pocket, in his mind.

He strode out down Lark toward Central Avenue with his suitcase in one hand and the beer sloshing lightly in his belly. He wore the hard black hat, tight brown pants, platform shoes-worn soft and not too high-with green tooled perforations on the toes, and a black furry coat. He was wet and mud-sprayed from the cars. But he felt ready and all right, leaving Beverly behind, looking ahead, nine blocks to Clinton. He would try Dinty's tonight, and see what Phil was doing. It was still early on a Friday evening, almost into spring, the day after April Fool's. He was still good for women. And he had $140 in his right front pocket. He reached down to see; the check was still there, all still there.

But he shouldn't keep so much, or he would lose it. He knew himself that well. If he began the evening with $140 he would end it with $7.50, if he was lucky. He would buy booze for the house, bet on faith that he was Minnesota Fats, and rent a woman for every pang. Before going out tonight, he should give his mother some; he owed it to her for all the meals and emergency lodgings. He would pay Joe's Grocery. How much did he owe them? $35? Pay back Phil Russell. Sam wanted to be clean, debt-free, when he went out tonight. He wanted the world to owe *him* one for once. He quickened his steps. It would be a good night for Sam Beau. He had left his woman; he would pay his debts; and then he would find himself a "piece of ass." Yeah. He liked the words. That was what he needed that night.

Meanwhile, walking up Clinton Avenue toward Joe's Grocery were two women who scarcely qualified as likely help for Sam. One was Elizabeth "Buddy" Goodhue; the other was her companion, Marianne Simberg. Lesbians.

Almost two years later, Sam and I were to go looking for "Buddy" on the street. It was twilight and the corner was in the distance ahead, but Sam thought he saw her in her usual place, a squat figure in many layers of brown clothing, flagging down cars to offer unknown services. As we drove closer, however, the khaki figure on the corner turned out to be a mailbox.

This evening, unfortunately for Sam, Buddy was no mirage. They met in front of Joe's Grocery, where Sam went to pay his bill and cash his check. Buddy accosted Sam on the street and asked him where he was going with the suitcase. Sam said it was laundry for his mother. Then Buddy proposed a party. The last time Sam had seen Buddy was the night of the fight at Deming's Tavern. But if Buddy wanted to make up, that was all right with him. He also noticed Marianne standing shyly by and though she did not strike him as the fulfillment of those dreams that brought him walking briskly the half mile down from the Lark Tavern, he identified her quickly as woman and white, which, he thought, were steps in the right direction.

Sam said he could not go to a party until he had cashed his check, paid the grocery, and given his mother some of the money. Buddy and Marianne were willing to wait. Sam emerged from Joe's Grocery after a few moments, then went across the street to give his mother $30 and dump his suitcase. He returned to the street five minutes later and the three went off together to Norman's Liquor Store around the corner, a small cubicle that specializes in Thunderbird, cherry gin, and cheap wines. Sam bought a pint of Canadian Club whiskey and Buddy got a half pint of vodka.

Coming out of the liquor store, Buddy asked Sam if he had eaten. She said she had a roast and was going to put on some rice. "Buddy was being real friendly," Sam said later. But he said he couldn't go up until he had done another errand. Buddy and Marianne waited while Sam went back into Joe's.

At that point, Sam ran into Phil Russell with Sandra in the grocery, and asked them to come on up to Buddy's. Phil said he would have to make a phone call but would be by in twenty minutes. Sam emerged from Joe's with a six-pack of Budweiser and hurried up Clinton behind Buddy and Marianne.

Back at 894 Clinton, Phil met his nephew Billy Grant, returned from the Parks Department printing room. He also was at loose ends on that Friday evening and Phil suggested that he come to Buddy's party. Billy said he would think it over, and after contemplating Dinty's and the TV schedule, he decided to saunter up to Buddy's. By the time he got there it was in full swing.

Buddy was playing a small pile of 45 R.P.M. records on the record player: soul music from James Brown to the Jackson Five, Aretha Franklin to Joe Tex. Phil was sitting in a tattered easy chair with Sandra draped decorously in his lap. Sam was sitting on the couch making uneasy overtures toward Marianne, who was not yet having a good time. She seemed to have higher hopes for her vodka and orange juice than for Sam. She had broken up with her boyfriend Eddie, she told him, and was "for the time being" uninterested in men. "I am unavailable," she said in a vaguely haughty tone. Sam found this a challenging proposition.

There was not much in Marianne that attracted him. But the idea that she was Buddy's, had "broken up with Eddie," and "for the time being was unavailable," yet at the same time sitting next to him on the couch, slowly glazing over with drink, looking sallow and soft, the very image of the possible woman—these coquettish contradictions led him to decide she would be his before the evening was out. Why the hell not? Sam leaned back on the couch and gave her a long stare which she returned evenly. On the record player, Joe Tex was rhythmically asking: "Who will take the woman with the skinny legs?"

Sam then poured himself more whiskey and thought of new approaches. Buddy was walking between the kitchen and the record player, making sure that nothing got out of hand, and washing down her whiskey with swigs of beer. She did not show any interest in the scene on the couch. At one point, she and Sandra reminisced about old times in jail. Both agreed that "there was some crazy women in there." But the liquor and the music prevailed.

Billy stood nervously, leaning on the edge of the couch for awhile. Then he decided that the only available woman was Buddy and she was not the woman for him; and he detected a lowering cloud of alcoholic menace. He left. He was to return later, having failed to find better diversion on the street. But Billy was a survivor on Clinton Avenue. Going to all the same places that Sam went, playing pool and cards against the same players, living on the same blocks among the same escaped felons and trigger-happy fighters, Billy managed every day to go to work and every night to avoid trouble. Broad-shouldered and softly heavyset, he nonetheless remained light on his feet, nimble and alert, looking often behind him, sniffing the air, skittishly gregarious, always ready to flee a crowd or bashfully concede a point when trouble threatened. Billy Grant sort of wanted to go to a party that evening, to relax after his week's work, but all that evening in his visits to Buddy's he never so much as sat down.

Although Buddy's party was to become one of the more richly chronicled social occasions of that Albany season, at seven o'clock when Billy left, it still seemed a bummer. Phil might have been enjoying himself with Sandra; Sandra's charms lent themselves to wordless pleasures. Sandra even gave Sam a dance. But no excitement seemed in store. It seemed likely that Phil and Sandra would soon enough decide to leave in quest of more comfortable furniture.

The only question of any interest was whether Marianne, sagging on the couch under the rising influence of vodka, would eventually go to bed with Sam, or with Buddy. It was not the choice, it seems safe to say, that she envisaged for herself as a little girl under the bowering maples in Colonie. Nor did it seem a romantic triangle of passion and intrigue sufficient to preoccupy two judges, several lawyers, two newspapers, scores of Parks Department workers and officials, hundreds of Albany lesbians and feminists, and inmates and guards in large numbers at the Albany County Jail, all through several months of the spring and summer.

Nonetheless, Sam was pleased, when at about eight o'clock, Marianne leaned back and nestled in his arms. Shortly afterwards, he tried kissing her. "She seemed," he said later, "to like it all right." Sam decided that the party was going acceptably well and called Buddy over and asked her to go out and buy some more liquor. He gave her a $20 bill. Bev's rejection was almost forgotten. Joe Tex sang out, "I guess I'll take her, skinny legs and all."

10

The "Rape"

When Sam left Bev with a suitcase in his hand, walking out angrily as if he would not come back, she felt a heavy pang of regret. She wanted him to leave, she wanted to feel her own power to make him leave, she wanted to make the point that he had to go when she told him to, but once he had rushed out the door and she was left with Melissa, she began to look forward to another of his sheepish returns.

This was the usual rhythm of their relationship: She could drive him out and he could burst in—yes, he could burst in, with a cold, blank excitement, resembling hate, in his eyes, that hardly acknowledged her. He could break in, and they would feel together briefly in warmth and love. But this was dangerous, because feeling warm and dependent on Bev, Sam would sometimes fairly ache with vulnerability, drink to quell the ache, then lurch into violence against her; and she could not always deflect it from her face, and into her body, could not always disarm his fists and summon his sex.

That was the horrible balance, the seductively exciting see-saw between them; her money and rooms and sexual power, his lurching sexuality and violence. He could burst in and out. She would stay, most of the time, around her home. She was where it was. She and her womb—and Melissa—were the family. Sam on the streets, bouncing from bar to body, could create nothing stable or lasting. Soon enough, she thought, he would have to come back to her.

She walked over to Melissa's crib. Bev was always amazed at the loveliness of her light tan countenance—a beautiful child, as if God had approved of Sam and her and revealed beneath all the ugliness and hatred—the bloodshed and brutality—the purity and loveliness of a little girl's face. Was that what she saw in Sam during those elusive moments when his features mellowed and grew warm and they held one another closely long?

She lifted Melissa by her legs in the crib—showing the other side of the little bronze coin—and changed her diaper. She would never get used to this chore, she thought. Sam, though, would now change her sometimes; Bev wondered how many men would do that. No others she had seen around, not her father, certainly. Only her little brother Roger, bigger than she was by then, but still little Roger to her, still not quite right in the head. Perhaps for a few bucks he would take Melissa for the night.

Bev decided that if Sam was going out on the town that evening, she could, too. She turned up the radio as one of her favorite songs surged forth: "Hey, boy, you're just a playboy, can't believe a word you say, boy." She tapped her toe, then took Melissa by her two hands and began prancing with her across the rug in front of the TV. "Hey, Lissa," she said, "you're a real purty dancer, you are. You'll really turn on the men. You got a natural sense of rhythm, don't you girl?" Bev smiled. "You sure din' get it from Sam. That's for sure."

She let go of the little girl's hands, and stepped back. Melissa teetered a second, took half a step, then tumbled to her knees, looking surprised, baffled, and on the verge of tears. Bev picked her up and continued dancing, rocking the girl in her arms, but Melissa burst out crying anyway. "You like to go see your Uncle Roger?" Bev said, "Yeah, tonight you get to stay with your Uncle Roger." Bev smiled at her daughter, and after a minute the little girl stopped crying.

Roger was home alone in Mr. Burden's apartment on Tenth Street when Bev arrived with Lissa. Little Roger was now almost 6' tall, stooped, round-shouldered and chubby, with puffy cheeks, and short-clipped blond hair, pinkish skin, and a peculiar frightened look in his eyes, as if he always expected a blow or a slap from the side or behind him.

"Wha' you wan'?" he asked Bev.

"Say hello to your Uncle Roger," Bev said to Melissa. "Hi Roger, how're you? You gonna let us in?"

He stepped aside and they walked into a disheveled room with a tattered brown couch and several worn chairs, all oriented toward the old black and white TV, on with a celebrity quiz show in the corner. It was as if the room was organized for an impromptu meeting, perhaps for a speaker to mount the box, except that the speaker was the box.

"How's Dad?" Bev asked.

"They's out," Roger said.

"They all right, though?" Bev asked.

"Yeah, they's all right," he said.

Bev sat down on the couch and Roger in an old chair. He looked dully at the fluorescent faces on the TV. "Would'ya like to make some money tonight, Roger?" Bev asked.

"Yeah," Roger answered without interest.

"Will you watch the baby? I'll give you three bucks," Bev said brightly.

"Yeah," said Roger. He did not remove his eyes from the gray glitter, or react to its hyperkinetic images. He just watched, mouth open, as if to be spoonfed gruel.

"She walks now, a little," Bev said, "and crawls. Don't let her get into anything."

"No," Roger said.

"I'll leave some Pampers on the table," Bev said. "And a bottle. If she cries, give her the bottle."

"She gonna shit?" Roger asked. "I don' want her shittin'."

"I don't know, Roger," Bev said sarcastically. She got up and bent down over his chair. "Why don't you hold her?" Roger reached up from his seat and took the baby at first by a leg. "You crazy?" she yelled. Melissa began crying as Bev pulled her quickly away.

"I thought you had her top part," he said lamely.

"You don't grab a baby like that by the legs," Bev yelled. Then she began rocking Melissa and smiling again. "You gonna stay with your Uncle Roger tonight," she said. After a few minutes, Melissa finally stopped crying. Bev lay her down on a cot in the corner and headed quickly for the door. As she went out, she heard the girl burst out with a loud, protesting squawk. Bev stepped briskly away down the street, thinking that Roger might seem a little funny but at least he was harmless.

Bev, however, had underestimated Roger. He is currently serving a sentence of twenty years to life for kidnapping, assault, rape, and sodomy. He pleaded guilty to raping and buggering a girl, after two female accomplices, who resented her good looks, had cut off her hair and seriously stabbed her several times in the breasts with their scissors in an apartment in the headquarters building of "Eckandahar—the Ancient Science of Soul Travel," on downtown Central Avenue, over a health food store.

That night, after leaving Roger, Bev decided to go pick up her friend Gloria and go drinking and have some fun. A plump Italian girl with a big smile and love of beer, Gloria lived on Clinton Avenue about four blocks below Joe's Grocery. But as Bev walked down the Avenue, she found herself worrying about Sam. She remembered how fiercely angry he was as he left the house. He would probably get into trouble, she thought; it was on nights like this, when she had kicked him out, that he most often got into fights. Maybe she should go look for him. She did not really want him to leave for any long period. If she found him and told him he could come back, he might not drink so much beer that night—might not sink into that dumb and desperate trough from which he so often lunged out in violence.

She went upstairs to Gloria's apartment and knocked. Glo came to the door and admitted Bev. Always there was the sweet, innocent smile and the off-color plaques on her walls: "Virgin : A woman without working parts." "Voulez-Vous Coucher Avec Moi Ce Soir?" A fat Puerto Rican with oily combed hair and a moustache sat watching television and did not turn to look at Bev as she entered.

"Watcha doin'?" Glo asked.

"I thought I'd go out tonight," she said. "Interested?"

"Where's Sam?" Glo asked. "Or should I not ask?"

"I ain't goin' with him anymore," said Bev. "Unless I run into him tonight."

"He's bad for you," Glo said. "Stay away from him."

"Yeah, but sometimes when he's bad it's my fault. I make him do it. He's really on a bad one tonight . . . I hope nothin' happens." Bev paused and looked dubiously down. "It ain't no concern of mine, I guess."

"Damn right," Glo answered, "after the way he's treated you."

"I guess," said Bev.

So Bev and Glo went out on the town and headed for The Guardsman, reversing the path that Sam had followed after leaving The Lark. "I'm serious," Glo said. "You shouldn't stay with him. One of these days he might hurt you bad."

They walked silently down Lark Street, where Sam had walked just an hour before. Finally Bev said, "I'm havin' another kid."

"You sure?" Glo asked.

Bev nodded, "I'm scared, Lissa hurt so *bad*. I'm scared."

"You don't have to have it, you know," Glo said. "How long you had it?"

"Two months."

"Is it his?"

"I think so," Bev said. "It's gotta be."

Suddenly Bev said, "Let's go find Sam. He's gettin' in trouble. I know it. He's mad. He's gettin' in trouble. I feel it in my gut."

"Aw shit," Glo said. "If he's in trouble, that's a good reason for you to stay away. What can you do? You done enough."

"No, I want to find him," she said.

"Look, we walked all this far. Let's get a drink at The Guardsman. We can find him later. You know where he'll be. He'll be at Dinty's," Glo said.

Beverly looked down. They were passing Woody's Bar before climbing the hill toward Central Avenue where The Guardsman was. "Hey, girls," a voice rang out from the door of Woody's, "come in here. I got somethin' to tell you. Whatcha doin'?"

Bev waved and smiled, quickening her steps. "Hey, where you goin'?" the man yelled out. "You lookin' for Sam, he went the other way." They couldn't escape Sam if they tried, it seemed. But the two girls kept walking up the hill.

"I guess he was headed for Dinty's," Bev said. "I guess he'll be all right."

Friday night The Guardsman was densely packed with a mixed crowd. Glo and Bev sat down at the bar and were soon surrounded with men. The hours passed quickly.

Meanwhile back on Clinton Avenue, Buddy and Marianne Simberg's party continued on its disaster run. One could say that on that evening of April 2, Buddy was conducting a rare experiment in cross-cultural relations. A kind of Clinton Avenue T. group: Let all the factions of the street just gather to talk, have a beer or two, smoke a joint together—yes, so might an amateur sociologist propose—and intergroup tensions might decline. The white lesbian from middle-class Colonie would gain a new appreciation of the trials and torments of the black street stud from Greenville. The 250-pound black lesbian pimp would find new respect for the middle-aged construction worker and his voluptuous, vixen, fully heterosexual white woman. The bashfully smiling state printing room attendant would enjoy the happy exchanges of views and sentiments among the others at the party, and might even in the end sit down to drink his beer. Buddy had failed only to invite a cop—every true experiment in urban group dynamics should include a perplexed policeman. But perhaps, as the evening proceeded, something could be arranged.

In any such experiment some tensions were to be expected. Unless the participants were to be wholly hypocritical, they would have to confess certain misunderstandings. They did not have to confess their profound sexual disgust, mostly, for one another. But certain points would have to be clarified. For example, Sam had arrived at the party with the strong and highly righteous conviction that the world owed him, that evening in particular, one "juicy white piece of ass." Marianne Simberg, however, had decided to withdraw from the "meat market" exchanges of men on the make and keep her body for the purer and tenderer ministrations of Buddy. She was perhaps willing to perform certain services for money, chiefly for whites. But she emphatically did not want to succumb to Sam that evening. In fact, if the truth were known, Sam's insistent beer-breathing demands and fondlings on the couch were beginning to make her feel physically ill.

On the other hand, Sam had had too much to drink; and in this situation, he, like his mother and his Aunt Sallie Bea, does not take no for an answer. Even though he fully reciprocated Marianne Simberg's disdain for him, the idea that this sappy, half-besotted lesbian, this white girl who lived in the grip of a smarmy woman like Buddy, would reject him at the end of this grimly humiliating day, was more than Sam could easily accept. He listened to Marianne as she spoke of her sickness but he did not really hear what she was trying to tell him.

So he continued, as he put it later, to "baste the chicken" and for some reason—fear, propitiation, foolishness, or some unmentioned plan—she continued to let him hold her and paw her lightly, while jerking nervously away whenever he tried any deeper probes below her layers of cheap men's clothing. "What was she doing here anyway?" wondered Sam. "If she doesn't want me, why is this schoolteacherish white girl here?"

About ten minutes after her departure, Buddy returned from Norman's Liquor with new reserves of beer and Canadian Club. It was just what the party needed at that juncture, to provide for more honest exchanges of views. But it boded no good to Billy Grant. "The party was bogging down. Bad moods," he said. "I could feel it." Sam was looking sullen; Marianne Simberg was looking sick; Buddy's jiving was losing its verve; and Billy saw her sitting there once like an exhausted and world-weary clown. Food had somehow been forgotten. Phil and Sandra were all right but they were planning a getaway. Billy left first. Then Phil and Sandra. Shortly afterward Marianne got up to go to the bathroom.

Sam, who remembered that Buddy still had more than $10 of his money, asked her whether Marianne was her woman.

"Yeah, she my woman. What you want wit her?" Buddy asked.

Sam took another swallow of Canadian Club from his glass. "What the fuck you think I want wit her?" he asked. "How much you charge anyway?"

"Nah," Buddy replied; "I keep her for white men." She paused, half smiling at Sam's intensity. "$25," she said.

"Well, you got ten from me already," he said. "I'll give you five more to take a walk."

"I'll go talk to Marianne," Buddy said.

Buddy left the room and went in to confer. Sam remained on the couch, holding his brow. He sat, gazing glumly at the nearly empty bottle of Canadian Club, then looking out at the room-waste of other bottles, glasses, and paper cups. He noticed that a cigarette, which he had balanced on a beer can, had burned down to a long cylinder of ash, much of which was about to fall onto the greeny-brown rug. He couldn't think of anything to do about it. It fell. There was a coffee cup with ashes and whiskey dregs, a crumpled carton of Tropicana, a bottle of Smirnoff's Vodka, two-thirds done—Marianne had really been putting it away, he thought—an array of discarded containers, perched around the couches and tables, on the arms of chairs, by the record player, like a flock of Hitchcock's avenging birds: bottles, butts, burned out and drained—dry pleasures; and over all, a strange repetitive sound: shush, shush, shush. Sam was sourly aware that this shushing had been preying on the silence. What was it? Shit! The record player. He got up. His head throbbed, as he walked over to turn it off. Then he became aware that the television was on in the next room. Maybe he should just leave. No. He had paid for Marianne; he should have her. He walked into the back room to find out what was going on and found Buddy and Marianne together on the bed.

"Hey, what's happenin'?" he asked. "I thought we made a deal," he said to Buddy.

"Just a minute," she replied. "Go back in the other room and I'll be out." He noticed Marianne lying dourly on the bed with her wrapper half open. "Shit, $15 would be a lot," he said to himself. He went back to the couch. *What the hell were they doin' back there*? How do they do it anyway? he wondered. What do they use? Vibrators, massage kits, dildos? He tried to envisage Buddy's huge yellowy black body, folds on folds of flesh, the breasts hardly discernible among the overgrown lobes and wattles of her stomach and shoulders, the fats of her chest, the hulks of her arms. He could not keep his mind away. If Buddy just rolled over wrong, in a drunken yawn, just kind of hunched over onto her side, without warning, would not the sudden shift of fats pose a very real danger of drowning or suffocating her friend Marianne? *What do they use?* If Marianne was almost sick already, what would happen to her suburban hoity-toits in the alcoholic stench and black greasy flesh in the next room?

Among his morbid fantasies, Sam found himself summoning large currents of physical excitement. Beside Buddy, Marianne, a reasonably proportioned white woman, began to present to him an occasion of arousal that ripened into a rich challenge at the notion that as a lesbian, she expected from him less pleasure than from Buddy with some plastic object.

He would get her and make her come, teach her the joys of men. But *what the hell are they doing*? he wondered again. Were they talking or was it only the TV? He sat glumly for long headaches of time. Then Buddy emerged, "You still here?" she asked offhandedly.

"Damn right, I still here," Sam said. "Whatcha talkin' about?"

"All right," she said, "Gimme $5 an' I'll take a walk for a half hour." She stood there, holding out her hand as if to be slapped in greeting.

"What you been doin' back there anyway?" he asked roughly.

"Jest watchin' TV," she answered.

"I bet," Sam said.

"Look," she answered, "you want me to go out or not?"

"You's gettin' kind of deep in my pocket," he said. "That'll be aroun' $20."

"I can stay here real happy," she said. "It's my house. Maybe you want to walk?" She slurred her words and Sam wasn't sure she could go far anyway.

"Yeah, I want you to go," Sam said. He gave her a $5 bill; where was the rest of his money? While he frisked his pockets, she turned and went through the kitchen and down the stairs.

As to what happened at this point in the evening, there opened a wide divergence among the stories of the various participants in Buddy's experiment. Marianne's story, we know.

Sam's story was quite different. In his rendition, she slackly succumbed to him and even seemed to "like it" some, even if issuing no screams of joy. Sam, for a moment, had fulfilled a contemporary sexual dream of glory. In his skilled hands, under his muscular body, the lesbian's man-hating grimace had given way to an ambushed gasp of pleasure, her dryly writhing body had frothed and smoothed with the sweats and oils of sexual surrender; he had made her feel, he imagined, in Aretha's words, and perhaps for the first time, like "a natural woman." Thus he had escaped, by this triumph, the usual perversity of purchased sex. He had won. Out of this dismal day, despite Beverly and drunkenness and Marianne's newly discovered lesbianism, despite Buddy's famous hostility, he had gone to her party and made her woman ooze and gasp. As Marianne lay flat and exhausted on the bed, still breathing deeply, he dressed quickly and walked into the living room to get a drink. His mouth had something of a musty feel.

He sat down on the couch and poured the last remains of the whiskey into the glass he thought was probably his. Then he became aware of a commotion on the stairs. When he went casually to the door, to see what was going on, Buddy burst in and hit him in the face. Six neighborhood policemen followed to hold back Buddy and handcuff him. At that point, Marianne rushed from the bedroom in bra and panties, yelling feverishly, "He raped me, he raped me." Finally, Buddy sidled over to return $5 to his pocket, but Sam turned away to avoid taking it.

The differences between the two views of Buddy's social experiment are immense in terms of the law. On what happened in that room hung a charge of rape, a felony in the first degree, with a sentence of from twenty-five years to life for Sam, or a finding of innocence and freedom. Albany's Rape Crisis Center mobilized its indignation and made demands for a full-cale rape trial and a heavy sentence. Assistant District Attorney Diane Dubiac prepared to prosecute the case. The city's newspapers called on their staff for full and detailed reports.

Sam was taken away to the District 2 City Jail for the night, where he was to be allowed one phone call before being put in his cell. Who to call? John Reilly's name came to mind, but John would disapprove. John might think he should stay in jail, John might tell jokes, might detect that he was drunk. Who did he know who had a telephone and who could help? Mark Lawton? It was too late to call Mark and it would be too embarrassing to describe the problem. He had not seen Mark much at the office anyway. He should call someone from the office, though, he thought, office people had telephones, houses to put up for bail, contacts with lawyers, long words to recite in courtroom testimony. Office people knew Sam as a worker, not a street man. Who? "Are you gonna make a call or not?" the guard asked.

"Yeah, I'm just trying to 'member the number," Sam said.

"The book's right below there," said the guard.

John Carter, Sam thought; good old John, a black man in his forties with a white fringe on his hair like snowflakes and a lot of contacts, talk, influence; clean short-sleeved white shirts, neat colorful bow ties, gray suits that fit, longevity with the state. And

he was a "brother" after all; a brother with a house in the suburbs, who had helped Sam in a crisis before. Sam called John
Carter. He answered and listened.

John Carter was "sorry" to hear that Sam was in jail but did
not know what he could do, but would "get back" to him. Sam
clung to the words, "get back"; get out? and hung up. He was let
back to his cell and the iron gates kept clanking shut behind him,
reclanking in his head, in a long echoing sound of metal, cold
and hard and sharp and pendulous, resonating in swings too,
too wide, too cold for the short, warm, beery synapses of his brain;
there was not enough room in his head, without stretching and
pain, for that sound behind him. He would have to get back.
Carter would get him out.

The cell was about 6' x 6' with a wooden bench in the middle
and a toilet. Sam lay down on the bench and fell asleep. It was
midnight.

Beverly and Glo meanwhile were getting bored with the
crowding men at The Guardsman and Beverly, for some reason,
continued to fret about Sam.

"I am goin' to have his baby," she kept saying to Glo. "Let's
go see if he's all right." Finally, Glo agreed and they walked back
down Lark and up the hill toward Clinton and Dinty's.

"Shit, we walking too much," Glo said.

"Yeah," Bev said, "I gotta find a man with a car."

"You found Jasper," Glo said.

"Yeah," Bev answered, "maybe some other man has a car."
As they walked into Dinty's, several faces turned to greet them.
They sat at the bar and ordered beers.

"You know Sam's in jail," said the bartender. "Raped one of
the lezzies."

"What you mean raped?" Bev said.

"What you think I mean? Buddy said he raped her. You know
that big fat lezzie?" the bartender asked. "Well, she says he raped
her."

"Shit, she's nothin' but a whore herself," Bev yelled out. She
was already flushed with rage.

"Calm down," the bartender said nervously.

"Calm down, hell," she said, leaving her beer untouched.

"Where you goin'?" Glo asked.

"To the phone," said Bev.

She crossed Clinton to a pay phone in front of Joe's Grocery and called the police. At first, they would not give her any information. Then she said, "Look, is it rape you're holdin' him for?"

"Yes," said the policeman.

Bev hung up. She stood on the corner where six hours before Sam had met Buddy and Marianne, and seethed until she thought of what she was going to do.

"I'm gonna get 'em," she said.

"What you mean?" Glo asked.

"I'm gonna get them lezzies. I'm gonna knock the shit out of 'em and go to jail with Sam," Bev said. "I'm gonna go to jail. I'll teach 'em rape."

Bev stormed off toward an all-night restaurant where she often saw the lesbians on a Friday night: Steve's Diner on Central Avenue. Glo could hardly keep up with her as Bev strode down Lark for the third time that evening and up the opposite hill. Like Sam, Bev knew of only one answer to a grievance—violence against those who inflicted it, or violence against their friends, or even, so it would seem when they arrived at Steve's to find one lonely lesbian sitting in a corner booth, violence against the class of particular offenders. Bev also could think of only one way to expiate the guilt she felt for evicting Sam that evening. If Sam was in jail, she would go too.

She walked into Steve's with Glo, dubious but not unwilling, in tow, and ordered a milk. Then she stepped over to the lesbian's table and poured the milk on it. "You lezzie shit," she said. The lesbian leapt up and hit at Bev and she grabbed her by the hair and pulled her to the middle of the diner, knocking chairs aside and scattering sugar bottles and salt and pepper shakers all across the room, as they tangled together, a mass of hair and denim and pink pants and popping buttons on the linoleum floor. Finally Steve managed to pull them apart and called the police.

Bev could have left with Glo but instead she waited until the police came, then slugged out again at the torn and battered lesbian. The police, however, drove her away toward the wrong jail. "Hey," she said, "I want to go to City Jail with Sam."

"Nah," said the policeman, "you didn't have no weapons. You ain't no dangerous weapon, are you? I guess we can keep you in the neighborhood."

"Shit," said Bev.

"Now is that any way for a lady to talk?" asked the policeman.

The next morning about 9 A.M., Sam was taken upstairs to police court with seven or eight other prisoners, most of them charged with public intoxication. The perennial star of police court was Judge Tom Keegan, a sandy-haired Irishman, with curls that hinted an Irish Afro, with the looks and charms of Steve McQueen, and with a tone of dimpled sarcasm as he addressed and sorted out the stream of Albany mischief and misdemeanors—intoxication and burglary and trespassing and drugs that daily came before him. Some cases he would dismiss with a lecture that usually ended with a heavy nasal emphasis: "Keep off the grass, Mr. so-and-so." Others ended more grimly, "I want that $100 here by next Thursday . . ." he would pause, "or else bring your toothbrush, Mr. Jones."

Keegan's lectures were highly entertaining both to the prisoners and to the flocks of spectators—mostly kin and friends of defendants; and the court was normally a cheerful place, full of smiles, on all of Keegan's big days. Most of the defendants pleaded guilty; a few did not. Some of the less serious cases, below felony level, that did not entail sentences longer than a year, Keegan would try in police court. The most important cases he would remit to County Court if he found a basis in the charges. Sam hoped that his rape charge would be forgotten and thrown out.

When he was brought into the low-ceilinged courtroom, however, he was depressed to see that Buddy and Marianne had shown up in dresses. Shit, dresses, it makes 'em look almost like real women, he said to himself, and felt a sudden pang of horror. Twenty-five years to life, is that the toll for rape? Dresses. Marianne's pinkish, Buddy's blue with flowers.

As Sam was led forth by a guard into the bull pen, Keegan was dealing with three elderly whites who had recently broken up after living together for twenty years: a bald, bent man on crutches, and two old ladies. One of the women, with gray hair still sallow from years of blond dye, loomed disdainfully tall and erect on dilapidated high heels. The other woman was a short, hunched figure with wire bifocals, a handkerchief over her head, and swaddles of dull flannels around her bowed body. The tribulations of a long and difficult life had finally overcome her and she was railing out her charges of treachery and theft against the taller woman.

"An' *he*," she then pointed with a palsied flourish at the man on crutches, as her voice leaked and squawked into still higher registers, "*he* chased me with a butcher knife." The woman's rage and indignation was of a pitch that could be satisfied only by immediate public torture of her two friends.

But Keegan somehow managed to keep cool. "Well, tell me, Mrs. Adderly," he asked in a mildly sardonic tone, "when he chased you with the butcher knife, did he lay down his crutches first?" The room broke into titters and smirks. Keegan looked up severely. Everyone immediately hushed; no one there wanted to miss a moment of Albany's best long-running cabaret entertainment. The woman looked flustered.

"All right . . . did he catch you?" Keegan asked.

"No, but I got scars," she yelled, "an' I want police protection when I go back to get my things."

"Let's get this straight," Keegan said.

"A butcher knife, he chased me with a butcher knife," she yelled.

"Shut up, lady!" Keegan snapped. He lowered his voice into a baby-sitter's warble. "Now Mrs. Adderly, why don't you tell me just what belongings they are that you say Mrs. Krimetz is keeping."

"What do I do about this phone bill?" interrupted Mrs. Krimetz, waving an envelope.

"The phone bill is a civil matter. If you think Mrs. Adderly owes you money, you go over to Small Claims Court and sue her for it." Keegan said this smoothly, ascending to that firmer ground on which every bureaucrat feels most comfortable: denying his own jurisdiction and authority.

"A butcher knife," Mrs. Adderly cut in. "He chased me with a butcher knife." The man and the tall woman turned toward the crowd in theatrical disgust, looking for support.

Keegan resumed his questioning of the smaller woman in a soft, sympathetic tone. "Tell me, Mrs. Adderly, about this butcher knife. Is it yours? You want it returned. Is that it?"

"No," she replied, "But. . . ."

"Just *what then* do you want returned?" he demanded in a crescendo.

Sam at this moment saw Beverly waving to him through the bulletproof glass in front of the gallery. She was pointing at Buddy and Marianne. Sam nodded grimly. The two lesbians looked stonily ahead.

For the next five minutes, Keegan negotiated the details of the exchange of goods. Then he proceeded to the case of a handsome young man from Loudonville who had been charged with disorderly conduct at a Johnny Winter concert in the Palace Theater. Sam looked on with interest as the entire complexion of police court changed; a large sleek construction magnate, who had come to like and admire the young man on ski trips to Stowe, prepared to testify to his good character and credibility. The boy's equally well-dressed parents sat intently in the front row. A handsomely gray-vested private lawyer with shiny black hair and glittering cufflinks passionately presented the argument.

During intermission at the concert, so it transpired, the boy had wanted to take a leak, but had found the men's room full of menacing blacks. He went back upstairs to the theater. At first, he had planned to ask a policeman to escort him to the bathroom, but the idea embarrassed him. So he asked a guard whether he could get out for some fresh air—he felt sick—and then return. The guard said, "No."

The boy was not prepared for this answer; it did not seem likely he had heard it often during his eighteen years in the suburbs. He protested loudly. The guard called the police and said, "This guy wants some fresh air; maybe you can help him out." The policeman roughly led him to the door and hurled him out onto Clinton Avenue. It was too much. After taking his leak, the boy returned to a side entrance to the theater—so he testified to Keegan—and broke in. "I had a ticket," he said. Keegan nodded. "Then when I got in, the same policeman was at the door"—the boy's voice was rising with indignation and shock—"and he grabbed me by my lapels and hit me . . . four times!" the boy said.

"No!" said Keegan.

"Four times," the boy repeated.

"No shit," said Sam to the prisoner next to him.

"I don't believe it," the prisoner responded.

"Tell me," Keegan asked. "Did you fall down?"

"It was the *policeman* who hit me," the boy repeated, as if Keegan could not have understood.

"What did he hit you with?" Keegan asked.

"With his fists. The policeman hit me with his fists," the boy said. Hearing laughter, he looked behind him. Nearly everyone in the courtroom was smiling.

The boy looked mystified. "Sit down," said Keegan. The boy sat down next to a black prisoner. "You had a real tough time, didn't you?" the prisoner said.

"Yeah, I'll say," said the boy, "and I don't think the judge understands."

"He understands," said the prisoner.

Finally the case was held over for later in the week and the names Marianne Simberg, Elizabeth Goodhue, and Mitchell Brewer rang out in the courtroom.

11

Keegan's College

Near the Albany County Airport, the dark, sooty brick walls of "Keegan's College" shudder several times each hour under low-flying aircraft splitting the sky overhead like power saws in raw wood. They give assurance that realtors will never covet the surrounding land even if Keegan should give it up.

The campus actually looks more like a high school, expanded to accommodate the postwar baby boom, with a few parapets and other ornamentation added as afterthoughts when parents complained that it looked too much like a jail. As he was driven toward the building, Sam thought it still looked too much like a jail.

Keegan does not run the jail. It is popularly named after him because he is the director and only significant member of the board of admissions. It is nominally coed, but relatively few women qualify; at any one time, there are apt to be about ten women and one hundred fifty men in attendance: a proportion typical of U.S. prisons, though it offends all the canons of affirmative action and most of the theories of soaring female crime. Racial integration, however, is complete. The student body is approximately half black and half white, and Keegan is regarded by applicants of both races as a fair judge. The chief complaint is that he gives excessive credence to the testimony of the police. This is understandable, however, since a judge in police court who doubted police testimony would suffer the approximate plight of a college admissions dean who was skeptical of both college boards and high school grades.

Handcuffed on each side to a white drunk, Sam arrived at Keegan's College in a windowed paddy wagon. They entered the jail through double-gated portals, in which the first closed behind them before the second opened. As the day went on, Sam had the sense of doors closing on him everywhere: *Buddy and Marianne arrive and are received as veritable women, worthy of deference and respect;* clank; *Keegan disallows all intense questioning; Sam's public defender seems timid and ineffectual;* clank. *They are taking the charges seriously. Rape. Ridiculous. Twenty-five years?* Click, on go the handcuffs. *Lesbians, prostitutes, pimps, all in pretty dresses and suburban moral poses, prim and feminine, with handsome lawyers leaping gallantly to their defenses. Shit,* Sam thought, I *gotta get out of this place.* Clank.

It was many months later that I first came to Albany County Jail and heard that echoless dead metal sound, that chordless terminal note. I came in the company of Nini, who for several years had served as a volunteer counselor at the jail and thus knew Sam both at work and in jail. We drove in, parked in the lot in front of the building to the left, and climbed up a flight of stairs to the visitors' receiving room. There a husky, young black-haired policeman with a dapper mustache officiously ignored us. Nini finally caught his attention sufficiently to tell him I had been approved as a visitor. After checking his file, he motioned us toward the automatic sliding door. It opened noisily and clanked shut behind us. We then signed in at another window. It resembled a teller's cage and was attended by a large, bluff reddish-blond policeman, also mustached. He told Nini that another prisoner, a Joe Gambino, wanted to see her. "You'll find him a really wonderful fellow," the policeman said with a sneer. I laughed nervously. "A great guy," he said.

Another volunteer visitor was already there. A pleasantly handsome professorial figure, with neatly clipped gray hair, a small neat mustache, and an undefinable calm about him, an almost palpable aura of liberal earnestness, he greeted Nini in a soft friendly voice and was introduced to me. Another automatic sliding gate of barred steel opened its jaws before us and we walked into the prison. Clank.

I had the feeling of being definitely inside. This, my first visit to a jail, made me suddenly uncomfortable and I felt gouts of sweat wash from my pores. There was no reason for me to be afraid. But there is something about a prison, about the helplessness and dependency it inflicts—*will they reopen the doors? Surely the guards often fantasize: If those do-gooders like inmates so much, why not give them a real dose?*—there is something about that echoless clank that reverberates long and morbidly in the visitors' minds. *Surely the prisoners consider them: possible hostages.*

We entered an elongated room containing a row of cubicles with desks, giving the effect of restaurant booths. One inmate followed us in—a mildly Afroed black with a green hat, jeans, and a denim shirt. As he approached, his dour face gave me a qualm. We, after all, three outsiders, were in the room alone with him, with no partitions or police between us. What was to happen? He was a *prisoner*, a different, menacing species, with behavior patterns—as we learned in the movies and on TV—erratic and dangerous. Nothing to lose.

It was he that put me at my ease. He smiled and began bantering with another counselor who came in behind him. He seemed very engaging, disarming. I was relieved. *Prisoners seem to be just folks after all. Fellow humans in trouble.* This surprise propels the pendulum toward sympathy and gratitude, a notion of innocence, a flare of rage. Why are they here? Why? The guard may answer. *Why that kindly black man you were talking to over there, he shot his wife dead in family court last week. That blond boy burned down an elementary school. The other two sold heroin.*

Then a white convict entered, a long-haired street person without visible graces or charms, who seemed not to have had a settled home or job since he stopped cleaning up at McDonald's several months before. But the professor warmed him with a smile of greeting and they entered the first booth together. The boy seemed merely pathetic. He was. He kept on robbing people.

Then Nini's charge, Paul, came—a New York City black who was in for fraud and forgery. We discussed Sam. Paul remembered Sam and was faintly disdainful of him. Sam was "kind of country," kind of inarticulate, kind of lower class for Paul. But, Paul made it clear, Sam was a good cut above most of the whites in the jail. "The blacks are cleaner, sharper than the whites in here, got more on the ball. The whites are really scuzzes—off the wall. The blacks are intelligent guys. They may have made bad career choices. But they do wash." I laughed. "Don't knock it," he said. "This is close quarters, man. Cleanliness is next to godliness in here."

Nini had visited the jail for several years and I was to come back many times. Both of us had to acknowledge the point. The blacks in Albany County Jail seem to be representative citizens; the whites, for the most part, were obvious losers. A smart black in Albany, appraising the opportunities before him, all too often seems to turn to crime.

Keegan's College, therefore, is another means by which Clinton Avenue loses some of its most nubile men—another reason why black women so often give up on having a husband in the house. Many of the best young black men commit serious offenses and go to jail, while comparably sharp and attractive whites do not. Within the welfare culture, the fatherless realms of the street, crime is a real possibility in a way it isn't in communities with more stable families. This difference is not a matter of police and courtroom racism, as is often charged. Murder is the one crime for which the statistics are reasonably dependable. Blacks are five times more likely than whites to commit murder. There is no reason at all to suppose that the figures showing a similar disproportion for robbery and assault are much out of line.

Regardless of race, the overwhelming bulk of violent crime in America, nearly 90 percent, is committed by single men. Many are youths under twenty-five. But in every age group, single men are far more likely to commit crimes than married ones. Although it is impossible to offer conclusive proof in sociology, I think it is safe to say that the chief cause of disproportionate black crime rates is the vastly disproportionate rate of family breakdown— and thus singleness—in the ghettos. Poor black males do not get brought up by fathers, socialized by marriage, or regulated by breadwinning. Detached from the continuities of family life, the disciplines of paternity, the link to the future uniquely conferred by children, single men of all races are far more prone to crime. They are twenty-two times more likely to be incarcerated in prison. Poor ghetto black men are less likely to be married and living with their wives than any other group in America outside the Catholic priesthood and the Mattachine Society. This is the central tragedy for which the jails of the land perform as often unconscious accessories.

The five prisoners with whom Sam was brought to Albany County Jail were a representative bunch—two winos, a drunk and disorderly white man, a nineteen-year-old pot possessor driving without a license, and Sam—all single. They were herded by a group of gray-clad policemen into a receiving room, where the handcuffs were removed. They were told to strip and raise their hands, open their mouths, and bend over to have their rear cheeks spread for police inspection of the contents of their colons. The guards moved briskly in suede hushpuppies from orifice to orifice like examining doctors. Sam's body was found to conceal no files, knives, hypodermics, plastic bags, suicide pills, or escape hatches. "Get dressed," the Sergeant said finally. Everyone seemed very serious.

They were moved into an adjoining room where Sam got to inspect his valuables taken at the police station—wallet, money, shoelaces, pen—before they were placed in a large brown envelope to be held pending his release. He picked up his blankets, sheets, pillow, pillowcase, and mattress and was led through the building, down corridors of sickly green and gray pastels, from one set of clanking gates to another. "Open one," the guard would say; then they would pass through into the pen between, then "open three," and so on, until they reached the first tier, East Wing, where stayed the men awaiting trial. Sam was shown to cell number 9, in which he was to live three months because Marianne and Buddy had accused him of rape.

At the time, Sam had little confidence that his defense was being pursued. His public defender had not encouraged him; stuck in prison with a $10,000 bail, he did not see what he could do to help himself. Since Carter did not, in fact, get back to him, Sam gradually resigned himself to the life of the jail.

"I acted just like I do on the street," he said. "Go my own way, don't cause no problems for nobody. Just try to have me some fun." The attempt to make the first tier into a kind of celibate side street off Clinton Avenue posed some difficulties, however. The cast was amenable: for example, L. B. Adams, who was called Pounds because he was so thin, had lived right off Clinton anyway. He had been convicted on a drug offense, but was kept in the East Wing with the men awaiting trial because his girlfriend's husband was on the other side and had threatened to kill him. Pounds thought the man was crazy. "I tole him I didn't like the girl none," L. B. explained, "I just wanted to put her on the street." There was also a black man named Eddie who did not commit either of the robberies for which he was charged after the stolen goods were discovered in his house. "I bought the stuff fair and square." To complete the table for games of pinochle and bid whist was Glen, a young white boy who had shipped a suitcase full of marijuana to Albany by bus and was caught when the bag split indiscreetly open in the Greyhound terminal.

Glen, L. B., Eddie, and Sam played cards daily on a card table set up outside L. B.'s cell. Soul music crackling forth from an old radio, and police periodically passing through, lent to the tier a faint air of Clinton Avenue on a hot summer day. All they needed, it seemed, was money to wager, beer to drink, junk food for snacks (the jail's schedule of regular meals inflicted a jarring change on the Clinton Avenue metabolism) and women to ogle and occasionally fight about.

It is testimony to the ingenuity of men in extremes that all these desires, except beer, were approximately fulfilled on Sam's tier. Cigarettes served everywhere as currency. Cartons or "crates" changed hands daily among the card players. They were earned at a rate of a pack a day by those with jobs, but Sam received occasional money from outside which could be deposited in an account at the front desk and drawn against for the purchase of cigarettes and other items from the commissary wagon that passed through daily.

Unlike earned cigarettes, cigarettes purchased from the wagon had tax stamps on them, valuable because they could be carefully removed in their cellophane, and applied to packages of jail cigarettes which then could be sent outside with visitors and sold. Jail cigarettes could be sold regularly to guards at a discount. In the card games, Sam at first got eight crates behind, but he soon learned the ropes well enough to fight his way back to parity.

He had enough currency, as well, to buy snacks from kitchen workers like Paul, who would filch cakes and coffee to sell on the tier and even at times contrive a juicy roast beef sandwich with tomatoes and lettuce. The kitchen workers would also sell spe-

cial treatment of food. Sam, for example, was willing to pay cigarettes to assure his hamburgers were well done. He also would
make his day by acquiring the ingredients to mix a "really great
salad." Occasionally, as a treat, the inmates would even come up
with a substance, made of vinegar, rotten fruit, and other now
forgotten matter that served as some sort of low-proof alcoholic
beverage. But the stuff made Sam sick the only time he tried it.

Sam also did not like the idea of doing his own laundry,
which was woman's work on the Avenue. After a week or so in
the jail, he made an arrangement with a worker in the prison
laundry to mix in Sam's clothes with the linen and even to iron
his shirts. Sam in jail thus satisfied most of his Clinton Avenue
needs as well as he did on the street, while at the same time, as
never outside the jail, he even managed to save a little money. "If
those guys worked as hard on the outside as they do in here,"
one inmate observed, "they'd be millionaires."

To complete the scene, one day in flounced a certain Billie
Washington. A flagrant homosexual, he was charged with murder after he and his friend Puddin', dressed as women, lured a
white man into a South End project stairwell to robbery and death;
they were both thrown into the briar patch of Albany County Jail
to await trial. "Billie was a real flaming *punk*!" said Sam. He,
along with his dear friends Puddin', also black and willowy, and
Billy Jo, "who had long blond hair and tits," served as the tier's
females. Paul recalled, "It was strange having him around. Talking to him was like flirting with a woman. Powerful stuff he laid
down, those big soulful eyes. Man, I started to wonder." Although
neither Paul nor Sam availed himself of Billie's sexual services,
Sam did get "her" to braid his hair, just as he did now and then
the women on Clinton. Skillfully braided hair on black men is
cherished as a public signal of the subservient affections of a
woman, and to come forth so coifed in the county jail was a feat
worthy of a Sam Beau!

After awhile, however, Billie became bored with the heterosexual group of whist players and Sam was perplexed to see "her"
roaming far and wide around the tier even after hours, and flaunting packs of jail cigarettes without working. A few weeks later
Billie brought charges against several guards for forcing him to
perform sexual services for them. In the jail, this claim evoked
much amusement, as if anyone had to force Billie down, but it
was widely believed that he might have been servicing some of

the guards in exchange for privileges and cigarettes. Nothing came of the charges publicly but reprimands for the guards were widely rumored.

Then one evening Sam remembers hearing on a radio that the jury was still out, after two days of deliberations, in Billie's murder trial. When Billie returned to the jail, however, just one hour later, there was no longer any question of the outcome. Sam remembers him then as a bent and broken teenager in the awkward age, jilted. Tears glowed amber in his large soulful eyes. He "didn't mean to kill nobody," he said, "never hurt nobody in my life. Honest." But he killed one and left some of the guards at the jail under a baleful cloud, before he went away to the far thornier patches upstate.

As the weather mellowed into warmer spring, Sam spent several hours a day playing handball or basketball in the yard, trying to avoid fights with "young punks" who tried to cause trouble. The rest of the time he played cards, discussed his grievances, and watched television. Sam enjoyed best the Saturday morning cartoons—"I don't know why; they just fascinate me"— and the evening police shows which taught him how to live. In them the winners were always the ones most effectively violent, and the men were always being forced by circumstances back against a wall, where they had "no choice but to fight"— Sam could understand this; as he saw it, it was the story of his life—"no choice but to make a stand"; no choice, sometimes, but to defy the rules and reluctantly take the law into their own hands.

In the television shows, the prisoners also learned that the real culprit was very often a businessman—Horatio Alger become a big shot crook—someone high up, well dressed, slick, often patriotic and moralistic, in executive suite. On Sam's tier, the inmates sometimes gathered on a bunk or around a card table, and talked of Rockefeller. They all knew, for sure, that he had got his money, the old man did, originally, as a member of the gang of Jesse James. I laughed when Sam told me that. But it was clear he believed it. Standard Oil was merely a front for the James brothers. That anyone in America—with the exception of an athlete or rock star—could get rich without stealing was very hard for the folks at the jail to accept. This is a kind of politics which is quite the fashion at Keegan's College and at Harvard.

On weekends Sam was often visited by Bev and Sandra. Visits to Albany County Jail are painful and frustrating for inmates and visitors alike. The speaking tube is about a foot below the thick murky window and transmits the voice in a squawky blur, as hard to hear as the glass above is hard to see through. The inmate seems to be floating in jaundiced fluid and talking on a long distance line from far away.

The result is that one has to decide either to talk and listen, or to look; one can hardly do both at once. Nonetheless, despite all the obstacles, Bev and Sandra managed to flirt enough one day with L. B. to enrage his woman. "You sure you want him?" Sandra said. "I could make him real happy." The woman, a young black, flew at Sandra, slapping and scratching, and Bev piled on, causing the eviction of all three and permanent banishment of Sandra and Bev.

Before she was evicted, Bev told Sam that she was spending much of her time trying to get back at Marianne, and had harassed her until the lesbian had called the police and charged assault. In court, Keegan had warned Bev to stay away and promised Marianne, once again primly attired in a dress, that he would not dismiss the rape charges. After that experience, Bev began attacking other lesbians. For some time, this was more or less the extent of the help Sam was getting from outside the jail.

After Sam had been in jail about a month, however, he began being called downstairs on Wednesday evenings to talk with Nini. At first, they scarcely recognized one another: Sam looked different and somehow menacing; Nini had never struck Sam as more than just another of the many stylish women who worked in Historic Preservation. But after a time they relaxed together and Sam began getting some good news. He learned that several members of the office staff were ready to give character testimony in his trial, and he learned that Joe Harris, Albany's Chief Public Defender, had decided to take personal charge of his defense. Nini also brought him some artist's equipment—sketch pads, erasers, and colored pencils—and the office was much amused a week later to see the result, a number of rather stilted-looking nudes. "Somebody up there ought to check out who it is Sam has got with him in his cell," Jack Waite suggested.

Sam was encouraged by Nini's visits. Back on the tier he found himself talking more freely about his own case and winning much sympathy from the other prisoners. Sam's card playing also had improved and he was regularly winning cigarettes. What he missed was letters—"letters make the bars go away"—he still didn't get many. L. B. got two or three a week from his girl, and a total of over one hundred cards, but Bev wrote only about ten times. Other people on the tier, including "college dude" Glen, would read. A "book fiend" Glen was, according to Sam, who remembered him spending several days on laws. L. B. favored the more visual arts of *Playboy* and skin books.

One day, after about two months in jail, Sam's discussion of his case took a new turn. He was standing by L. B.'s cell, talking about Marianne once again, as L. B. wearily leant back on his bunk, nodding patiently. He had plenty of time, and he would want to discuss his own case soon enough. Then L. B. suddenly had an idea. "She was a blond girl, huh, with those thin metal granny glasses?"

"Yes," Sam said, "that's what I been sayin'."

"Short. Dirty blond hair, curled up sometimes. Calls herself Marianne. That's right," L. B. said.

"You got it," Sam said without enthusiasm.

"She's nothin' but a whore," L. B. said, sitting up in the bunk excitedly.

"I been tryin' to tell you that for two months," Sam said. "I paid for her."

"Yeah, Sam, I know what you been sayin'. But if this girl is who I think she is, she used to work for Eddie. Eddie pimped for her. And she's a fuckin' witch," said L. B.

"A witch?" Sam asked.

"Yeah, she used to live with my old lady, on State Street. She used to have garlic hanging all over to ward off evil spirits," L. B. said. "Hey, I bet you could get Al Love on the other tier to testify. I know for a fact he paid to fuck her."

"And your old lady, would she be a witness?" Sam asked.

"Shit," said L. B., "we'll have everybody testifyin' about that broad. It'll be a fuckin' This Is Your Life. She'll wish you never went near Albany County Jail."

L. B. and Sam slapped hands. It was the first big break in the case. But they did not know that under New York State Law the previous sexual history of the plaintiff might not be admissible in court.

12

Clyne's Court

Monday June 23, 1975, dawned warmly at Albany County Jail, but Sam turned over on his bunk and resisted the day-breaking bells. It was the day of the trial and his mind throbbed with the threat of twenty-five years in prison. It would be decided—it would begin to be decided, the jury would be chosen—on that morning in June. "Get up, Sam, time to face the music" said a guard outside his cell. "I hope it's soul music," he said. "No. Judge Clyne's music," the guard said.

John J. Clyne was a name that struck fear in the minds of all Albany's court-bound men. Tall, thin, tight-lipped, nasal-voiced, with eyes that sometimes squint in a demonic V behind owlish glasses, from a small face deeply creased, sinewed, and shadowed; Judge Clyne, demonstratively impatient with the strategies of defense, but willing to remand to the county jail for contempt a D.A.'s witness who balks or recants on the stand; Judge Clyne, heavy in his sentencing of what he always calls, as if insects, the defend-*ants*; Judge Clyne, faintly hunched in his black swirling cape, slinking stride and posture; a man often dismissed by critics as a "narrow-minded" product of a "political machine."

It was Clyne, for example, who gained the murder conviction of Billie Washington from a reluctant jury that had resolved on a count of first degree robbery but seemed to balk at the ver-

133

dict of murder. Clyne refused to accept the partial result, even after jury deliberations, which ran from 2:30 on a Wednesday afternoon for 11 ½ hours, until 2 A.M. in the early reaches of Thursday, and then, beginning the next morning at 9 A.M, churned on all day until 5 P.M., all without agreement on the charge of murder. Between 5 P.M. and 7:40 P.M., someone on the ten-woman, two-man jury broke down, as perhaps the judge expected.

Clyne's special role reaches even into the office of the city's Public Defender. There, prominently displayed on the wall, is one of the Judge's campaign posters. "He understands," is the slogan below his swarthy features. On the picture, someone has disfigured his close-cropped head with a pointed beard and horns; no one in the office has ordered the poster removed. Clyne's devil-decorated countenance serves to rouse the defense teams as they head off to do battle in County Court.

No less does the reputation of Clyne and his harsh sentencing concentrate the minds of prisoners, like Sam, awaiting trial at Albany County Jail. In the jail, in fact, one is given the distinct impression that Clyne's chief professional regret, which accounts for his consistently dour demeanor, his air of frustration and failure as he faces a world of insolent defend-*ants* and unrequited crimes, is that he is denied in New York State the more lasting relief and solace of imposing capital punishment.

Nonetheless, there is little evidence, for all his sneering, all his pretense of toughness, all the hostility he arouses, that he is significantly harsher or more draconian than judges who smile. It is possible that in his own way he is more honest and fair. It is possible, after all, that he is hated merely for doing without cosmetic graces the job that the good crime-fearing citizens of Albany, of all sexes and races, want him to do.

In any event, when Sam was brought before him on June 23, Clyne did not look down with an avuncular smile, nor, on the other hand, did he seethe ferociously. Sitting on the bench under the marble-faced, roman-numeraled clock, between the furled flag and the crotchety-seeming stenographer, hunched there in his flowing judicial robe, his large, black-framed glasses propped up in his short dark hair and catching the summer light like big tin ears; bringing the court into session in a flat twangy voice, he evoked the feeling of a sly summer-stock Richard the Third, with a self-deprecating hint—that twang, those perched, protruding spectacles—of Mickey Mouse.

By the time Sam entered the crowded, high-ceilinged room, with the rows of white Ionic pilasters along sky-blue walls, his case had already seen much litigation elsewhere—none of it in his favor. First there had been an extended trial before Keegan in police court. Then a grand jury proceeding in County Court. Then a bail-reduction hearing before Clyne.

The pretrial hearings had focused on the testimony of Buddy and Marianne alone. Marianne emerged as an employed beautician (between the police court and the Grand Jury hearing, she got a job at the Loudonville Beauty Room); as an abstemious drinker of grapefruit juice and Kool-Aid on the evening of April 2; as scarcely a participant in Buddy's party (except for a brief siege of repulsing Sam on the couch, she spent much of the evening watching television—"To Tell the Truth," "Concentration," "That's My Momma," and the beginning of "a movie with Peter Graves in it"—before Buddy left her to Sam's devices).

To her previous account of the evening, Marianne added the image of Sam rising from the rape and asking her expectantly, "Well, did you like it?" as if interpreting her screams and protests as the usual female applause for his virile technique. Then she depicted him requesting modestly, "Would you do me a favor? Would you please put back on your clothes?" But she also said that when Sam heard Buddy on the stairs, he boasted: "I'm going to get her, too, you just wait and see." Marianne described Sam as scrambling out to position himself "behind the door, supposedly to get her as he threatened," though from the bedroom where Marianne said she stayed, she could not have seen him. Marianne also denied that at any time between 5:30 and 9:30 P.M. on April 2, she had conferred privately with Buddy. She described Buddy as in terror of Sam when she left the final time, with Sam yelling, "Get out! Get out!" and she said that Sam's attacks left scratches on her arms, black and blue bruises on her arms and legs, and purple bands on her neck.

Buddy's testimony in the previous court proceedings was less direct and coherent but it did not radically diverge from Marianne's. She admitted accepting in fear $5 from Sam to take a walk "cause he had a record of cuttin' a lot of people," and "if I didn't leave, there would be a lot of trouble." But she said she did not ever leave the building because of the terrible screams above.

Cross-examination of the two women failed to shake any of their key contentions. Buddy expressed mystification at what had happened to the bottle of vodka, since Sam had been drinking only whiskey and beer with her. But it was possible that someone other than Marianne had drunk the vodka. Buddy also refused—on muddled grounds of self-incrimination—to answer the question, "Did you ever employ the complainant as a prostitute?" This was a crucial moment in the pretrial proceedings, but the question was so confused by objections from the D.A. and counterobjections from the defense, that it remains uncertain whether Buddy ever understood what was going on. She may not have known the possible implications when she accepted Keegan's advice that she consult a lawyer before answering. Nonetheless, her testimony can be read as resort to the fifth—refusal to answer on grounds of possible self-incrimination—when asked if she had ever pimped for Marianne.

Buddy's account contained one demonstrable untruth and one highly questionable claim: she denied trying to give back Sam's $5 bill when she came in with the police (the police saw the attempt and she admitted it after the trial); and she said she had returned to Sam his change for $20 after her trip to the liquor store for the beer and pint of C.C. (Sam began the party with at least $50; was arrested with less than $10). She also provided intriguing details of atmosphere. She said she was "havin' a fine time, talkin' with everybody there"; she described Sam in the kitchen helping her with the rice and the roast; and as if fearful that her good repute as a Clinton Avenue hostess was being besmirched in the trial, she firmly denied "any physical conflict between any parties at the house at any time from 5:30 to 9:30 P.M." She ascribed to Sam merely a "nasty voice" in ordering her out. This testimony tended to undermine both her claim of near terror as she was driven from the apartment and Marianne's descriptions of early tussles on the couch with Sam.

All Buddy's testimony, however, was so swamped by her tales of tippling that it is hard to understand how she or Sam could remember much of anything. Phil Russell and Sandra—neither of whom testified in early proceedings—both said later that their drinking was confined to a small shot of whiskey and a beer apiece during the fifty minutes or so that they spent at the party. Billy Grant did not finish a beer. Most of the purchased alcohol, therefore, was drunk by Sam and Buddy, and presumably, Marianne.

As the trial began, though, Marianne's story remained essentially intact. Buddy's corroboration was hazed with drink, but strong on atmosphere and screams. The prosecution's case was to acquire powerful new support as the days passed. Presenting the arguments, moreover, would be La Passionaria of Albany prosecution herself—the perfect foil for the sinuous glooms of Clyne—the clear-eyed and candid glamour of Assistant District Attorney Diane Dubiac.

With her dark auburn hair brushing with graceful curls her fine straight shoulders, her lips full and luminously red, her carriage elegantly erect, her body at once lithe and richly feminine, her step brisk and commanding despite lofty high heels, her diction clear, her manner mostly confident and unruffled, her suit slate blue and sleekly styled, with the pink blossom of a gay bow at the neck, when Sam first saw her, from his chair facing the dour judge, all he could think was, "Wow—she sure as hell ain't cooked." But maybe, after all, *he* was.

She was a woman for whom the prosecution of Sam could be a fitting venture. From a relatively poor family in the industrial suburb of Green Island, with no man in the house from infancy, when her father died, she had always had to make it on her own in the footsteps of a mother who for nearly two decades did not remarry. Diane breezed through the State University course in business education in three years, working in her spare time occasionally as a filing clerk. She is recalled by friends as a "vivaciously incompetent filer" and a woman obviously preoccupied with other things.

Thus Diane Dubiac did not need feminism to tell her she had to succeed by her own efforts alone. But she must have welcomed the feminist message that the fault was not hers but the male-ruled world's that women like her have to struggle. Then single and thirty-three, she had created by herself an independent role and style. In her twenties she had run for the state assembly from Colonie, and her veteran Republican opponent, who won handily, remembers her as an active, articulate candidate, both dynamic and dignified. Now appointed to be Assistant District

Attorney, she had developed into a spectacular forensic performer, an elegant and commanding woman, who brought to bear all the wiles and radiances of an actress on this stage—Clyne's court—that she had come to know and master.

Moreover, as a woman often alone in an era of feminist fashion, as the first woman in the county to be named Assistant D.A., and as a favorite of local women's groups and a member of NOW, she had come rather to specialize in rape cases. She had served as a consultant in the founding of the Rape Crisis Center. She had chosen this one—Sam's case—and she believed in it. It was hers, and she seemed in her prime, ready and resolved to put Sam Beau away.

Sam, however, would not go easily. Joe Harris, his public defender, was perhaps the city's most eminent defense lawyer. A leading Albany Democrat, a year later he would be elected judge, to take his place with Clyne on the county bench. Though Harris faced no opposition in the general election, he raised large sums of money and conducted a lavish campaign, speaking more widely and eloquently than any other Albany politician of the period.

Harris was a large shambling bear of a man, perhaps 6′ 4″, who unlike Diane Dubiac never seemed to have his papers, or his arguments, exactly under control. He was anything but stylish, favoring plaid jackets, thin gray ties, and whatever shirt happened to be at the top of the pile. (As judge, he is the best argument for judicial robes as a way of raising the dignity of the bench.)

Harris's hair was gray and thinning, his eyebrows dark, his eyes peering from shadowy hollows. He was a "gut liberal," with the emphasis more on the ample gut than on the liberalism, which was the vintage and texture of his tailoring. Unlike Diane Dubiac he did not appear to keep up with the latest fashions in social thought. He had simply never heard, for example, that a refined and liberal-minded man would never allow to pass his lips—in public reference to women who chance, in the enlightened exploration of their sexuality, to become female homosexuals—the word "lezzies." Unlike Diane Dubiac, and like Judge Clyne, he did not know the difference between the words "flaunt" and "flout": both men spoke of "flaunting" the law. Unlike Diane Dubiac he let his voice and syntax drawl and slur. In addition, he clearly understood that the effective prejudice in an American jury today is in favor of, not against, a young black man like Sam. Indeed, Harris might not always have been fair in fighting his fair lady opponent, but he could sense the real weaknesses of the prosecution and exploit them as well as any lawyer in the city.

Thus the battle was joined: the old liberalism against the new, in a courtroom governed, in the person of Clyne, by the old morality. It was a contest that seemed at times to pit the old demagogy against the new moralism: the view of the courtroom as an arena for the architectural display of evidence and law, a *case*; and the view of the courtroom as a democratic crucible of emotion, in which the public, through the jury, expresses its view of the currently applicable bounds of behavior. This is not to say that the lines would be so clearly drawn; that Harris would not effectively attend to evidence, or that Dubiac was not a grand master at playing to a jury. But in general, Dubiac would coolly apply herself to building a stable structure of argument, and Harris—working in that treacherous gulf between the letter of the law and the spirit of the time—would huff and puff, sweat and storm, and try to blow the damn thing down.

Sitting in front of the courtroom at the beginning of the first day, Sam looked up at Clyne and saw first his long artist's fingers weaving themselves sinuously together in a way that suggested to him a pit of snakes. He felt his stomach turn, his palms perspire, his heart pound, and he remembered the words of his gym teacher many years before: he took four or five deep breaths and felt himself relax. But as the jury formed, with staid white, middle-aged men succeeding elderly retired women with little round faces and stout bodies, with not an interruption in the parade of the Caucasian middle class, Sam's fears rose again. A black man and a white woman—rape—those words would inflame their minds; how could he possibly win? "I gotta get out of here," Sam said to himself in the old familiar way and then smiled grimly when he remembered where he was and saw the fat, gun-laden sheriffs at every door.

Then he turned and saw Nini and his mother behind him in a front row of the court; and Harris asked him whether he would pass on a tall, white-haired man who worked as an unemployment claims investigator. Sam didn't have the slightest idea. "Sure," he said. No objection, Harris said. Sam had influence; he had friends around; he might be safe.

That night back at the jail, inmates crowded round to encourage him and harangue against the wiles of lesbian whores. "They all hated Marianne for what she had done to me," Sam said. "It was like she had done it to them." When he left the next morning, they all called out good luck, or gave him deep soul handshakes and slapped his back. Even the guards joined in the warm wishes.

But all too soon, Dubiac was in the courtroom again, building her case remorselessly. An Albany police matron, Helen Di Domenico, testified that while at the police station describing the incident, Marianne vomited several times. Dr. Ajay Maitra, the young Indian gynecologist who examined Marianne afterwards, said he found evidence of sperm and detected bruises on her right breast and on the front of her neck. The bruises were small and the doctor admitted to Harris that he did not know what had caused them. But bruises were bruises, evidence of violence, not of smooth business between prostitute and client.

Then Diana Smothers, a tall, gangly, young black woman from the second floor of the apartment at 925 Clinton Avenue, said she heard screams that night when Buddy came to her door—screams that surely echoed in the minds of the jurors long after Harris secured her admission that screams were not unusual at all in that third floor apartment; screams that surely survived in their memories despite Miss Smothers's agreement that it might even have been a James Brown record playing upstairs.

The most dramatic moment was the arrival on the witness stand of Marianne's mother, a respectable lady in the midst of a nightmare, fighting back her tears. Her child had been battered and bruised, she said, when she saw her that night at the hospital. Dubiac showed her pictures. The woman said, sobbing, yes, that was her daughter. Mrs. Simberg, Sam sensed, in her neat brown suit, graying brown hair, routinely made-up face, cultured pearls, would fit without the slightest friction into one of those square boxes where the jury sat. A chilling thought.

Then Marianne herself came to the stand in a blue dress, and again she told her grim story, while Diane Dubiac framed her questions slowly and carefully, dwelling on the innocence of Marianne and the brutality she suffered. Dubiac worked systematically, in the jargon of the court: "Did there come a time, Marianne, when you went into the bedroom?"; "What, if anything, happened?"; "Did there come a time?" "Use his exact words, Marianne." And Marianne was answering: "Grapefruit juice"; "To Tell the Truth"; "nothing to do with him totally"; "repulsed him"; "pushed him away"; "feeling ill"; "robe, shirt, vest, jeans, underwear"; "fuck me"; "kicked him"; "threats"; "cut"; "penis"; "strangling"; "choking"; "screaming"; "rape"; "Elizabeth too." The words and images piled up, quietly and clearly evoked by Dubiac: Marianne was an innocent woman who had been "horribly and brutally raped." What could Harris do? Sam wondered.

He could ignore those images and come to the heart of the matter. "Miss Simberg, have you ever practiced witchcraft or voodoo?"

"Objection," cried Dubiac in her resonant tones.

"Sustained," roared Clyne.

"Miss Simberg, do you know the meaning of the term 'goofer dust'?"

"Objection, your honor."

"Objection sustained. The jury is ordered not to consider the question."

"Miss Simberg, is it true that you go to cemeteries and sit there all day long?" And so on, with Clyne's anger rising to cold rage and Dubiac leaping repeatedly to her feet. Then Harris changed his tack: "How many beds are there in the third floor apartment at 925 Clinton Avenue?"

"One," said Marianne.

"You have said you often stay overnight in this apartment. Where do you sleep?"

"Objection," Miss Dubiac said.

Harris and Dubiac both approached Clyne. The defense said it was urgent to establish the relationship between the two women. Clyne frowned long, and then assented. Dubiac walked back from the bench tossing her handsome tresses in frustration and annoyance, but all the same looking defiantly sure of her ultimate triumph. Harris proceeded with his line of questioning.

"Where do you sleep, Miss Simberg?" he asked.

"In the bed," she said.

The entire courtroom was hushed in expectancy as Harris launched his irrelevant but nonetheless crucial inquiry.

"Miss Simberg," he asked, "have you ever had sexual relations with your friend Miss Goodhue?"

"Yes, I have," she said quietly. In its way, it was a noble moment, the statement of a hard truth and the expression of a rare trust in the adherence of a trial by jury to the evidence that pertains to the charge. It also might be considered as a sign of a high credibility: "If she would not lie about lesbianism, why would she lie about rape?" Diane Dubiac would later ask the jury. Harris, however, pushed on, with a series of accusatory questions about prostitution, all denied by Marianne or disallowed by Clyne, that indicated the defense's plans for the rest of the trial.

Buddy then came to the witness stand. Wearing a pink dress, she did not look obviously masculine, obviously alien to the world of black women of her size and corpulence, common on Clinton Avenue. Under Dubiac's artful questioning, the case was yet again constructed. The party, the drinking, Marianne's indisposition, Sam's fierce demands, the screaming on the stairs, the call to the police. Buddy seemed a good witness.

But she and Harris immediately established some strange rapport: the ruddy-faced lawyer whom everyone called Irish, despite his Jewishness, had had a drink or two in his time, and under his questioning, Buddy chose to regale him with common experiences in the realm of booze. The two women, so it turned out, had spent not only the evening but also the afternoon consuming drink. About the party of the evening, Buddy first denied it was a party at all; then as she recounted the tippling and fun, defined her own capacity for beer and Canadian Club—bringing a smile even to the face of Judge Clyne—and as she listed the six persons who ultimately came, she had to acknowledge to Harris that a party it was: a party of liquor and music and dancing, a party at which money repeatedly changed hands, always moving from Sam to her, rarely back. Then she denied that she had tried to sell Marianne's body, but like Marianne, she did not deny the lesbianism. When Harris asked Buddy if she had ever had sexual relations with her friend, she replied: "Not totally." Buddy had had a good time with Harris, but Harris had had a good time too.

The third day was the day of the defense. Harris chose to put Sam on the stand. Sam tried to remember what he had been told: "Glance at the jury from time to time, but do not stare";

"remain calm and polite no matter how angry or untrue Dubiac becomes"; "speak slowly and clearly"; "mention the Marines and Vietnam." Sam had been frightened and nervous throughout the trial. But somehow "when I began getting the questions, I felt calm and cool and ready. Like everything would be all right. Like I knew all the answers and no one could break me." Indeed, the newspaper reported that he "was on the stand for about two hours and appeared composed the entire time."

The story seemed simple prostitution. "I was sitting on the sofa and Marianne came over and sat close to me . . . she was laying with her head in my lap and then she got a drink and laid down with her feet in my lap. We were kissing for awhile. Later she got up and went to the bathroom. She said she had to throw up.

"About ten minutes later she came out of the bathroom and went in the bedroom. I gave Buddy some money to go get some more whiskey and a six pack of beer. . . .

"Marianne called me into the bedroom and asked me to lay down on the bed with her. We were kissing and hugging and she asked me if I wanted to buy a trick. I said 'sure' and she said she wanted to get rid of Phil and Sandra and I'd have to ask Buddy if it was all right, make arrangements with her.

"I came out and spoke to Phil and she spoke to Sandra and they left. About fifteen minutes later, Buddy came back and I asked her if Marianne was her woman. She said yes and I asked her if she was selling it.

"Elizabeth said yes, but she usually only sold to white guys for $20 or $25. I told her I only had $10 and she said that was all right. I gave her the $10 and she said she would speak to Marianne.

"Phil and Sandra came back. I was in the living room and Buddy spoke to them in the kitchen and then they left. They were only there for about two or three minutes. Then Buddy went into the bedroom and later I looked in and saw her there on top of Marianne and they were kissing. So I waited in the living room. After awhile Buddy came out and said that for $5 more she'd get lost. I hesitated but I gave her the money.

"When Buddy left I locked the door and went into the bedroom and asked Marianne if she was ready. She said 'yes' and we had sex for about fifteen minutes."

Sam had answered Harris's questions with quiet and earnest confidence. There were gaps and inconsistencies and no accounting for bruises or screams. But it worked well enough. It seemed that he was born to testify. He seemed handsome, precise, careful, sincere. He only forgot to mention the Marines. Harris would make up for that error later.

First, however, Sam would have to face cross-examination by Diane Dubiac.

By this point in the trial, Dubiac had reached a pitch of coolly suppressed anger that could even be termed a rise in consciousness. She had a new fire in her voice and flush in her face. Though it lent her an intense feline beauty, it also led her into a dangerous temptation: an assurance of righteousness that would offend the jury if it did not share her risen knowledge. To Diane Dubiac, with her command of the law and her respect for its traditions, with her deeply inculcated sense of professional tradition and integrity, it was obvious beyond query that all the talk about lesbianism and prostitution was completely irrelevant—even outrageous if it were true that Sam had taken intercourse with Marianne without her consent. Rape is rape, whether it happens to the Happy Hooker or to the Flying Nun. In theft, there might be varied charges and levels of criminality dependent on the value of the items stolen. But in the law of rape, there was no scale of values, no concept of grand larceny (the act of a stranger against a little girl?) or petty theft (the ill-compensated entry into the grand central plaza of a working street walker); no sense that certain forms of rape are less culpable than others. The law is clear—rape is rape—and Diane Dubiac felt sure in her righteous indignation. She launched on an attempt to destroy Sam's credibility.

Pacing back and forth before the stand, striding up within feet of the witness to ask the question, then walking reflectively away to frame the next, dramatic in her concentration and assurance, Diane Dubiac scored point after point against Sam.

"Mr. Brewer, is it true that you have been known regularly to hit your common-law wife Beverly Burden?" "Objection," Harris would bellow. "Sustained," Clyne would fiercely chime. But as much as Harris's questions to Buddy had done before, Dubiac's now seemed to have served to discredit Sam. Then she went on and got him to admit inconsistencies in his testimony, to concede his record for fighting, to acknowledge the possibility of his lying. It was a brilliant feat of cross-examination, and it deeply shook Nini and the other observers from the office. But on the other hand, it offered an extended display of Sam at his best: direct in his answers, pleasing in his demeanor, intelligent but not obtrusively clever in his manner of speaking.

There were other witnesses for the defense. L. B., for one, down from the County Jail: Marianne's rep? "Reputation as a prostitute," isn't that right? Inquiring brows.

Eddie: "yessir, Albany County Jail." Marianne? A common prostitute, no doubt about it. "That's her general reputation in the community, that is, sure."

Leone: Absolutely. Furrowed brows, studious, thoughtful look. "Her genul reputayshun, I'd have to say, you askin' me. A prostitute. Right." He nodded.

Then Isaac Cram. About seventy years old, with a voice too low and crabbed to hear, but according to Harris, and why not?, he said that Marianne had a bad reputation for promiscuity, in the general community, that was.

Then came L. B.'s old girlfriend, who spoke as if in an English recitation class; no problem hearing her: "As far as I know, her general reputation in the community is bad for prostitution." ... "Yes, I said a bad reputation." "Thank you, Miss Spence." "In the community." "Yes, Miss Spence, thank you."

Sandra Collins was next. Diane Dubiac later confessed she was glad to see her because she had been worried that Sandra was the pretty and very credible-looking girl sitting next to Sam's mother at the front of the room listening to all the other testimony. Finally Dubiac had demanded that all scheduled witnesses leave the courtroom and Harris had agreed. Phil Russell was not scheduled but he got up anyway. Dubiac glared at the girl in the front row next to Sam's mother. During a recess, she asked the girl fiercely if she was Sandra Collins. It was Nini.

Sandra had tried to find decorous clothes for court. She wore a bra and eschewed her usual décolletage. But her only full-necked jersey was much too tight and her breasts swooped out with all their usual drama. She wore a short skirt, fashionable a few years before, which happily exhibited her fine thighs. She had her usual expression, sullenly sensual. As she spoke, she leaned back and folded her arms below her bosom complacently.

She was potentially a key witness—the only person other than Buddy who had actually attended the party and was available to testify. She was very good, perhaps too good. Marianne had been making out with Sam on the couch; then after an hour or so, she asked Sandra and Phil to leave in order to allow her and Sam "to turn a trick." The next day, Sandra said, she met Buddy and Marianne at a bar and took Marianne aside to ask her "why she had put Sam in jail for rape." According to Sandra, Marianne replied that "it wasn't my fault, Buddy made me do it."

Sandra told her story with cool aplomb and responded to Dubiac's questions with a quizzical, insolent frown. Dubiac suggested that there was a conflict between Sandra's account and Sam's statement that it was he and Buddy who arranged her and Phil's departure. Sandra managed for several minutes to misunderstand the question in several different forms. Dubiac finally gave up in disgust. Sandra shrugged, memorably thrusting forward her chest. Then Dubiac asked if it were not true that she had visited Sam several times at the jail. "Yeah," Sandra said, "he's a friend of mine." "And did you not prepare testimony then?" "No," Sandra said.

Overall, Sandra managed at least to break even with Dubiac. But there was an air of slight unreality in everything she said. She seemed a little too pat and sure in her answers. In her testimony, that murky evening became too clear and calculated a case of prostitution used in order to take Sam's money and set him up for an arrest. Conceivably it was true. But it failed to convince Sam's best friends, and might not have much impressed the jury.

Sandra and Dubiac confronted each other as bearers of two modes of white female power. Dubiac with brains and style and accomplishment; Sandra with pure sensual magnetism, sinister in its radiance but nearly as strong in its way as Dubiac's learning and status. As the exchange approached its conclusion, Sandra seemed to be looking down at her antagonist with something close to raw contempt. Dubiac responded with a more refined and artificial disdain.

Finally Harris called four witnesses to Sam's good reputation and character. After resorting first to the street and the jail to discredit Marianne, he turned to the high reaches of the Mall to exalt the reputation of Sam. Lined up in the hall outside were

Kathleen Kearney, a pleasant and intelligent Irish girl from Albany, with long blond hair and an earnest and believable tone of common sense and skepticism. She had worked beside Sam in graphics for his entire second stint with the state. Next to her was Ed Moore, Sam's boss, middle-aged, well-spoken, and eminently respectable. Also there was Ron Santz, Sam's old gym teacher, crusty and sincere. But the prime exhibit would be Mark Lawton, then First Deputy Commissioner of the Department of Parks and Recreation, a top floor man at the Mall, the kind of official that any jury from Albany, New York, would understand and appreciate.

Ed Moore went first. He gave his name and position as head of the graphics division, and Dubiac rushed to the bench, calling forth her objection. "He just knows the defendant at work," Dubiac said; "he can't testify to his reputation in the general community." Clyne sustained the objection and the testimony was disallowed. But Harris went through the others anyway, including Santz, who was shown to have no knowledge of Sam since 1968, and Lawton, who probably, despite himself, had seen all too much of Sam in his habitat, but was disallowed anyway.

Harris, however, did get to display Lawton on the stand long enough to elicit several times a statement of his official status.

"You said Commissioner Lawton?"

"No, First Deputy Commissioner of Parks and Recreation."

"Well, Commissioner, tell me. . . ."

"No, *Deputy* Commissioner." And so on.

At that point, late on Thursday, the defense rested. Diane Dubiac, however, decided that if Sam's character was to be the issue, she would call testimony from the police. Clyne agreed to extend the trial for another day and the defense faced the prospect that the last testimony the jury would hear before summations would be policemen telling of Sam's "assaultive character" with women and of his reputation in the community for violence.

The next morning, however, only one policeman turned up. He said Sam had been arrested for fights five times during the previous two years. But he admitted that this record was not at all unusual for a young man on Clinton Avenue. The second policeman, who was to tell of Sam's reputation for assaulting Beverly, did not show up, though Clyne recessed the court in order to wait for him, while Dubiac paced anxiously back and forth. Then she leant back onto the table on the left side of the courtroom with her arms straight behind her, and glanced repeatedly toward the door. Her eyebrows twitched up and down. The man didn't come. Sam was fully aware of what was at stake. He told Harris that the cop could really tell some heavy stories. Dubiac muttered something to a court official and walked out to look for her witness. Five minutes later, after Clyne had reconvened, she returned, angrily hurling a pile of papers down on the table. Clyne looked up in annoyance. Once again he conferred with Dubiac. Finally, he announced that the summations must begin.

"Whew," said Sam. Harris wiped the sweat from his brow, walked over to the jury and began his speech. After the usual pleasantries for the jury, he launched his argument. "The key to this whole case," he said, "is was it rape? Was it simple prostitution? Or was it a setup? . . . Reasonable doubt not only permeates this case, but there is no doubt at all it was a setup."

At this point, the lost policeman walked into the back of the courtroom, only three minutes too late. Diane Dubiac shook her fists in undisguised anguish.

"Miss Goodhue had a motive since she and Brewer had had an argument some weeks earlier. . . ." Dubiac trilled her objection, and Clyne sustained it, but Harris was on his way.

"Everybody agrees on one thing. There was a party, full of drinking. But after that nobody seems to be sure of anything much until the police came. They bought a lot of booze and after that all we have is a lot of obvious reasonable doubt," he said. "The key prosecution witnesses have a reputation for lesbianism and prostitution . . . money changed hands all through the evening. . . . Sam began the evening with $140 and ended with $9. *He* didn't go out. The prosecution has not told us where the money went. . . . The two women saw Sam with the money. They knew where the money was. They wanted it. They set him up.

"Screams and bruises. The prosecution talks of screams and bruises. But the prosecution's witness, herself, living downstairs in the building, testified that screams and fighting were usual in that house. I guess that's how some people make love." Dubiac objected continually during Harris's recitation, and Clyne usually sustained. But Harris would only retreat momentarily before launching another salvo. "The prosecution questions the credentials of our witnesses to the character of the complainants, calls them criminals. Well I say that to get the reputation of a streetwalker you've got to talk to street people. In a case like this you can't expect the witnesses to come in business suits from Colonie."

Finally he got going on Sam's character—"the only person in this whole cast of characters with a permanent job and no criminal convictions. And for a young black man in Albany to get to be twenty-five years old," he said, "without getting in trouble, is something." Dubiac's objections were again sustained. Harris barged on. "An ex-Marine who honorably served his country. A man admired by his fellows at work. Are you going to believe him, or are you going to believe the dream couple . . . Buddy and Marianne. If you *think,* you will realize there is only one possible answer. You believe Sam and you acquit."

By the end of his speech, Harris was drenched with sweat, but his statement had been effective and in control. Dubiac listened without expression between her outbursts to object. Clyne looked bored, between his routine motions to sustain the objections. Then Dubiac got briskly to her feet and launched her own summation, with all the unruffled coolness of a woman sure of her game, and with all the drama and intensity of a masterly actress who has found her best part.

Once again she went through her architecture of evidence—the doctors, Mrs. Simberg, the police, Miss Smothers; all the testimony, the photographs, the proof of screams and bruises. Her voice was slow, clear, and pleading, her hands out and open, her head forward and respectful. "It *all . . . fits . . .* toge*th*er. The puzzle fits together. . . . Did you see Mrs. Simberg? Did you see that lady? Do you think she came here from Colonie to *lie* to you? She said her daughter was bruised and battered; she said her daughter was hysterical; she said her daughter had been raped. This is testimony that cries out: This must be the truth. And if you believe it, you must convict. It is your duty to convict." She paused, then implored: "But we gave you *more* evidence than that; the *people* gave you more evidence. We gave you a doctor! The testimony . . . of . . . a . . . *doctor* that the woman had been bruised, that the woman had been beaten, that she had sperm in her vagina. It means she must have been raped. And there is only one man who could have done it."

Then Dubiac stood up suddenly straight and shook her fists. "And what did the defense give you? The defense gave you that man"—her lip curled—"and his incredible story of a setup and his incredible friends from jail—criminals who say that the complainant has a reputation as a prostitute." Here she moved into a crescendo of rhetoric, volume, and emotion. "Yet there is no one on this planet who has more reason to lie, no one with less interest in telling the truth, than Mitchell Brewer! But he wants you to think he's the only one telling the truth!

"But there is only one side in this case that makes sense, only one side that holds together, only one side that commands expert medical testimony, and that is the *people's* side.

"Now this is a rape case," she said. "A man doesn't commit a rape in a crowded room. We cannot give you ten witnesses to a rape. We cannot give you a rape on a motion picture screen. But the *people* do not have to remove all *possible* doubt; we have to prove guilt beyond a *reasonable* doubt. And we *have.* We *have.*" She spoke with such pleading emphasis, her hands again up and open, her brow furrowed, her voice so full of the throaty feminine appeal of a woman in distress, alone with her truth and her beauty, captive to a tribe of corrupt and hostile, yet perhaps reachably softhearted men, that even Sam might have wished he could give her what she wanted as she pleaded the cause of all women, against him.

"You cannot walk away," she said. "After looking at the pictures and hearing the testimony, you cannot walk away from Marianne. She has come here and bravely, near tears, told you the truth. She has done her part, the most painful and difficult part. She has suffered anguish and humiliation. Do not fail her now. Now you must do your part. Tell her you trust her. Tell her you believe her. For the sake of *de*-cency . . . for the sake of *just*ice . . . for your own sake and the sake of your women, your community, you cannot turn away coldly from the scene of this terrible crime, this horrible beating, this brutal rape of a woman while she suffered and screamed for help. No one helped her then. But now you can give her *your* help. Give it now. Return, as you must, a verdict of guilt."

Until this point, Diane Dubiac was in command. But then she deepened her voice, enriched her language, and propelled her argument to a level of higher purpose. She spoke not for the people but for the rights of one of America's least understood and appreciated minorities—the community of lesbians.

"This has been a downright nasty trial," she began. "It has been very cleverly twisted about to be a trial of the sexual behavior of Marianne Simberg. . . .

"Maybe you and I don't like lesbians. Maybe you and I aren't homosexuals. But lesbians have rights too. And no one has the right to rape them." She waved her arm indignantly toward the defendant.

"This *man*," she said with a sneer that made Sam cringe. "This *man*," she positively shouted, "thinks he can get away with raping a lesbian because who'd ever believe a lesbian? But Marianne Simberg is telling the truth. Lesbians can be raped. Any woman can be raped. And we must stop it here and now. It is your duty not to make a judgment on her as a lesbian.

"This trial has been crazy. What has happened is that Marianne has been publicly *humiliated* and *disgraced* because she was brutally and violently raped.

"You of the jury must right that wrong now."

She spoke as if it were hardly conceivable to her that a jury, being presented openly with the issue, could decide, in defiance of the law, that lesbians do not have quite equal rights. But that elderly jury of conventional Albany citizens—not peers by far of the ambitious young Assistant D.A.—were not modern men and women. They believed, most of them, that to rape a professed practitioner of strange sexual experiments is an act significantly different and less fully serious, less deserving of high felonious levels of punishment, than to rape a normal heterosexual woman. In the murky world of perversity and prostitution, it may well be that a jury will not enforce the same standards that apply in the world of heterosexual lovers and families. Diane Dubiac had made a serious cultural mistake.

The jury chose to believe Sam. Sam was taken to a caged room in the rear of the courthouse, prepared for a long wait, ready even to sit for days as Billie Washington did. But Sam had hardly settled himself in his cell when he was summoned back to the courtroom to hear, standing and with eyes closed, his fast acquittal.

Sam ran out and embraced his tearful mother warmly. The jury looked on with smiles, as if Sam in that act had vindicated his freedom. One juror, a little old lady with thick glasses, herself began to cry. Harris stopped by and shook hands with Maybelle. She thanked him fervently. "We're just doin' our job, Ma'am," he said. She gave him one of her fragrant hugs, and he detached himself as quickly as he could, waved gingerly, and walked away. Sam walked out onto the street with his mother, into the empty silence of late afternoon on a hot summer day.

They returned to Clinton Avenue, where Sam met some friends on the street near Joe's Grocery and decided to have a party. Sam said he could get some C.C. and beer at Norman's Liquor.

As he celebrated, however, with thankfulness for Harris, and Lawton, and Sandra, and Nini and Kathleen, and L. B. and the others, and even allowed a sneaking glint of gratitude for the humorous, smarmy testimony of Elizabeth "Buddy" Goodhue, he failed to recall the real hero of his victory. More important even than his own unshakably dignified demeanor, more important than the final excesses of Diane Dubiac, was—amid all the rulings upholding the prosecution—Clyne's one key decision in favor of the defense.

Let us return to that vital moment in the trial. Harris and Dubiac had rushed to the bench. Clyne had shown anger at Harris for his long siege of questions on voodoo, goofer dust, and other staples of the defense. Now Harris was demanding that the court allow him to present evidence about the previous sexual activity of the complainant with Buddy, another woman. It was clearly irrelevant and immaterial, as Clyne so often declared about less questionable evidence. Moreover, the state legislature was even then about to enact by overwhelming margins a law that would tend to make such testimony altogether illegal. The new statute would be interpreted as outlawing all testimony about the previous sexual history of the complainant except material relating to intercourse with the defendant or a record of convictions for prostitution. Thus, most of the case for the defense would have been excluded—all the testimony about lesbianism, all the claims about a "reputation as a prostitute" unconfirmed by any pertinent convictions.

The debate over rape law was surely known to Clyne. He surely knew that no court of appeals would ever question a decision to exclude these materials. Nearly everyone in the courtroom expected Clyne to rule, as usual, for the prosecution, as he very often did. Nearly everyone expected him to vent his alleged hostility against young black defend-*ants*. Sam surely did.

But Clyne, for whatever reason, curiosity, or favor toward Sam, hostility to sexual experiment—or was it a simple belief in fairness, a feeling beyond the technicalities of the law that the lesbianism and alleged prostitution of the complainant and key witness are proper concerns for a jury in a rape trial, appropriate indices of character and credibility—whatever Clyne's reasons, it now appears in retrospect that when he said "objection overruled, the defense may ask the question," he resolved the case in favor of Sam and earned his full measure of gratitude that happy evening on Clinton Avenue, a street where gratitude very rarely redounds to the person of Judge John J. Clyne. And if today in America, people like John Clyne are not real enemies of young black men like Sam Brewer, who are his enemies? It is a question worth contemplation beyond the reaches of Clinton Avenue.

13

False Fathers

S am was free again: back at work, back with Beverly, back on the street. Free as he had always been free, ever since his father left Greenville for the service; free to shape again a suitable manhood from the molten substance of a moldless youth.

Fatherless boys all suffer the gnawing void of freedom. At Maybelle's breast he was warmed and fed; in Ella's arms he was cared for, strengthened; in the thrall of remembered teachers, women all, he could learn and love. But none could show him how to be a man. In fact, he sensed, as every boy senses, that his mother's love can finally become a threat if it is not balanced by a father's teaching and example. A girl can evolve, as she grows, into the image of her mother; a boy must break away from that first embrace, move into a frightening psychic space between the sexes, before he finally attaches his identity to a man's. The impulse to break away is as strong as it is shapeless; if the father is not there to give it form, the impulse moves to the street.

In adolescence, the force reaches a crescendo, with male hormones of aggression and sex, growing muscles of strength and movement, bodily changes resolving in no clear role or ritual: impelling only violence. Without strong fathers, random street boys or boys in gangs become the arbiters of manhood, and in the gang these drives are multiplied but not refined, intensified but not matured. Being a man becomes something very different from being an adult.

The fatherless rooms of Clinton Avenue are often crowded with men. But the exposure to men—to "male role models" as they are clinically coined—does not suffice. The boy at large, tottering, then lurching beyond the reach of his mother, needs a man who loves as well as disciplines him. A Fats Botson passing by with an ironing cord, a Joe Lewis one year at Christmas and Halloween, an Uncle Horton for a weekend on the farm, such temporary men cannot give a boy, could not give Sam, the kind of steady compass and ideal—attached and tempered by male love—that will not dissolve in the hormonal heats, among the taunts and challenges, the sexual games and gropings of the gang.

What Sam lacked was the phased and affirmative sense of growth and change from childhood to fatherhood. He lacked knowledge of the links between the love of his mother and the feeling of a father who loves and serves her. The fatherless boy accepts love from women; it is what he expects from them. But he is at a loss in returning it.

Every study of fatherless boys reveals this ignorance of the nature of manly love. On Clinton Avenue, the boys expect to be received by girls as if by mothers. "Nah, I won't pay part of the rent," said one young tough at Albany County Jail. "If she wants me, she'll pay." The father who earns his right to a woman's love by supporting her and helping raise her children has been nearly obliterated by the welfare state.

The most attentive father on Clinton Avenue often seems to be the television set. Incomparably more impressive than school or church, teacher or cop—or the men who furtively frequent the welfare mothers' rooms—is the male image that beckons from the hearth-warming screen: he is a man with a gun, most of the time, or a basketball now and then. He is rich without a regimen of real work, a fighting, swashbuckling familyless man, who swoops into the arms of sultry women and out, talks tough, and is responsible only for a glamourous, drudgeless job. The butt, or villain, much of the time is the businessman.

On Clinton Avenue, I often have the feeling I am in the midst of a TV Western. The kindly, intelligent black man of forty—Benny Williams—tells me in jail that he had no choice but to shoot the man who was approaching his house with a gun; it was the only thing a man could do. A man doesn't leave, or call the police, or hide. He steps out on his front stoop and risks his life to shoot and wound an enemy on the street. Benny was exonerated in this case—self-defense. But he was later, by a horrible accident, involved in Sylvester Smith's beserk sally with a shotgun against the police, and Benny was nearly convicted unfairly of assault largely because of his previous exhibition of frontier manhood with a gun. Men who don't identify manhood with supporting families tend to reduce it to sex and shooting guns, and never shrinking from a fight.

That is the essence of manhood to Sam. It is the essence of manhood in a world without fathers. What is most poignant about Sam and his Clinton Avenue friends is their sense that something is missing in this role they perform: something that has to do with children. They are proud of having children and proudly play with them; Sam baby-sits, and changes diapers. Beverly acknowledges freely that Sam is a good "father." But he still cannot comprehend why none of his women will keep him for long if he does not support them. He cannot comprehend the contempt that every woman eventually feels toward a man who refuses to be a breadwinner.

They sit around, these men, on stoops in summer or on the lawns of Washington Park, in bars in all seasons; they watch hours of television every day. They know what a father does. Sam knows; they all do. But because of welfare, they think it's optional, this business of earning a living and supporting kids, something one does when the *right* job comes, the right women. But they never come. So the remaining agenda of manhood is the knife and gun. "No way," says Sam, says Benny, says Sylvester Smith, "no way I'll let him do that to me, say that to me." There is no idea that there are other ways of being a man.

Joe Lewis, Fats Botson, Will Farmer were Maybelle's men, each available to Sam at best for a matter of months. Even John Reilly could briefly serve. For the last five years—by far too late, too little—his most fatherly figure has been Pops Smith, kind and interested, seasonally at work. Of his childhood men the most vivid was Will Farmer, who took Maybelle and her child North and stood tall for Sam during an impressionable year or so. But Sam lacked the signature, the final tie of paternity, and, lacking it himself, he could hardly inscribe it for his own children.

Dinty's, the neighborhood tavern that figures so often in Sam's affairs, now stands boarded up on the corner of Concord and Orange. The police closed it down late in 1976 for holding fights every Friday and Saturday evening without a permit. Sam was the star—the man whose fists would finally knock out Dinty's bar.

If Sam had pursued elsewhere his alcoholic batterings—his red-eyed rages that blundered on bloody, long past the bell, after even the moment when life and limb were left in the balance—well might Dinty's still be plying beer to its usual clientele: the gaggle of white lesbians, in tight Levis, loose work-shirts left just ajar, breasts untouchably braless, an insult or incitement to all the neighborhood blacks; the men strutting and sweating along tightropes of weekend money and desire, all night long, until one by one they start to fall, to leave, conk out, or fight. The Dinty's scene meant sexuality as a theater; no mothers and fathers allowed. Sam has fought there twenty times in five years; nine times he attracted the police.

It was his ability to draw police that distinguished Sam—his felonious fists. When Sam has a fight at Dinty's, attacking in the blinddozer style of Joe Frazier, someone usually leaves feet first, headed for Albany Memorial by Medicaid ambulance, waking all the neighbors.

Ambulanced, about half the time, is Sam himself. Under a flurry of Sam's fists, flung from a retreatless Frazier crouch, Sam's victims and provocateurs often reach for short cuts; they pull knives. This was what happened on August 3, 1975.

On the surface, it seemed a fairly typical Dinty's scene. At the bar, Alice, a dark-haired lesbian, was sprawled over two seats. To any but the most discerning eye—which would see that her hair was too short for a boy of the 1970s—she seemed to be a white teenaged male, of unremarkable appearance; except that the appearance of any white male lounging at the bar as if he owned it would seem remarkable enough at Dinty's to bring further investigation; and no one was investigating Alice. She was known.

At the beginning of the evening, she talked with Gordon, the owner and bartender—whose height brought his bald head scarcely above the counter—about horse racing, which is the passion of Gordon's life. Later Louise, a heavyset black lesbian, would come in, and Gordon would be left to attend to business. But at this point early in the evening, Alice was chatting with innocuous men.

Alice's voice is a bit high for a boy of her apparent age, and Alice is a girl's name. Under the name of Alice, she could ascend to a most desirable status in the bar. As a woman, she avoided the fights that her territorial claims might have otherwise provoked. As a lesbian, she escaped the sexual attentions that any lone woman would attract. She sat there at the bar like a boy regent. Sometimes she would be joined by others of her ilk, driving most of the neighborhood men to the surrounding tables.

At the tables this evening proceeded a hypertensive argument on the subject of blood pressure and the consumption of salt. Since high blood pressure accounts for perhaps 40 percent of the Clinton Avenue mortality rate, it is an important matter. Phil Russell has a problem of "high blood," and Sam, just twenty-five years old, registers just below the high blood pressure threshold.

The chief source of recognized expertise was a thin, intense black man of light complexion, named "Professor Sidney," who had worked five years at Albany Medical and seemed to know what he was talking about. He declared that the higher one's blood pressure the better. "High blood is good, man. It's low blood you gotta worry about, man."

"That's right, Sidney knows," said a red-napped man at another table. There was a general nodding of assent.

Phil Russell, however, felt somewhat uneasy with Sidney's analysis. As Phil recalled it, his doctor had told him that he had *high* blood pressure and therefore—his memory grew hazy on this point—he should either increase or diminish his consumption of salt. Like Sam, one thing Phil loved was salt. Whether pizzas or hamburgers, spaghetti or salad, the first thing either of them did to any dish was to smother it in salt. Phil would have been relieved to hear that he was "correctly" treating his malady. But he was confused. Perhaps low blood pressure was his problem and salt was making it worse.

Sidney, on the strength of several beers and wide public approval, began getting belligerent. Phil's confusion seemed a challenge to Sidney's status as Dinty's medical authority. He spoke in a tone of stridency and passion that was set either to end the argument or start a fight, one or the other, and he had a pool cue in hand. "I done worked at Memorial for nigh on five years. Don't tell me 'bout salt and low blood. Salt's bad for you, man. It makes your blood lower, all salty and slow, man. You get low blood, Phil, you should cut down on salt, unnerstan'?"

Phil said he thought he had high blood. "Then you're all right. Eat all the salt you want," Sidney said, looking fiercely around the room for dissenters. None arose, so he returned to his beer. Phil Russell lit up a Camel.

In the back room, there was a pool game going on. Sam was among friends. Pops, his mother's man, was there with Billy Grant, Phil's nephew, whom Sam had brought into the Parks Department printing room and who had for some reason renamed himself Bill Crosby. Others on Clinton Avenue often forgot the change, but everyone normally called him Billy anyway so it didn't matter. The key thing was that Sam remembered Billy as a pool player he could easily beat. He bet with Pops on each game.

This evening, however, Billy was having a streak of remarkable luck. Sam would dispose of a few balls, and then Billy would rise to the table and, moving swiftly on the soles of his feet, looking unlike the shambling Billy of the printing room and Clinton Avenue—Good Old Billy—he would shoot with startling grace and efficiency. He won one game after another, smiling bashfully afterwards, as if to say, "Aw shucks, it's jest me, must be some mistake." Each time Sam would just know he could beat him. He had always beaten Billy, and he would place another bet with Pops, all or nothing, until finally all his money was gone. In an hour, Sam managed to lose more than $15 to Pops.

Pops is probably Sam's best friend in Albany. Pops's face lights up with affection whenever he speaks of his tempestuous "stepson." But he was enjoying Sam's predicament that evening. The Billy whom Sam remembered was not the Billy he was playing that night at Dinty's. In the interim, Billy had practiced long and hard and had become something of a shark. Sam had been drinking long and hard and had become something of a flounder.

When Sam finally was wiped out, his mood turned surly and he demanded his money back from Pops. Pops said hell no, he won it fair and square, but he would return him half. Sam said all. Pops noticed Sam was glazing over into one of his beer-eyed fugues. "Calm down, Sam," he said. "I'll give you half your money."

"The Hell you say. You give me all of it." Sam then picked up a billiard cue and stepped angrily toward Pops. By this time Billy, no lover of violence, had beaten a quick retreat to the bar and was behaving as if he had never met Sam and Pops. Gordon, the little bartender and owner, detecting a possible mismatch above, was calling the police. Sam was holding the billiard cue in both hands high in front of him, ready for a hard downward stroke, as he had been taught in the Marine corps in wielding a bayonet. He struck out at Pops once, but Pops was scrambling back and away and the blow missed. In his haze, Sam failed to notice that Pops had pulled a knife. Sam lunged with the stick and Pops quickly dirked, and Sam fell off to the side clutching his stomach. "You stabbed me," he said.

"Shit, I didn't mean to," said Pops, standing stunned with his small silver fishing knife bloodied 1½ inches on the blade.

At that point, the police arrived and rushed forward with handcuffs. First they approached Sam, recoiled at the blood, then saw Pops with the red knife. They ran over, shoved him against the jukebox, and started to apply the manacles. Sam yelled out, "No, it wan't his fault. I won't press charges. Get me to the doctor."

"That means we will have to set this man loose. You understand that," said the officer. "I understand it. Set him loose. Get me to a doctor."

They carried him out to the street where he awaited an ambulance, stabbed by his stepfather and best friend in the city. This was not an unusual event. It was often friends who stabbed Sam, for Sam most often attacked the people he knew. He was stabbed once before in the stomach by one of his favorite women, when he told her he wanted to go out to a party at eleven o'clock at night. She stood at the door with the knife and he walked into it.

After being stabbed by Pops, he was rushed to the emergency room of the hospital, where he was shot with Novocaine that numbed the outside but not the depths of the wound. The doctor, a Japanese man, then inserted tubes in Sam's stomach that hurt far more than the stabbing—first a large tube, then a smaller one. Sam began puking a green fluid. He thought the doctor was killing him.

Then the doctor said he would need an operation. He had a slight oriental lisp and thick glasses. "No," said Sam. By that time Beverly had come and the doctor said Sam would die without surgery. "No more tubes," Sam said. In a little while, another doctor gave him a shot. Sam sank away into sleep. When he woke, he was bristling with plastic pipes. Later he was told that the surgery was exploratory and the tubes were needed merely to infuse the wound with a substance visible on the X ray. He said that he would never trust a doctor again.

It was a day after the first operation, and a few hours before a second one, when I met Sam for that first time, in a near coma, in Albany Memorial, and it was one month later that I first interviewed him with his mother and Nini.

When he left the hospital, he moved back in with Beverly. She was approaching the end of her pregnancy and therefore about to enlarge by some $60 a month her welfare check. Sam did not go back to work. They lived tensely together at 540 Madison Avenue.

Sam stayed away from Pops. He understood why Pops had knifed him, but he still was not at ease with him. Pops was one more man in Sam's life who had betrayed him. It didn't matter that Sam had almost forced the knifing. "I could have been killed, you know that," Sam said.

"Yeah, so could he, I guess," I answered.

"Nah," Sam said with vehemence, "I was just trying to scare him some." Sam seemed to believe it.

"I guess you overdid it," I said.

"Yeah, I guess I did," Sam replied.

After leaving his job with the state, Sam found his life with Beverly increasingly combative. Now bulging with a baby, she did not go out at night with Sandra any more; she stayed home and complained to Sam that he wasn't giving her any money, that he drank too much, that Melissa was difficult, and that childbirth was terrifying. "Oh, I wish the men could have the babies," she would moan. "Never again, never again." Sam would spend most of his time in front of the TV, smoking Winstons and nagging Beverly to give him welfare money for beer.

Finally, after a long evening of bitter nagging and sniping, she told Sam he had to go. It was about 11 P.M. He refused. Beverly called a friend from next door to help her. Sam continued watching television. When the TV shows expired for the night, Sam and Bev argued briefly again: the heavily pregnant Beverly feeling strangely more self-sufficient as she prepared to give him another child, making him yet more unnecessary, still more unable to compete with welfare; Sam feeling ever more angry and alone. It was to be *his* child; yet its arrival would force him out. Was that how it was to be?

"No, Sam," Bev said, "it's just I don't want you around me, drinkin' and stompin' all over the place, not workin' while I got to have this kid. It makes me upset. The doctor say it bad for me to be upset." At 3:30 A.M. Sam left the apartment to return to Clinton Avenue: to move back in on the couch with his mother and Pops.

But as he crossed Washington Park, he decided that this was the end for him in Albany. This moment, that night, was the end of the road: Beverly "upset" and resentful, Pops guilt-ridden and unhappy, Maybelle more and more puling and alcoholic. He would go back for his father, maybe Will Farmer, whom he had heard was in Newark. Maybe he could put something together in New Jersey. Newark, perhaps the single most downtrodden of all American cities, lifted for a moment to Sam as he crossed the Park that night—a beacon, a job, a father—something. He would go to Newark.

He went to Clinton Avenue, woke Pops, and demanded $10 to go South. Pops readily gave it to him. He then trudged back across the park toward Madison, feeling exhilarated, as dawn slowly creamed through the coffee dark. Newark. He could find Will at least; he had an address for Will; Will with the fancy cars and warm feelings for Sam; Will would set him up in Newark.

At 540 Madison, he told Bev he was leaving for good. He piled his stuff into a brown paper bag—two pairs of pants, underwear, two shirts, some socks—and left for the bus station. The bus fare to New York had gone up to $8, he noticed. The bus to Newark would be 88¢. That meant he would have $1.12 left over when he arrived. "I sure as hell better find him," he said to himself, "him or somebody."

There were seven or eight people on the bus. Sam walked quickly to the back, sat down, and in a minute fell asleep. He awoke as the bus left the Lincoln Tunnel and headed through heavy traffic for the bus terminal. As Sam stepped out into the dense fumes of the entry area, among the barging and elbowing travelers, he thought for sure that he had passed the point of no return.

A guard directed him upstairs to the New Jersey lines. Sam soon found himself waiting next to a tall black man with thick glasses and a blue denim suit. Sam asked whether they were right for the bus to Newark. The man said yes. Sam then asked him if he knew Will Farmer. He didn't. Sam sat next to him in the bus and they talked—about Newark and jobs and the dangers of New York City. In the end the man gave Sam a dollar and five cigarettes. Sam would have $2.12 and five cigarettes with which to sustain his search for Will—a man who did not expect him and had not seen him for years, a man he knew only in the rose-ate memories of a grateful child, and in the fragment of an old address: South 10th Street, Newark.

But the encounter on the bus lifted Sam's spirits. "A friendly dude," Sam said, "no roughneck." Sam was relieved because he had heard there were lots of roughnecks in New York and he didn't want to take any chances.

When they arrived in Newark, the man took Sam to an elderly bus company official to get a bus schedule and then disappeared. Sam found himself alone outside a Dunkin' Donuts and a Florsheim shoestore, waiting for the 24-46 bus to South 10th Street.

The bus stopped and Sam got aboard. Having asked the driver to tell him when he reached South 10th Street, Sam went to a seat in the front. The bus went down 11th Avenue for a long way, into steadily more dilapidated neighborhoods, "not missing any of the bumps, an' there were plenty; my head told me 'bout every one. And I was feelin' so hungry I could faint away." Finally he reached South 10th and was left off.

On the corner, he had a sudden sense of the immensity of the city compared with Albany; it stretched off in motley monotony in every direction, broken fragmentary neon signs with missing letters limning a pidgin language of city decay—the my an Navy Sto, Second-Han Shoe, talian Cusin, estaurant, iquors—down a cluttered street, bars, reject clothing shops, "Adult books," fast food outlets, spreading out in a pattern governed by no principle that he could see, without a range of commanding central towers to define the city and his place in it. Going to get a cup of coffee, he asked a man standing by the door how far South 10th extended. The man said five or six miles. Sam gagged and did not think to ask him if he knew Will Farmer. Sam had a cup of coffee and noticed that he had only a few cents more than a dollar left.

All this time, there had been, in fact, near at hand, a cheap, simple, and efficient way to reach Will. It would have been the very first resort of any of us arriving in a strange city. But since leaving Greenville, Sam had only rarely lived in a house with a telephone (Bev had one in her name on Madison Avenue), and he knew few men in the book. Before he called information, he was to walk up and down South 10th Street between 11th and 12th Avenues, growing increasingly desperate, for almost an hour. After standing next to a phone booth for several minutes asking a group of men loitering near it if they had heard of Will or Botson or Joe Lewis, Sam finally thought to call directory assistance. Soon he was talking to Will, who no longer lived on South 10th at all but was then less than a block away from the booth at 547 11th Avenue.

There were three men together, Will, a huge blimp of a man named Deacon, and an old friend of Deacon's, all of whom Sam recognized from his Greenville days. They seemed pleased to see him, Sam thought, though they had heard from someone in Albany that he had been in trouble for rape. "Keep that thar thing in yo' britches," Will had said loudly, and everyone laughed uproariously, including Sam.

It was a three-story house, owned by Will, with a balcony off the second floor. The three men were working together, in a general flow of Gordon's Gin, to repair the top floor apartment for rent. Although plastering work had eluded Will in Newark, he had managed to purchase some dilapidated real estate and was making a living off the rentals. He had two cars: a 1975 brown Ford sedan with a tan vinyl roof and a 1973 green Buick Le Sabre.

Will lived on the first floor with his wife, Edith, and he brought Sam downstairs to be introduced. Edith seemed a bit cool to Sam, and after asking, "How's your mother?" with no interest in Sam's answer, she managed to lure Will into a back room. Sam sat on the front couch in the neatly kept living room, feeling hungry and planning to ask for food when they came out. Occasional spatters of angry words spilled through the door. "Rape . . . police . . . he's runnin' from somethin'. . ." After awhile Will came back, looking somber, and before Sam could say anything, told him that Edith did not want him to stay.

"You ain't in trouble up North, is you?" Will asked offhandedly as they walked out the door.

"Nah," said Sam, "I haven't even talked to the cops, since I got off on that rape case. That's the truth."

"Well, maybe Deke or Fats can put you up for the night," Will said nervously. They went back upstairs to pick up the other two men and then went out to buy essential provisions for the afternoon, chiefly three more pints of gin. When they got into the green Buick, Sam said he could use some food.

"Well, I can't take you to my place," Will said. Then he turned to Deacon. "You got any food, Deke? Sam here is hungry."

"Sure, I got somethin' for him. Sam you want to eat now or later?" Deacon asked.

"I would like to eat now," Sam said.

Will drove by Deacon's apartment and dropped them off, and Sam and Deacon went in to eat.

"Cube steaks be all right?" Deacon asked.

"Yeah, anything would be good right now," Sam said. "Got any milk?"

Deacon had a small two-room apartment with a bed in one room and a couch in the other and a small attached kitchen. He began frying the cube steaks. The sizzle of the grease and the savory scent of the meat made Sam feel at home for the first time in Newark. Although Deacon was living by himself, he had a comfortable apartment, and the presence of this huge man, only slightly aged since Sam had known him in the South, was reassuring. Then Deacon turned from the stove and said, "Hear yo' in real trouble up North."

"Shit, who tol' you that?" Sam said angrily. "Is that Edith?"

"No, jest heard it from a friend of Will's," said Deacon. "I don't mean nothin' by it," he said.

He brought Sam a plate with the two steaks on it.

"I got off. I didn't do it. The jury got me off. I ain't been in any trouble since," Sam said.

"But if you was in trouble," Deacon said, "it don't do no good to run. 'Tickly down here. Ain't no work in this city to speak of."

"I ain't stayin'," Sam said, realizing as he spoke that he would return to Albany that very night if he could.

" 'Course if you want a place for a couple days or so, natchly you could use my couch here. . . . Edith don't like outsiders sleepin' on her upholstery," Deacon said.

"*I know* that," Sam said with a grim laugh. "She's sumthin', that woman. I don't like her," Sam said.

"She all right, you gets to know her," Deacon said. "She sho' sticks up for Will."

"Oh," said Sam, making a circle with his mouth. He finished up the steak and felt better. He took out his last cigarette and lit it.

"'Bout time to be gettin' back," said Deacon.

"I guess so," said Sam.

Will and the others had been sitting in the car outside, drinking gin and orange juice. When Deacon and Sam got to the car, Will asked Deke if he could put up Sam for awhile.

"Yeah sure," said Deacon. "Whatever Sam wants."

"I called yo' stepfather," Will said. "Tommie, he'd like to see you."

"Old Fats down here too?" said Sam. Sam was relieved. He knew he would need money but for some reason he hesitated to ask Will, who seemed nervous around him. Perhaps Botson would help.

They filled their glasses again. Will talked about the different brands of cement mixers, their advantages and defects. He was going to buy one, he said. They talked of the lack of jobs in Newark. Now and again, Will or Deacon would ask indifferently about Maybelle. At 6:30, Tommie Botson came by in a green Volkswagen to pick up Sam. Will seemed relieved to see him go.

Botson said it was good to see Sam again. "I hope you ain't in bad trouble?" he asked. "Don't do to run from trouble."

"My main trouble," Sam said, "is I ain't got no money to get back to Albany."

"I don't got no money," Tommie said. They were silent for a minute. Then he added, "I guess I can get you some though. How much you need?"

"Ten dollars and sixty-five cents," said Sam.

"I think I can find that much," he said. He drove over by his apartment, near a park, and told Sam to wait in the car while he went in.

"Don't want no trouble with the old lady," Tommie said. About ten minutes later, he appeared back at the car. He gave Sam $10.65.

"Thank you," Sam said. "I'll take you to the bus stop," Tommie said.

Before Sam was dropped on the street, Tommie asked him if there was anything else he needed. Sam said, "No." But as he got out, with his brown paper bag still in hand, he thought of something.

"Yeah. Could you call Beverly and tell her I'm coming back?"

"Sure," said Tommie, taking down the number. Then the Volkswagen pulled away from the curb and away, leaving Sam on the corner of 11th Avenue at the bus station for New York. He got back to Albany by Trailways at 1:30 A.M., sitting next to a pretty blond nursing student, "built," who told him all about her boyfriend and blood cells and how she usually didn't talk to strangers. She did not give Sam her name.

Sam walked all the way from the bus back to 540 Madison, stopping only for a ginger ale at the Lark Tavern on the way. When he returned, the woman next door told him that Beverly was out with Sandra and a newly occasional companion, a somewhat unctuous and shifty-eyed black man named Clarence, who had been taking an interest in Bev. But Beverly was without a man when she and Sandra burst in at about 2:30, finding Sam asleep in front of a vertically dissolving television image. Beverly actually smiled when she saw him. She said she had missed him. But, no, she had been in the apartment until nine and had received no phone calls from Newark.

"I figgered," said Sam.

"Why you ask me?" Beverly said.

"Never mind," said Sam.

Never mind, Botson wouldn't call, any more than Will would welcome him, any more than Pops would protect him, any more than his real father, Lewis, would track him down. The men of his past had dissolved behind him; the ties had always broken. The ties. Links of chance and sex and sperm, common needs and destinations—links once hard, then limp, now gone. Sam was left between Maybelle and the street, struggling for a foothold with Beverly, a fatherhold with Melissa and the new child. But how can a man hold?

He got up and fiddled with the TV, then turned it off. They went to bed together, but Beverly took almost all the space. One week later, she would give birth to Daisy.

14

Panama Joe

I don't like this place," Sam had said, standing near the St. Paul Baptist Church in the Carolina moonlight, with unrequited memories aswarm below. We were in Greenville, to "complete" my story. Sam, rebuffed by two girls he had solicited for help in finding old landmarks, old friends, had been staring down on the little scar of earth where once Aunt Ella's house had alone stood firm amidst the pains and losses of his childhood; where she had died, and her funeral, for him, tearless, had stuck, a splinter in his mind, not fully sealed by new flesh, during the agonies of growing up in alien places.

He had decided not to probe those scars, that scar of dirt. It would not do morbidly to restir the past, renew the nostalgic ache, find the crowded cemetery, pray for forgiveness to the worn memorial sliver of stone with the name washing away in the poisoned air from the new factory chimneys, revisit the schoolyards now erased by huge banks and billboards. "It's Good to be Home in Greenville," said a smiling cartoon black boy on the Chamber of Commerce ad that blocked the view from the old A&P. "What's the point?" asked Sam.

He was almost ready to leave Greenville that night, ready to abandon the search for other childhood places that might free his memories from the weight and distortion of the years that followed, piling up in a silt of new pains and perplexities, nearly crushing in him the recollection of love and freedom of a boy on a bicycle riding home to the house on Parker Street: unknowing that Ella soon would go, that all would end, as the house now was gone; Parker Street now half-paved and named Viola Alley. "It ain't no alley," Sam had said, "why they call it an alley?" He had looked up at me with a hard-eyed anger. "There ain't nothin' here for me," he had said. "Everything been done tore down and changed."

"Well, maybe we should go back and get some sleep," I said. "In the morning we might be able to trace down Ella's old bank account, get you some money anyway."

"Money, shit," he said. I had to turn away to hide a smile at my sense that Sam had at last, long after his departure from the state offices, become an advocate, and expense be damned, of historic preservation. "That's right," he said, reading my thoughts. "Why don't they *preserve* some of these buildings?"

In the period before she died, Sam and Ella had made frequent expeditions to a little brick bank, where she had often shown him her dark blue account book with both their names on top. This was his assurance, she had said, that he would inherit her money when she died. Sam's mother had said there were some thousands of dollars in the account at the time of Ella's death, but Maybelle could not remember who took the book. "Maybe those cousins from Philly," she had said. "But that money is Sam's; nobody could get that money but Sam!" Maybelle also thought that Ella had owned at least two little houses. "Them's Sam's too," she said. Sam decided that, after all, he wanted to find out what happened to his money and houses.

"Yeah, we'll look tomorrow," Sam said. We drove back to the Sheraton Hotel where we were staying. "I can get my bearings better in the light anyway," he said.

The next morning we discovered the little brick bank building had been taken over by an ophthalmologist and that, in all likelihood, the bank had been subsumed by either Greenville National or People's, which in turn had been taken over by the First National Bank of South Carolina, or else Bankers Trust. So Sam and I spent hours that morning sitting nervously in plush pastel chairs, while coiffed women in stylish dresses applied to computers for the whereabouts of a fourteen-year-old account, exact number and bank unknown, in the name of Ella King and

Mitchell Brewer. By visits to six different offices, we finally assured ourselves that no such account had survived the convulsive transformations of Greenville finance, which had overflowed all the small remembered buildings, merged and combined and compounded, boomed and blasted into a panoply of skyscrapers and sleek modern cubes, with possibly forgetful computers in their bowels and mock primitive sculptures on fountained plazas in front.

We also visited the courthouse to explore the deed to Aunt Ella's property. As we arrived in back, we encountered what I had understood to be a common Southern scene: a long line of some thirty prisoners chained together, herded by a sheriff. A sombre warning for the Northern visitor, they were being taken through the very entrance that we were approaching. We pushed on by and upstairs to the Registry of Deeds, remarking only that the sheriff was black, and every one of the prisoners white—the harvest, said *The Greenville Piedmont,* of a crackdown on the city's drug traffic. For some sorts of dope, it was rumored, land-locked Greenville is the Gateway to the South.

After much searching with a briskly helpful Southern lady through large leather tomes containing photostats of old deeds, we at last found the properties of Ella King. They consisted of one house on a small plot of land. The place was described exactly as Sam remembered it. But it had been left, so read the deed, not to Sam but to Ella's in-laws, who had sold it to the St. Paul Baptist Church for $1,500. Sam, it was clear, did not have a large inheritance in the South, of either money or land. We had completed in failure the first planned project of our trip.

Sam, however, decided to set out and see if he could find any friends or cousins remembered from his Greenville years. His expectations were not high. He knew that most of his family would be dead or gone now—in Newark or Philly or New York, or in the remaining Greenville cemeteries—but still he thought he should make one further tour before leaving his childhood home finally behind him. With his mother's list of possible survivors in hand, we returned to the car.

We drove back to Parker Street, so Sam could get his bearings again. I had long since reached the conclusion that the old Greenville which Sam remembered had been almost completely destroyed. He had been lucky even to find St. Paul's still standing so near the center of the booming downtown city. I guessed, in fact, that the little cluster of houses had been saved only by some geological peculiarity hostile to big building—perhaps the steepness of the ravine. But Sam still thought that by beginning from Aunt Ella's space, he could eventually work his way back into that childhood world, once traversed so freely on his orange bike.

But the remembered proportions had been so wildly distended by highways and four-lane streets, so outlandishly stretched by skyscrapers, that Sam, returning by airplane to his past, through the smooth and shiny surfaces of the Greenville-Spartansburg Airport, had been forced at first to pursue his childhood image as through a looking-glass, to step dwarfed and disoriented into a landscape vaguely recognized, yet drastically, radically, inscrutably awry.

On our first night we had driven, down highways unknown to Sam, below huge towers, motels, and hotels erected during the last ten years, along new commercial strips nearly unbroken by a franchise name older than Sam's Michelle, all the newly minted neon of market research—Pizza Huts, Burger Chefs, Cash & Carry, Colonel Sanders, Exxon, BP, Stuckey's, Church's Fried Chicken—*déjà vu*'s for Sam, mostly because many of them also fringed Albany.

It had been nearly midnight by the time we found our way, by guidance from firemen, to St. Paul's and Parker Street, the entrance to which, so it turned out, we had been driving past, over and over again, for several hours. But even that night when we had managed to find Parker Street, the little porched bungalows and pinched dirt roads of Aunt Ella's old neighborhood seemed tiny and misplaced, not enough part of a larger fabric to lead anywhere except back to the maze of the new Greenville.

The next morning, however, Sam believed that by an effort of will he could recover the old dimensions, drive from Parker Street the right distances and directions and find the houses and landmarks he sought. So back we drove, down the little hill. Sam spied again the reassuring pecan trees behind the old A&P, now a warehouse, and then saw the old general store. After parking in front of the church, we returned to the little shop.

Still on the front was a bent Doctor Pepper sign, and inside there was sawdust on the floor. We each took an orange Nehi before confronting the fat, elderly lady in the back.

"You know the Reverend Cunningham?" Sam asked, producing a dollar bill from his pocket to pay for the drinks.

"*Old* Reverend Cunningham?" she asked. Sam nodded. "I *did* know him," she said, "couldn't miss 'em. He daid now."

"I used to come from here," Sam said. "Did you know Ella King? I lived with her down by the church."

The woman looked at Sam with greater interest. "I *heard* of her but. . . . "

"How about Brewer, Mrs. Brewer? Or Lewis. Do you know any Lewises?" Sam asked.

"Look I just bought this store a few years ago," she said, "but I'll call Mrs. Mitchell. She goes to St. Paul's, been goin' for years. She might could help." She sent a small boy across the street to get Mrs. Mitchell, who turned out to be a short, elderly lady with marled, graying hair and bright eyes.

She remembered both Ella and Reverend Cunningham well, even recalled a little boy. "You Ella's little boy?" she asked. "No, I was her nephew," Sam said.

She hesitated, then burst out, "You Sam!"

Sam nodded.

"Old Ella, she was crazy 'bout her Sam," she said. Then she took a couple steps back to get a fuller view, "I declare. You done grow'd up big!"

Sam had at least found evidence of his earlier existence; not testimony sufficient for the South Carolina Department of Vital Statistics, perhaps, but nonetheless a sign enough to make him smile. "Yeah, I grow'd," he said. "Now do you know where any of Ella King's relatives might be? Any Brewers or Botsons or. . . . "

The little lady looked sadly down. "Well, Ella she done died," she said and paused, glancing up as if she might have inflicted pain.

"*I know* that," said Sam laughing impatiently, almost rudely.

"Yah, she died . . . so did the Reverend. . . . Her folks . . . her niece, that crazy niece . . . they didn't live roun' here. Lived 'cross town. I *think* they did," she said.

"Where 'cross town?" Sam asked. Her brow creased. "Somewhere roun' Sullivan Street," she said. "Sullivan Street."

"That's it," Sam said, "Sullivan Street. I went to the Sullivan Street Elementary School. How do I get there? I should be able to get over there."

I half expected to hear that Sullivan Street had succumbed to the banks and bulldozers. But the store owner said it was easy to reach. "You go up the hill and turn right on Rutherford, and then you go straight down Womack, don't turn down Amsterdam, keep straight, y'unnerstan'?" Sam nodded. "Then you cross the railroad tracks an' turn sharp right down Stern Street till you come to a T. Then turn a kind of half left on Douglas. Go down Douglas for two or three traffic lights til' you get to the Amoco Station—it's Amoco, ain't it?—yes, Amoco. Then take a sharp right, almost a U-turn back along the tracks past Sullivan Street School. Go three blocks and you're there. Sullivan Street. It's easy once you figger it out," she said.

"Got that Sam?" I asked humorously.

"Yeah, I think so," he said. "I'll be all right when I get to that school." Sam thanked the woman and left for the car. I walked behind. "You sure you got it, Sam?" I asked. "Maybe we should go over the directions again."

"Yeah, I think I remember. I know where the tracks are anyway," he said vaguely.

"Both sets of tracks?" I asked.

"Maybe," Sam said. He seemed distant, his mind wandering.

But, when we got into the car, he began giving me confident directions that corresponded in no way that I remembered to the ones given by the woman in the store. He looked perplexed now and again, but then he would suddenly penetrate—burst through the surfaces to some earlier signs and shapes, some earlier map in his mind. Finally, he said "Stop! Back up!"

I backed up and he turned me down another dirt road, resembling the ones around Parker Street, and we found ourselves within another cluster of little wooden frame houses with porches and pitched roofs. "This is where I rode my bicycle; this is it," he said.

Once again Sam seemed to consult some interior map, and a few moments later was pointing to the elementary school he had attended before the move to Aunt Ella's. Then we passed down a group of narrow streets that led to Sullivan. Sam had me park on the street next to a brown clapboard house on dilapidated brick stilts. "That there is my gramma's house."

"Your mother's mother?" I asked.

"No, my father's," he said.

"How old would she be?" I asked.

"I don't know," he answered, as we got out of the car, "but she had sugar . . . an' high blood. . . ."

We walked up a steep dirt hill, cluttered with old toys and grocery wrappers, and went around the back to a screened porch. Sam knocked on the door and called. After awhile a sleepy and disheveled woman shuffled out and looked impatiently toward Sam.

"You know Mrs. Lewis?" he asked. "She used to live here."

"When?" she asked bluntly.

"Ten years or so ago," Sam said. "I used to live here too sometimes."

"Well, I don't know no Mrs. Lewis," she said, closing the door. Then as Sam turned away, she added, "Why don't you ask at the store?"

We went down the street, followed by a brown dog and a couple of expectant little boys in big worn sneakers and outgrown jeans. We soon reached a small general store, similar in stock and decor and in ostensible management by a large elderly woman, to the shop on Parker Street.

Sam went to the counter followed by the two little boys. "Can I help you?" she asked. The little boys went to the candy counter and gazed at it lecherously.

"Well, I used to live near here an' I'm lookin' for some of my folks. . . . Do you know a Mrs. Lewis?" Sam asked.

"I don't think so," she said.

"How about a Mrs. Jones . . . or Sharna Jones . . . Molly?" he asked. "Horton Brewer . . . any other Brewers?" She kept shaking her head. "No Lewises?" Sam asked. "Mrs. Lewis used to live right up the street . . . on the corner there at the bottom of the hill . . . Mrs. Joe Lewis. . . . How about Panama?" Sam suggested, a new name to me.

"Pana who?" she asked with a note of sarcasm. "I ain't been here too long an'. . . ."

"Panama," Sam said more distinctly.

The woman looked bored and shrugged.

"Maybe we should try somewhere else," I said. Then one of the boys spoke up from the candy counter. "I know Panama," he piped self-importantly.

"Ya do?" Sam said turning to him. "Can you show me his house?"

"Sure," said the boy proudly. "Panama has a big white Cadillac."

"He sounds like a good guy to know," I said. "Who's Panama anyway?"

"He's my father," said Sam.

"Your real father?" I asked.

"Yeah, my real blood father," said Sam. "Where's he live?" he asked the boy.

"In the white house at the end of the street," he said. "Panama's my uncle."

"Yeah," said Sam, "that means we're some kind of cousins."

"Kind of an uncle," said the little boy.

By that time we had reached the white house at the end of the block. The boy pointed up the path to the porch in front.

"That's Panama's house," he said. Sam stood and looked at it. It was slightly bigger and better kept than the other houses on the street, but still a modest place, with one story and a small porch. Sam walked up to the door and knocked. In a few moments, a handsome young black man, about Sam's size and complexion, came shirtless to the door. He looked about sixteen and he had a sinuous intensity about him, and a sharp challenging expression, that reminded me of Sam's and told me at once that in this white house on Sullivan Street Sam had found a brother.

"Is Panama in?" Sam asked.

"No," the boy said without much interest.

"What's your name?" Sam said.

"I'm Robin Lewis," he replied.

"I'm your brother . . . Sam," Sam said.

"*No shit,*" said Robin in some enthusiastic disbelief, and they shook hands formally. Then they looked into one another's eyes. Something caught. "No kiddin'," said Robin. They smiled and then embraced, with an awkward arrangement of arms and bodies, the unpracticed, imperative clutching of brothers, blood-tied, mind-torn, elbowed, reaching out for closeness only to find another sprocketed, uncomplementary male. Robin summoned Sam into the house, leaving the little boy standing forlornly on the street. He wandered off and we did not see him again.

The front room was well furnished and immaculate. Before a large couch stood a coffee table bearing in neat piles the more recent copies of *The Ladies' Home Journal, Good Housekeeping*, and *Sports Illustrated*. To the right of a fireplace was a bookshelf containing the *Encyclopedia Americana* and Art Linkletter's *Encyclopedia for Children*. Like most of the front rooms I was to see in Greenville, this one displayed a brightly colored poster with photographs and quotations of Martin Luther King, John Kennedy, and his brother Robert over black bunting. There were also several reproductions of paintings of oddly distant and unrelated countryside—Vermont in maple season and the English lake country. Unlike all the other front rooms I would visit, there was no TV.

"Well," said Robin, still standing awkwardly, challenging. "Where you been anyway?"

"Oh, I been to New York, all over . . . Vietnam," Sam said.

"You want to see Panama?" he asked. "I can take you to him."

"Yeah, take me to him," Sam said.

"Let me get my coat," he said.

We then walked off across a rough patch of weedy land behind the house toward a group of stores.

"I'll just leave you there. I ain't getting along with him too good," Robin said.

"What's the matter?" Sam asked.

Robin shrugged his shoulders. "I don't know. You should ask *him*."

We walked in silence to the front of a dilapidated liquor store. Robin accosted an old wino in front. "Where's Panama?" he asked.

"Down in that car," he answered, pointing fifty feet farther along the block to a tailfinned Dodge of green and chrome. Sam looked. He could see four or five figures in the car. "There he is," said Robin, "in the front seat." Robin immediately started back across the road toward the house.

Sam headed with somewhat strained nonchalance down the sidewalk toward the car. When he reached it, he went around the front and looked in the window on the passenger side. A handsome black man looked out inquiringly. He had short hair and angular features, with high cheekbones and a faintly Indian look. Panama, as it turned out, is one-quarter Cherokee.

Sam stared at him for a moment. The face was smooth, still young-looking, and a hint soft. It was a face that had not tightened its sinews in self-denial through the years. Compared with Sam's scarred features peering in the window, Panama offered skin that had been exposed to razors only under the auspices of Schick or Gillette, the face of a man who made his way among women without fighting their men. There would have been many women, it seemed right away, who had basked deciduously in that too quickly blooming, too sweetly radiant smile.

But as Sam kept looking, the smile began to wilt and the face assumed the somewhat slack sullenness of a man whose devices began to shrivel at the moment when his smile did not suffice. "You lookin' for somebody?" Panama said.

"You don't know who I am, do you?" Sam said finally in a tone of measured belligerence.

The man squinted, racking his memory. "Can't say that I do," he said. "Who the hell are you?" He returned the note of masculine nerve.

"Look again," Sam said.

The man again looked at Sam. He seemed impressed by Sam's air of gravity. "Well, you do look a little familiar," he said, "but I sure don't know. . . . "

"I'm Sam, your son, Sam," he said impatiently.

"I'll be damned," the older man said, getting out of the car. "Let me see you. You lookin' good." He smiled and the two men embraced warmly for several seconds.

Unfolding from the car, Panama turned out to be a big man, lanky and wide-shouldered, well over six feet, and inches taller than Sam in his embrace. Panama had to lean down slightly. But when they parted it became clear that it was Panama's normal posture to bend attentively down, to hear the nice things in soft tones that his women would say, or the concessions to be offered by shorter men, or the orders from the boss; while Sam's natural stance was straight and hard, and if he bent forward from the neck it was with chin thrust out in defiance. They had lived different lives, but the flesh was essentially one—the same rich brown with the strange hints of purple in the shadows, the same glints of shine on the cheekbones. They were father and son all right, struggling to define the meaning of the common blood, filial words.

"I'll be damned," Panama said. "I only saw a part a you . . . with that goat you got." Panama pinched his own clean-shaven chin. "Where you been anyway?"

After Sam told him, in a limited way, where he had been, Panama introduced Sam to the men in the car and to a couple of men by the liquor store and to the owner of the store and to a policeman walking by, and to the wino on the steps. The wino tugged at Sam's arm as he was leaving and asked, "Could you gimme a little hep? Twenny cent?"

Sam turned to me suggestively and I gave the man a dollar. Then we set off with Panama to get his white Cadillac. "You seen any your brothers and sisters?" Panama asked.

"I seen Robin," Sam said, "How many more I got?"

Panama looked at him with a smile. "Six," he said.

"Yeah?" exclaimed Sam. "Six. Man you been keepin' busy."

"Have you seen your Granma or Granpa yet?" Panama asked.

"They still 'round?" Sam said.

"Sure they 'round, an' your uncles an' cousins. In fact," said Panama, "all of Maybelle's relatives are still here too. . . ."

"I don't believe it," Sam said, "I thought everybody was dead or gone to Philly."

"Some of us went North," said Panama, "an' some of us was smart enough to come back. I was in New York for eight years. I came back in 1971. I'd had enough. Driving trucks." We walked down another street and into a back lot. "How is Maybelle?" Panama asked.

"She's fine, I guess," said Sam evenly. "She works evry day."

We had arrived at a large white Cadillac, from the years when Caddies were veritable yachts, about 1969. Clean and shiny on the outside, it showed signs of wear on the seats and one of the padded door handles had a vexing way of coming off in one's hand inside. Nonetheless, it was a big, comfortable car—leathered and cushioned, with power windows, brakes, and steering—that carried us off on our expedition into Sam's remaining family. We needed the cushions, for the tour was long and exhausting, his bloods widely parceled, mixed, and scattered through the city. Panama was determined that Sam meet every one of his some forty-five kin, including children and excluding several relatives who weren't at home when Sam arrived on their doorsteps.

They all claimed to have had premonitions of Sam. "We was jess talkin' about you lass week, jess wundrin' 'bout Sam and Maybelle," said Grandma Millie from her rocking chair; said Aunt Anna Lou, who years ago had made Sam fat, again now giving him squash pie and ice tea in her immaculate front room; said Aunt Sally Bee Jones, Maybelle's older sister who had downed a pint of Calvert Special Blend in the Caddie, without anyone seeing her take more than a swig, in the half-hour drive to the apartment of her daughter; and ebullient Sharna with her sexology magazine and hanging plants, who had also just been talking about Sam. All but one or two of the older relatives, in fact, professed themselves to have been speaking or dreaming or wondering about Sam during the Christmas week before he came, and all exulted in seeing him then: "Sam," "Shownuff, Sam *Beau*," "How you grow'd," "Where you been?" "Charlotte I heard," "the Army," "Vietnam," "daid . . . we thought you was daid," "thought I never live to see the day . . . of Sam again . . . a man," "I cared for him, he ole 'nuff now to care for me."

As we drove between the little houses, Panama apologized. "It looks better in the spring," he said, "when the trees are all green and the folks clean up their yards. Now some people, they throw somethin' out, let the wind take it, let the dogs play with it." He paused thoughtfully, "'less you put lead on the top of the can, the dogs will get in anyway. . . . You should come back in the spring."

But it looked fine to me. There was very little trash compared with Clinton Avenue and the houses were well kept inside—neat, with clean floors and bathrooms, and family photographs and souvenirs—houses full of people mostly who owned them and cared about them. And among all of Sam's aunts and uncles and cousins I didn't meet one who was on welfare. Almost all of them worked: Sharna from eleven at night to eight in the morning at Burlington Mills; Sally Bee's man as a brick-layer in this town of brick houses; Aunt Holly cleaning up at Holiday Inn. Sam's uncle, Robbie Lewis, had been an attendant at Greenville Memorial for twenty-one years; Uncle Horton, tall, proud, and strong at sixty-seven, with thirty-two grandchildren and six great-grandchildren, had just retired to Greenville after forty some years on his farm and is "looking for work"; and Sam's grandfather, owner of a handsome red house, luxuriously furnished in velveteen chairs and couches and with glossy walnut paneling and plush carpets, and with a view overlooking a tree-filled ravine, Sam's grandfather won't stop working at seventy, would hardly stop for Sam; and after smiles and embraces, he returned to repairs on an askew front door, "Gotta keep the air off my young wife, Rose." Even Sam's great-uncle, Willie, deaf, dumb, and something of a genius at pantomime—he did a continuous mime commentary as we talked—works on a garbage truck in the city; he is presumably the one garbage man in Greenville who himself can perform in a living room all the gyrations of an automated disposal truck.

Only Panama is at present unemployed. After four years of tearing down old buildings for a New York demolition company, five years of driving interstate trucks for Continental Contractor and Heldon Hall Enterprise, and two years with Greenville Sanitation, he is taking a little unemployment in his white sloop of a car.

There is a good reason why I didn't meet people on welfare in Greenville. In South Carolina, they don't give welfare allotments that seriously compete with work. In fact, the levels in South Carolina are approximately one-third the levels in New York, and only 15 percent of the officially poor avail themselves. There is a reason why blacks in Greenville are more likely to own their own homes. The government does not build public housing projects for which you qualify best by leaving your man or your job.

It seems that the values of work and regularity are being passed on in some degree to the next generation, though it is hard to be sure. Sam's cool twenty-year-old half-brother Paul is working in construction; cousin Sharna is at the mill. But we met Sam's nineteen-year-old half-brother James at 2 P.M. on Tuesday, handsomely groping his way from sleep in a red velvet wrapper and talking about women and grass. Even he, though, is "looking" for a job.

Then there was the revelation of Sam's half-sister Yolanda, sixteen, quiet and dignified and lovely, warm and articulate, star and captain of her basketball team at a nearly all-white school and resolved to go to college. She works every night at a local television station as a camera girl. I do not suppose that even Albany could have kept her down, but one never knows.

After the rote enthusiasm of the greetings, Sam's brothers and sisters seemed to take him for granted. It was a big family, larger in number, perhaps, than all of Sam's close acquaintances combined in Albany. Relatives, one gathered, cropped up and disappeared regularly in Greenville, just as Panama had often come and gone.

Sam and Panama, however, realized that something momentous was happening, something that should have been transforming, a meeting between the lost father and prodigal son, from which each should have taken a deeper vision of himself and his possibilities. Instead there was a certain tension and a shifting of focus.

They arrived at the home of one of Maybelle's younger sisters. After the usual screams and embraces of cheer and recognition, Panama noticed that her twelve-year-old daughter's bike was broken, the wheels and sprockets, chains and gears all askew. He had tools in the back of his car, "But I can't figure these ten-speed jobs," he said.

"Let me see it," said Sam abruptly. "I can fix that." While Panama and Sam's Aunt Holly and Sally Bee and her husband reminisced ("the last time I saw Maybelle, she was at the bus station *toe down*." "Yeah, if she wasn't drunk she was feelin' kinda mella." "Oh shit, she was lit." "She was *fired* up."); while they talked in honor of Sam, Sam worked intently on his little cousin's bicycle. The little girl looked up at him trustingly as he loosened all the bolts and realigned the various gears and wheels and bearings, then tightened the bolts again, "Now I see what's wrong," reloosened them, retightened them, until finally the bike was back in shape and Sam could bask in a cousinly glow. That was easier, somehow, than discussing the past with Panama.

Sam and I went out that night with much of his immediate family—Panama, Paul, James, Yolanda, and Ruby, his pretty youngest sister—to a local discotheque called the Showcase in a shopping center on the edge of town. "Do I need to bring a blade?" asked Sam, sidling up to his brother. "Nah," said James, "it ain't that kinda joint." We went off with Panama in the Cadillac, with

Albert King and Bobby Blue Bland singing blues on the tape deck and vindicating the invention of the electric guitar—"It's an Up and Down World," "How Blue Can You Get," "I Don't Want to Be Right"—and the kids demanding rock and soul, which sure enough at the Showcase they got.

While Sam sat and drank beer or went outside with James, presumably for something better, and Yolanda danced decorously with her brother, and Ruby danced less, and more sensuously, Panama told the story of his three families of children: his affair with fourteen-year-old Suzie Blake, the mother of Yolanda and Ruby, his brief candles with Maybelle and Sam, his sour, tempestuous marriage with Mary Mae, producing five children, including the dashingly handsome boys, James, Paul, and Robin, and two younger girls whom I scarcely saw.

At nineteen, he had already broken with Maybelle when she became pregnant, and he was already enlisted in the Air Force when Sam was born. He dropped off money at the hospital before he left (enough to pay the bill, said Maybelle) and departed the day before she gave birth. By the time he returned from the service, after three years overseas, Maybelle was married to Tommie "Fats" Botson and interested in Will Farmer. So at twenty-four, Panama married Mary Mae, a pretty woman who became more ambitious and demanding as the years went by. And Panama philandered, chiefly with Suzie Blake.

He met Suzie at a dance hall and immediately fell for her without realizing that this radiant and bosomy girl—as bright as she was pretty—was just fourteen years old. In a rebellion against overbearing parents, she ran off with Panama, got pregnant with Yolanda, and then with Ruby, at the same time that Mary Mae was producing Robin and Sam's younger sister.

Years later, Panama would want very much to marry Suzie, but by that time, she was no longer willing. She married Leander Baker instead and Panama was left grudgingly with Mary Mae. But he did not let marriage crimp his style . . . until one day the Sheriff came by and arrested him on a claim of non-support from Mary Mae. Panama remembers leading the Sheriff to the refrigerator and opening it to an array of food, asking, "Does that look like non-support to you?"; then taking the Sheriff to closets crowded with his children's clothes. The sentence was suspended, but two months later he was arrested in a dragnet as drunk and disorderly and was hauled off to a chain gang for eight months, an experience that banished any remaining magic from his marriage to Mary Mae.

When he got out of jail in 1964, he went North to New York where he socialized with Sam's young cousin Sharna and began his succession of well-paying but peripatetic jobs. He did not return until 1972. He remembers that some of his trucking runs out of Providence and Syracuse took him through Albany in 1970 and 1971, but as far as he knew, Sam was still in Charlotte.

At that point in his story at the Showcase, Panama got up and asked his daughter Ruby—who was being left out some by the boys in favor of her older sister—to dance with him. It was a slow number, and they shuffled awkwardly cheek to cheek under the strobe lights, with elbows out, much to the derision of the boys, who regarded the posture archaic. Shortly afterwards, at 1 A.M., the place closed for the night.

After leaving the younger group at their homes and saying a warm good night to Suzie Blake and a cold one to Mary Mae, Sam, Panama, and I went out for late food and drink at one of Greenville's after-hours clubs.

It was in a dark building on an open lot. From a distance, it looked silent and closed. But the door opened into a long room, moderately lighted, with a large jukebox of glinting kaleidoscopic purples and rhythmic, emotional music. There were advertisements on the walls with sleek black models pushing cheap sweet drinks: "What's the Word? Thunderbird"; "Get *Tickled Pink*, great new wine from Boone's Farm," and "delicious malt duck." We played "Misty Blue" by Dorothy Moore, on the jukebox because Sam remembered it coming out when he was in jail. Then Sam turned to face his newfound father, alone together, nearly, for the first time in their lives.

Perhaps it was the light, the gilded haze that suffused the place, free of fluorescence, from plain, yellowy bulbs; perhaps it was the sense that everything in the bar was real and functional— the clean counter and basic wood stools, the plain board floor, the shadowy stalls, the undisguised jars of catsup, sugar, salt, the array of liquor bottles—all without decoration or frill. The smell too, must have helped—a mist of mellow fumes from the skillet and the wood heater over the counter at the end—the voices, too—an effervescent rhythm of gruff yet musical conversation, the melting flow of warm, buttery, beer-bubbling talk after the cold outside. Perhaps, too, it was the sense of illegality in "after hours," the glamour of the speakeasy; perhaps all fused in the notion that I was somehow privileged to be there—a white man in this nocturnal haven of Greenville blacks. The music itself, the pleasing sentimentality of "soul," stagey and routine of manner and rhythm, yet in touch, all the same, with real emotions. It was the right music that night, our last in Greenville.

There were four men behind the counter. One was a large young black with a round butterscotch face and braided hair projecting in all directions. He had a cool air about him, with a hint of the oriental, a sulky suggestion of menace. He weighed perhaps 250 pounds and was said to play football. He could handle, it was clear, any trouble that might arise, or that he, in his vaguely sinister way, might see fit to provoke. Helping him was another almost equally large man. Both of them were much involved in low chatter with the customers, lending the scene a conspiratorial tone; we were outsiders, in from a wasted field of the city on a cold, dark night; they were part of the glow.

The owner of the place, a short, neatly dressed man with a triangular Afro, close-shaven by the ears but expanding to a flat top like an aircraft carrier, greeted Panama as an old friend. Classmates in high school many years before, they had kept in touch. They jibed at each other about their ages: "I'm goin' on twenty-nine," said the owner. "What are you? 'bout fifty?" "No, I'm twenty-nine too," said Panama. He stepped aside to introduce Sam. "Hey Albert, you meet Sam, my oldest son?" The man shook Sam's hand cordially. "That means he was born when you were three, right?"

"I was advanced for my age," said Panama, "in some ways."

"In some ways you were," said Albert. They both laughed. Panama turned to me. "That's the way I got my name. I didn't tell ya. When I was a little kid—hell, a baby—that song, 'Panama Joe' was a hit. Whenever they played it, I used to kind of shake on the floor like I was dancin' to it. Couldn't walk, but like I could *do* it. . . . The name stuck to me."

We sat down at the counter and Sam and Panama ordered beers. Sam said, "When you first saw me out there you weren't shook, were you? Like I might be comin' back to jump on you or somethin'. Come back and get you like the Man named Sue?"

("The Man named Sue" is a song by Johnny Cash that tells the story of the eponymous son who returns to kill his father for naming him Sue and ruining his life.)

"You might have jumped on me but you'd a jumped off quick." Panama's face and tone reflected in a minor key his son's.

"You think you could take me?" Sam said. Sam was going through one of those mysterious changes in mood that called up all the soured chemistry of his lifelong resentments. It happened only under drink, and did not always happen, even after long alcoholic stints like this evening. But now and again like his mother, or his Aunt Sally Bee., he would stick his neck out—let his lips go slack, his eyes go dull—and demand something: drink, money, sex. It wasn't necessarily happening yet in the glow of this place, but I could feel the tension rising in Sam after a full night of beers at the Showcase, and Calverts with Sally Bee. before, and now another beer at the counter. I thought that a fight, in fact, was remotely possible, that Sam would end his day of familial revelry by striking out at his father, conveying a sodden sense that he would never forgive anyone, anything, because of what happened in 1951.

"I don't take no shit from nobody," Sam said. "I know I can fight and I don't take no shit. I wouldn't take no shit from you either, I stay down here. I might figger you was to blame for my bad times and I'd come back and jump on you. . . . Man I don't take no shit, that's one thing I learned since I left here, a man got to fight for what he wants." Panama looked coolly back at his son. So this is what Sam was like, sometimes.

"Like I said. You'd jump on maybe, but you'd surazhell jump back off in a hurry, I'll tell you that," Panama said.

"She-it," said Sam.

"Damn right," said Panama, "an' if you cut me you'd never cut anybody else, either. I'd get out a piece and cool you off."

"You'd do that, would you?" Sam said. "To your son."

"My son would know well enough not to jump on me; he would never try it. An' neither would you."

Sam looked doubtfully into his beer, then fiercely at his father. "You better not mess with me, that's all I say."

"Well, I ain't messin' wit' you, Sam," he said with a flicker of wry amusement. "It seems to me, though, that other folks done messed with you plenty." He pointed to Sam's neck and the side of his face where Sam was scarred. "I just hope they didn't mess up yo' mind too."

"What you sayin'?" Sam said roughly, raising his fist.

"You know what I'm sayin'," Panama said. There was a long silence. Panama ordered two more beers.

"Let's talk 'bout somethin' else," Sam said glumly. "You got any womens around here? Why ain't there women in here?"

"I gots me lotsa women. All I can handle, to tell the truth," Panama said. "I never had any trouble gettin' women."

"I don't see none for me," Sam said.

"Well if you'd maybe told me you was comin' or if you could stay a couple days, you could get all the women you want," Panama said earnestly.

"I could get women here. I could get 'em tonight," Sam said.

"Where you think you are?" Panama replied laughing. "Vietnam or New York? This is South Carolina, Sam. But as I say, if you wants to find womens, I can help you tomorrow."

"Tomorrow, shit!" said Sam. "Let's get outta here. I need one tonight."

"Yeah, let's get out of here," I said. I was happy to leave. The tensions were rising and my energy was flagging after some eighteen hours of visiting with Sam's family. My whole body ached for the bed. "Yeah. Let's get back," I said. "We got to leave the hotel at 6:30 tomorrow morning. Our plane reservation is at 7 A.M." We walked out into the moonlit night and headed for the Cadillac.

Sam turned to me sullenly. "Gimme $50," he said.

"Whattya mean $50? I've spent all my cash Sam. We gotta get some sleep," I said.

"She-it," said Sam. "I wanta get some more drink. I want a woman."

"Sam, at this time of night in Greenville, there are no women and no liquor open period," said Panama.

"What you know about women?" said Sam. "Don't tell me about women."

Sam knew about women. Women were the way out, escape from the rule of father, don't tell Sam about women; he could get himself a woman whenever he wanted—beg, borrow, steal a woman, burrow into her warm body, hide away in the folds of her breasts, beat on her with his hard loins, until she cried uncle, daddy, Sam Beau, the man; and Panama could have no claim. Don't tell Sam about women; surely you remember he spent his life with women. With Maybelle first, Maybelle toe down, fired up, lit, stoned, feelin' kinda mella; black girls and women, from Greenville and Aunt Ella, on up to Albany and Babydoll Bev. Don't tell Sam about women; he knows the way in and the way out, white women, black women, juiced up and sand dry, pregnant and well-pilled, lesbians and prime foxes, cooked and kinda raw. He had nothin' to do with Panama, fatherly talks, disciplines: "Ain't none. All closed. Tomorrow maybe. Next week. Keep off the grass, Mr. Brewer. Keep off the street. Curfew. No booze." Father Keegan, Father Clyne, Father Panama. Teachers, cops. Fuck 'em all. "I'm gonna go get me a bottle and some tail." Sure, Sam. That's all you need. Don't need no father, if you got a bottle and a broad. Don't need nothin' else. "Don't tell me there ain't no women. What the fuck you know 'bout women? What the fuck. Fuck."

Panama looked quizzically over at his son. "You crazy, Sam? It's three in the mornin'."

"What you know about women?" Sam said with a disgusted look. "You ain't nowhere, you know that?"

"I know more 'bout women than you'll ever learn, Sam," Panama said. Then he smiled. "Sam, your daddy's a rich whore's cream and a poor whore's dream."

"An' he can't get nuthin' after 2 A.M. in his own home town," said Sam. "Shit on that."

Panama laughed. "Like I say, I do all right. . . . " He paused, then continued. "Sam, your daddy's fresh roasted to a golden tan, drenched in creamy milk chocolate and covered with . . ."

"Shit," said Sam, "full of shit." But he half smiled.

"Drenched in creamy milk chocolate and covered with a thin candy shell," said Panama.

"Shit," said Sam. "Where you goin' anyway? I don't wanna go back to that hotel."

"I don't care what you do, Sam . . . until 6:30 tomorrow morning. But I am going to have to get some sleep," I answered.

"I'm gonna get me some tail," said Sam.

"OK," said Panama, "but there ain't nuthin' open but the ho tail."

"Shit," said Sam, refusing to smile.

"Pretty bad," said I.

We rode silently back toward the Sheraton through streets as dead as the moon above. Sam glowered into the night, looking ready to wring its neck and shake it down for stars. Panama turned into the Sheraton parking lot. I got quickly out of the car. I had had enough. Sam followed sourly. We walked across the lobby under the skeptical eye of the night clerk and stepped into the elevator with two laughing white basketball players who towered above us.

"You guys lost?" said Sam. "You laugh like you lost . . . stupid."

They looked at him with a mixture of irritation and anxiety. "Yeah, we lost," one said; he held out a trophy designating third place. Sam looked as if he might spit on it. But we thankfully reached our floor first. "Good night," the basketball player said.

"Fuggit," said Sam. We walked down the corridor to my room and opened the door. I plunged head first down on the bed and instantly closed my eyes. Sam turned on the TV to a police movie with Broderick Crawford.

"Gimme one of them $50 checks," Sam said.

"Nah. What do you want it for?" I asked.

"Just give it to me," Sam said. "I need it. I'm goin' out. I gotta go out," he said. He was not in a mood to discuss anything. I had become someone from whom he wanted something in one of those late night binges that he so often ended in trouble, in a fight or a sexual rage, and dead-ended in jail.

"Shit, Sam, you can't cash these things in the day half the time. How you gonna do it now?" I said.

"Just give it to me, I'll worry about that," Sam said.

"Nothin's open," Panama commented.

"All right, if nothin' is open I guess I got nothin' to lose," I said. I got a pen and filled out the traveler's check. Sam took it and looked at it. "I'll use it all right. I'm gonna go get me a woman."

I felt I was making a bad mistake, letting Sam go off, full of booze, about three hours before the plane would leave. I was half afraid I would not see him again, that he would jump his probation in Albany, or at least show up late, making it more difficult for me to take him anywhere again. "Just be sure you're back by six," I said.

"Yeah," said Sam looking at the check as if it were a bare breast. "I just gotta go out, get me a drink, a girl . . . you ready, Panama?"

"I'm ready," said Panama, and they headed for the door. As they went out, Panama turned to me, "Don't worry about Sam. He'll be back. I can take care of Sam."

"You better," Sam said. They left. An hour later, Sam came back, somewhat sobered. He hadn't had a woman or a drink. He had had to make do with Daddy and a big Whopper.

"What you do?" I asked.

"We rode around," he said. "We had a good talk."

Sam rolled over, fell into a loch-deep sleep, and swam in his dreams with monsters. Every now and then I would hear him moan or cry out. The next morning I had to shake him hard for some time to wake him and we made the plane to Albany by minutes.

But he was glad to go back, glad to return to those spalled, familiar streets, those scratched and gouged familiar bars, those women he knew. If Sam was going to make it, it would have to be in the only town he knew: his hard, black cul-de-sac, sucking on a bottle in a brown bag on a stoop on Clinton Avenue; waiting to win a lottery; or else, at last, to find something that he had to do, find among the welfare cushions a hard place to begin an uphill climb, find in the middle of the American mush of paupering charities from the state a real edge of poverty, a hard edge of reality. What poor people need most is their poverty. You take it away, and they stay poor forever. It is necessity that is the father, not only of invention but also of character. The welfare state takes away far, far more than it ever gives. The problem is not wasted money; conservatives talk too much of the waste of money in welfare. The problem is that welfare wastes people.

15

Washington

"All's fair in love." I said. I was trying to reassure Sam on the subject of Beverly and her "new black dude." "She's not worth it. You should say the hell with it, to hell with him—he doesn't have any picnic coming anyway. You know that; taking Bev from you will be its own revenge. Let 'em stew in their own juice. As I said, all's fair." Sam looked at me through blood-murked eyes. "I don't believe that," he replied in full inebriated gravity. "I kill."

"Well, in that case, let's get out of here," I said. "I am driving to Washington today." "That be fine," he said; "they got colored cops, and lots of jobs, and foxy women, and warmer weather, and the President"—what more would Sam want?—so South, that same day in January, in my orange Pinto car, sweeping down through the shining Mall that Sam so liked—"I worked there; I'm gonna miss this place"—and spiraling off onto the Thruway South—"it's Rocky's revenge, I said"—we began again the old argument on Rockefeller's money and Jesse James.

"Didn't you know that?" Sam said. "His money all came, originally, from the James brothers."

"Shit, Sam, that's ridiculous," I said. "The money came from Standard Oil."

"That's what they *want you* to think," he said. "Standard Oil was a front for the James Gang. I learned that in jail."

Of course, he's sure, I said to myself, and changed the subject. "What you gonna do in Washington?" I asked.

"I hope I can get a job," he said. "Maybe someday I can open up a butcher shop. I think I could learn to be a butcher. Phil Russell was a butcher once."

"Good luck," I said. "I hope you can find somebody to apprentice you."

"One thing I know," he said, "I want to get rich enough by the time I'm thirty-five so I can retire."

"Shit, I'm thirty-five, Sam, and I can't retire," I said.

"Well, maybe forty," he said.

"Most people can't retire 'til they're sixty-five," I said.

"Most of the folks I know on Clinton Avenue, they retire around forty. Go on disability, welfare, wine, or somethin'," he said. "You know that."

"You don't want to retire that way, do you?" I asked.

"I guess not," he said. He looked solemnly down.

Early that evening we checked in at the Diplomat Motel on the edge of the city. Sam took his bag of clothes from the car and a bottle of Brut, and the first thing he did on entering the room was to flick on the TV. The robbers were having a mid-show rally to stir up tension before the final crescendo of police fire and Sam was quickly hooked for the night. I went to sleep.

The next day I left Sam at the Diplomat watching a recipe show on morning TV and drove off to find an apartment. I got an efficiency on Calvert Street, across Ellington Bridge from Connecticut Avenue over Rock Creek Park. We moved in that afternoon. At about five o'clock, I left Sam with some money to buy some food and a hot plate, and prepared to go to my office across town. "I'm gonna get me a woman," Sam said. "Well get the hot plate first," I said, as I went out the door.

I had finished my research for the book and written several chapters, and I didn't want any more episodes. I thought maybe I could set up Sam in Washington, bring him into the middle-class world of government workers, and save him from the bottle in the brown bag, or jail. My plan was to fail, due chiefly to Sam's homesickness, and three days later he was to be on a plane headed back to Albany, where as yet he has not killed anyone, won the state lottery, found a job, or scored, for me, a happy ending. But he is still only twenty-five, still young and looking good.

I left my office about two hours later and returned to Calvert. As I opened the door off the street an avalanche of angry voices—righteously raging, indignantly denying, implicitly threatening—a seething tangle of alcoholic whines and shouts burst down upon my ears from a second floor apartment. Not as quiet as advertised, this place, I thought. I started up the stairs. Amidst the uproar of invective, I heard with a falling heart the plaintive protests of Sam. I heard the shouts of women demanding money—several women and a boy, too, perhaps—and mention of prostitutes and sex, and Sam saying he had had a lot of money early in the evening but it was all gone. I hesitated on the steps. Sam had evidently found not one woman, but two, and a pimp perhaps to boot, and was embroiled in a fierce verbal battle, just frailly confined to words.

To hell with it, I said to myself. He would have to get himself out of it, I decided, even if the racket meant I would be ejected from the apartment on my first night there. It was a nice neighborhood—racially mixed and by the park—right down the street from where Carl Bernstein and Nora Ephron would shortly buy a house. The other tenants would not long put up with cat-fights among whores and their customers. But there was nothing much I wanted to do. I had already given Sam $100. If he had really spent it all, that was too bad. I decided to cross the street and have some dry couscous on rice and raisins at Madame Ayesha's Calvert Café.

The Calvert is famous in the city for its large servings of good Middle Eastern food and pleasantly informal atmosphere, suffused with the smell of seasoned lamb and the sound of Middle Eastern music or soul from the jukebox. One enters into a bar-room ebullient with chatter from the battered wooden bar and its polyglot patronage.

I sat down alone in one of a row of low-backed booths along the wall, between two groups of bearded faces, lumber jackets, and Army surplus greens on braless girls who spoke in a quaint mixture of suburban polysyllables and percussive "fucks." I diverted myself by listening in to what turned out to be a counterpoint chorus of the Washington left: "Oh wow!," "the CIA," "you dig it," "and Oswald was in Mexico at the time, for Chrissake," "vegetable couscous," "Julian Bond is selling out, OK?" "the fukkin' Mafia," "fuzz," "down at the Institute, Mark said," "stuffed grape leaves," "right on, baby," "kofta kebob," "Duane Allman was a saint, man," "mainlining meth," "beautiful cat," "you dig?" "sexism, racism, it's the same thing, OK?" "FBI," "Title I," "Africa," "he's into fascists like Proxmire," "Art Waskow," "outtasight," "fukkin' war criminals, OK?" It was a continuing colloquy of the radical mind, all subsumed by the overriding question, everywhere in the air: Is our theory quite funky enough, crazy Jewish Afro enough, wiry-haired terrorist enough, bloody-handed revolutionary macho enough to please the blacks? "In junior high, they're ready to kill, man. Any day." "In my neighborhood. Shit, man you got a car? They own the streets already, man." "Right in broad daylight, stabbed nine times. OK?" "The fukkin' cops took twenty minutes." "Let's take a taxi." "Hey dig that cat coming in now. The scar on him." "Oh, wow!"

I looked up and saw Sam standing coolly at the door with not one but three women, one white, two black; uh oh, the bastard's got himself hooked up with another group of lesbian prostitutes, I thought. One was a light-skinned black girl with a full figure, heavy dark clothing, and a small mustache. Her face was strangely pocked and flaked, as if scarred from short razor gashes, an effect sometimes produced by dope. She was smiling at Sam. The other black was shorter, very heavyset, with a round darker face and warm brown eyes. She seemed drunk. She wore jeans with a visible zipper down the front, a navy blue parka, torn and faded, a sweater, a long dark coat, layer on layer of clothes that she opened but did not remove in the hot restaurant. She looked like a small, swarthy, long-unemployed longshoreman, dressed for the cold winds on the docks. The white girl was about the same height, had a sullen look, slightly adenoidal, wore granny glasses, a long black coat, and some kind of dull red and green garment underneath. Her figure was not discernible, mostly concealed by the coat. Her hair was blond, tinted a little silver, cut short. She had a bruised look and a gray, but mottled, complexion. I waved them over, and in much confusion—as we moved together to a long table in back by the jukebox—they told me the story of the last two hours.

The first thing Sam did when I left, after he dumped his stuff in the room, was to saunter down Calvert to the crossroads of 18th Street and Columbia Road, where he crossed the street and entered the first available bar. It was a dark basement cave called the Showboat Lounge and Mattress Company ("used pillows and bedding wear, deloused and sanitized"). During the day, it sold second-hand bedding and at night it offered a band and dancing, but at six that evening when Sam entered, it was nearly empty. He ordered a beer from a Puerto Rican bartender and thought without enthusiasm of his impending weeks in this strange city. Maybe he could send for Bev and the kids, he mused, get a bigger apartment. Maybe he could find some women here. A job. Maybe. *What's this?* A match, in his face, *get it away*, who is it? "Hey it is, it's *Sam*! Whachadoin' here?!"

Shit. Buddy. Marianne.

Sam at first was terrified. How had they found him? Marianne's voodoo, had to be; it would curse him, gain an unescapable revenge. Buddy and Marianne thought Sam had come down to kill them. How did he know where they were? They were just coming up from Palm Beach, Florida, where they had been staying since the trial; came in to get a beer. Well, have a beer. Sure, why not? No hard feelings. Well, some hard feelings, no forgiveness from Marianne, but Buddy was in control. "Come on, you come too, we're goin' to see Sam's apartment, drink there." "I'm not going," Marianne said in a whine. "Yes, you are, come. And here's Opal, our friend down here; Opal, remember the guy I was tellin' you 'bout? One that raped Marianne? Mitchell Brewer. Sam. Well, this is him." "Nice to meet you," said Opal, no sweat, no hard feelings, "sure let's see Sam's apartment." "The guy is writin' a book about me," said Sam. "No shit," said Buddy. "Shit," said Marianne.

The uproar I had heard when I came back from the office was no new affair, just a high-dudgeoned rehash of the same old case, same trial, that had preoccupied me, and Sam, for all these months, but with Marianne and Buddy nowhere to be found—to my considerable distress, as it happened, since the characters did not spring vividly enough alive in the testimony.

I had given up on them, though; decided to write the book without them; driven off to work in Washington alone with Sam; and chose that very day to live on Calvert Street. Voodoo or not, something had brought us together; mindflows mingling mystically on the routes of coincidence, South, like migrating birds that mysteriously go without maps or memories to the place their parents had always wintered before them; bodies moving unconsciously, ignorantly, mindless, and thus open to the guidance of a higher mind, a deeper control.

Most of the time, our souls, our individual gifts of spirit, are sucked up by the roots of consciousness into the great neural tree of our photosynthetic brains—the enlightened gallery of thoughts and senses—and held there in beauty and pride, in science and faith, in the ramifying, foliating glory of imagery and words, reasons and ideas. But there is also communion. We may always, and without warning, flow darkly back, our minds sucked with blessed gravity down into the phantasmal dream flood, the eternal, all-knowing river; the universal unconscious; where distant minds and spirits brush together in the supreme coincidence of God. Thereby we can know things far beyond the ken of our individual minds and senses. Thereby we experience the miracle of coincidence more frequently by far than any science of probability would allow.

By whatever providence, that very evening we found ourselves—Sam, I, Buddy, and Marianne—all sitting, quite intentionally together, at the Calvert Café, back on the case.

"Justice," Marianne said, "was not done."

"Three months in jail not enough?" I asked.

"Two-and-a-half months, that's all. I'll never tell the truth in court again. It ruined my life. I'm not saying more. All I want to know, if I'm such a big prostitute, why didn't I have any arrests? I tell you, no money in the world bring me to sleep with *him*. And I'm not talking to you, either. You say you're writing a book? Well, not with my help you aren't."

Her words poured bitterly forth. She was a "trained hairdresser," but there were no jobs. Bev harassed her, until Keegan said he would never drop the charges because of it. Her girlfriend told lies. Everybody lied. She would never tell the truth again.

"I don't think like her," Buddy said. "She hated me at the time of the trial." The black woman twinkled across the table at Marianne, who looked grimly at the table. "But she likes me all right now," Buddy said flirtatiously. "Don't you? I like *her* pretty good too." Buddy smiled. "I really go for her now."

"But at the trial, I ain't a revengeful person. It all turned out all right in the end. Nobody won. I could have testified good. I could have gotten lots of witnesses, friends to tell 'bout Sam. But after the first time, the prosecution rested. I didn't want to press it. I thought Sam had had enough. I told jokes. Sam had had enough. An' besides, he been drinkin' and he went to jail." She then looked very mournful. "But he did it," she said. "He was guilty. You should have heard the screamin'. They called the police downstairs. He scared her by chokin' her. It was awful, it was. But I don't have no hard feelins. Sam gave me money for drinks an' I kept some. An' he gave me money to take a walk. But I couldn't walk. The screamin' was so awful."

"Shit." Sam said, "I gave you $20."

"For drink, an' takin' a walk. You didn't say nothin' about havin' Marianne," she said.

"What you talkin' about?" Sam said. "You said she's your woman but you'd take a walk."

"I couldn't take no walk. There was too much screamin'. It was terrible. The neighbors." She mumbled.

Marianne abruptly stood up at the end of the table. "I'm feeling sick," she said. "I've had enough of this."

"See, George, what I say?" Sam said. "As soon as the truth starts to come out she wants to leave. I paid and that's that. Over $20 an' Buddy took a walk. Said she'd take a walk."

"I did," said Buddy.

"I'm leaving," Marianne said.

"All right, just a minute," replied her companion. Buddy looked back at us and shrugged. "What can you do?" she said. Then they went out together, the fair white girl with the hairdressing degree and the refined voice, and the plump black woman, with the slurred unsyntaxed Southern way of speech, out into the night of Washington, D.C., swaddled in layers of wools and flannels, to sleep, they would not say where. Opal stayed back with us.

"That Buddy's full of shit, you know? Palm Beach. Shit," Opal said.

"You don't think she's been to Palm Beach?" I asked.

"Do they look to you like they's comin' from Palm Beach? Shit," she said. "Potomac Beach maybe."

"What are they doin' down here?" I asked.

"Well, I heard that Marianne's been turning tricks. But I ain't seen it. I don't know," she said.

"You want a ride home?" I asked.

"Sure," she said. "Thanks. It's cold out there."

The next day we found Buddy and Marianne at another bar down 18th Street, with country music on the jukebox, pinball machines surrounded by Spanish-speaking players, and a Maryland basketball game on the color TV. When Sam and I came in, Buddy waved us over to her table and Marianne got up to move away to a booth. Buddy and I began talking, but it quickly became clear that this was not a bar in which a single white woman could sit alone without being harassed. Two swarthy Latins immediately went over to sit with Marianne. Buddy got up and moved over to protect her woman. She stood up erect, all 5' 5", cocked her head to the side, and looked one of the men in the eye. "You lay off her, or you'll have me to deal with," she said.

"So what," the man said.

"Stop bothering the woman, she's mine," Buddy said.

Marianne said, "I'm leaving."

"Siddown," Buddy said, "I can handle this." Then the manager came over and began to pull Buddy away. "Just stop these men from bothering the white girl. I'm just drinkin' beer. Make them stop."

The manager told the men to stop, directed Buddy back to the table with me, and returned to the bar. "Come on over an' sit with us," she told Marianne.

"I'm leavin'," Marianne said. "I won't sit with Sam, either of them."

"Go siddown then," Buddy said, "an' don't bother us either." Marianne walked over and sat morosely at the nearest table. Buddy began telling me the story of her life—her childhood in Newburgh, her athletic triumphs in school, her move to Albany, her courtship of Marianne.

"Why did you become a lesbian?" I asked her finally.

"Shit. There ain't no men," she said simply. "Black men, they worth a shit, they go for white girls. Sam too, he like white 'uns, don't you Sam?"

Sam smiled. "Sometimes," he said.

"Well, I do too," she said. "Ain't no harm innat. I figger they must be sumthin' good if all the men like'm so much. So I git some of it myself." She looked challengingly at both of us.

"Ain't no man worth a shit," she said. "Drunk, in jail, outta work, sniffin' 'round white pussy. I do a little sniffin' myself. Ain't no harm innat," she said. She fell silent.

"I's sorry what happened to Sam," she added, looking into her beer. "But in a way he had it comin'." She looked up. "You unnerstan'?" she asked.

"Maybe," I said.

Sam said nothing.

Buddy then jumped up. The two Latin men were whispering something at Marianne. What was it? They were leaning forward in their chairs looking up at her with bright-eyed oily faces, small black mustaches, slackly gaping mouths, hands held forward, palms up, rubbing their thumbs and fingers together; that was it. "Here pussy. Here pussy. Pussy, pussy, pussy, pussy. . . ." Buddy walked up to one and put her hand roughly in his face. The other man leaped to his feet and began calling the manager. The first man knocked Buddy's arm aside and got up, but Buddy pushed her padded body up against him, jutted out her lower lip, and said, "You lay off her or I'll cut you, don't you think I won't." His lip trembled. "I didn't mean nothin'," he said.

"We better get out of here, George," Sam said. "I don't want no trouble down here."

"I guess so," I said, "it's not our business." As the manager came up and prepared to throw out the two women, Sam and I stepped out onto 18th Street.

"I want to go back to Albany," Sam said. "See my kids. I've had enough of Washington. I'm thankful an' all that, but it ain't gonna work."

"We'll discuss it later," I said. "Let's get back to the house."

"OK. But I'd like to fly back today, George. I want to make it in Albany. Albany's my home," he said.

"Won't you get in trouble up there?" I asked. "You won't fight Clarence?"

"I was drunk when I said that," he said. "I wasn't thinkin' right. But if I get workin' up there, I think things will turn out. An' George, I gotta be with my kids. I don't feel right down here."

So I took him out to the airport and bought him a ticket back to Albany. His trip to Washington had evidently fulfilled its purpose, and he could feel nothing more to hold him there. I watched him walk down to the waiting area for the Albany flight, carrying only his bag of clothing and his bottle of Brut.

I never saw Buddy or Marianne again. I don't know where they are. But I was left with Buddy's lingering questions. Where *are* the men on Clinton Avenue? What is a black woman to do, faced with their flight, their drink, their lack of money and racial pride, their macho posturing, their final retreat to the bottle in the brown bag. What the women do do—many of them—is clear. They resort to welfare and raise their children alone, with their mothers and aunts and grandmothers, and any men who choose to stay around. A few of the women, like Buddy, give up on men altogether, live as lesbians, even fight back as pimps. On Clinton Avenue today very few get married and stay married.

Last year in America almost two-thirds of the children born to young women on welfare were illegitimate. In 1970, only 56 percent of American black women between twenty-five and thirty-four, compared with 82 percent of whites, were living with a husband. The situation today is worse.

"Where are the men?" Buddy asked. Where are they? Not one of the men in Sam's life in Albany, old or young, is married and living with his wife and children. Not one. Phil Russell left his wife years ago, lived for a time with Sandra, and now sees a number of black women from time to time. Benny Williams just got out of jail after being exonerated for Sylvester Smith's berserk siege with a shotgun. Benny's wife and children live on welfare in Cleveland. Sylvester Smith is dead at thirty-five, shot by the police; he had children by several women. Billy (Grant) Crosby lives with his mother. Dave Smith and Eddie Harris drink wine. The list could continue, but the point is clear. Clinton Avenue men are not marrying and supporting families. Some are in jail, some are dallying with white women. Some spend time with various black women. Few stay. They are not needed; welfare is a better provider by far than a Clinton Avenue father.

The situation is not essentially different among whites involved in the welfare trap. Bev can no more marry a lower-class white man than she can marry Sam; and she can no more marry him than can the black women on the avenue. Nor can Kathy or Anna or Judy or any of the other white welfare mothers who have passed through his life. For steadiness of income and variety of benefits, no normal man, white or black, on Clinton Avenue can compete with welfare as a provider. Therefore, few try. Who can easily blame them? Who of us anywhere works hard without a system of constraints and necessities, whether social or financial pressure, normally combined in the demands of women?

We work, nearly all of us men, because we are forced to work, by our image of manhood imprinted as a child or by our profound need, as deep as any purely economic necessity, to maintain our status and prestige in the higher classes. If all our women had leisure incomes that could support them better than our jobs, few of us could marry or stay married any more than Sam. Welfare, to an uneducated lower-class man, is wealth—wealth beyond the dreams of all the immigrants of our history, wealth beyond the ken of workers around the world. Illegal aliens swarm our shores, ignorant of the language, to earn the livings—the positions on the ladder up—that our own poor citizens disdain in order to qualify as fatherless, workless, disabled, impotent, lost.

The situation today on Clinton Avenue is complicated further for blacks by the large number of available white women with their siren skin—the gloss of TV desire—and welfare, or whorefare, money. Cities with larger black communities, more isolated ghettos, thus may be easier for black families. But the general point is clear and should not be misrepresented. The poverty-stricken black family, in bad shape a decade ago when Daniel Patrick Moynihan studied it, is in chaos today—abandoned, for one reason or another, by most black men.

I am not talking about middle-class black families; they are just as solid as comparable white ones. I am talking about the poor black families and communities in which "welfare rights" movements, "poverty" program organizers—all the vendors of "poverty" aid—have lavished their baneful attentions. All the sociological prattle about the tradition and strength of black matriarchy can not obscure the tragedy of a culture where the vast majority of children grow up without fathers: the tragedy of Clinton Avenue in Albany.

We can explore some of the sources of the tragedy by examining the other city in Sam's life: Greenville, South Carolina. In the 1970 census, there were 19,145 blacks in Greenville compared with 14,132 in Albany. Of the men in Sam's life in Greenville,

most of them are living with a black wife and many are supporting their children. Beyond Sam's kin, this impression of greater
family integrity in Greenville is supported by the 1970 census
figures, adjusted for the difference in the sizes of the two black
communities.

Poverty, statistically measured, was clearly worse in
Greenville. Median black family income was more than 20 percent higher in Albany than in Greenville, and the proportion of
black families in poverty was 45 percent lower in Albany. Yet in
Greenville the men were tending to stay with their families and
there were only half as many poor female-headed families with
small children. In proportion to size, Greenville had 17 percent
more black husband-wife families overall. The men were only
half as likely to remain single.

Contrary to the theory that it is chiefly poverty that causes
black families to break down or men to abandon their women
and children, Greenville had both 50 percent *more* black poverty
and 50 percent *less* abandonment of women with small children.

This disparity, moreover, began in the mid-sixties of the war
on poverty. Before then, female-headed families were just as common in Greenville as in the North.

Observation and interviews in Albany lead to the conclusion that black family conditions there have steadily worsened
since 1969, when the census data were collected. The advantage
of Greenville may well have increased. Poverty itself has little to
do with it. Comparison of Albany blacks with rural South Carolina blacks who are poorer still than the Greenville ones, shows
an even greater Southern advantage in the indices of family formation and stability. The statistics of poverty simply do not cor-
relate with statistics of family breakdown. The correlation is
between family breakdown and *welfare* poverty.

As might be expected, the chief statistical difference between
the two cities is welfare. Forty percent of Albany's poor black
families were on welfare in 1969 compared to only 18 percent in
Greenville. In Greenville, in fact, welfare itself was almost negli-
gible. Only about 350 black families were on welfare and they
received only $676 per family. In Albany in 1969, welfare fami-
lies received almost 2 ½ times that amount. Since 1969, Albany
welfare coverage and benefits have soared. When income in kind
from Medicaid, food stamps, public housing, and other poverty

programs is included, the gap between the public assistance received by poor families in the two cities becomes greater. Although
conclusive proof cannot be given in matters of sociology, it is clear
to those who have studied the reams of data on the subject that
our current welfare programs both cause breakdown and prevent formation of families.

The reason is not the administration or regulation of the system. For one thing, the rules are very similar in the two cities.
The reason is that we are giving more welfare, including in-kind
programs for the poor, than we can afford. The welfare that a
society can afford, however, is not determined by its tax rate or
budgetary capacity. It is determined by the society's wage
rates, which in turn must ultimately be determined by its pro-
ductivity. As long as work is compensated less than non-work,
the "generous" welfare levels maintained in Albany and in most
of America will only demoralize and deprave the poor,
destroying their families, draining their energies, and stultifying
their lives.

We must face the fact that today it is the North, Northern
liberals—in a spirit of charity, fatally corrupted by a spurious sense
of guilt—who are enslaving blacks. The Northerners argue that
it is the low benefits in the South that cause the incompetent poor
to migrate to the Northern cities. But Southern blacks leave for
the North chiefly in search of new opportunities and much of the
time, surprisingly, they find them, doing the work which the
Northern poor in the welfare culture reject.

It is not the migrants from the South who cause the problems of the North. In fact, census department studies show that
the migrants do much better in the North than the men blessed
from birth with Northern generosity. It is Northern welfare generosity that ultimately blights and maims their fatherhood and
families, their motivation and character.

Today on Clinton Avenue, the celebrations of marriage and
reunion, the compassionate care of children, the faith and love of
fathers, the dignity and strength of labor, all the rituals of family
and community are rapidly dying out. In their place is a conge-
ries of Human Resources Departments, Daycare Centers, Counseling Services, Welfare Offices, Food Stamp Registration Centers,
and Medicaid Bureaus, all designed for one clear effect: to re-
ward the people who manage not to marry or work. Yet work

and marriage are the crucial ways that men grow up and become responsible citizens.

Sam still wants to marry and work. He wants to support his children. He would if he had to. He would if they needed him. Instead, welfare takes care of his children while he does the circuit of veterans' counseling offices that tell him he needs some five years' worth of high school equivalency studies—a so-called "pre-vocational" course—before he can qualify for a real pre-vocational program. In effect, they "counsel" him that he is dumb and his situation hopeless. Every Thursday, he checks in with a probation officer, whose only significant role is sometimes to stop him from getting a driver's permit or going out of the city for training or work. Or he passes by the Comprehensive Employment and Training Act Office which cherishes the silly conceit that it can "create real, permanent jobs" by diverting college graduates and other easily employable types into CETA projects. CETA isn't interested in Sam until he makes up those five years of high school.

Even in Albany, outside the high walls of civil service and the other bastions of fake meritocracy, there are innumerable jobs that Sam could do with a little time and training. There are many jobs that he could get and do immediately. They are the sort of jobs termed menial. Some of them might serve as entry jobs. They are the sort of jobs that cannot begin to compete with welfare. He would not consider doing them as long as welfare pays more.

So he spends his time chasing pretty welfare mothers and part-time prostitutes, drinking beer, playing cards, and watching television shows that glory in violence and the beauty of white women. After a time, he usually gets into a drunken fight. If he wins, he may go again to jail. There in a month he will show more resourcefulness and ingenuity in accumulating large caches of cigarettes, snack food, and other small indulgences than he shows in a year on the street among the pretty lifetime pensioners of his community.

My book is finished now. I will have to leave Sam there on Clinton Avenue among the street stud paraders, blue-denimed lezzies, the pretty pimps and prostitutes, the home relief remittance men, the winos, the welfare chatelaines—all rocking away their lives as they await the green tide of government checks.

Like Sam, many of them are attractive. Many have considerable potential to contribute to their country and community. A few of them are of the sort who would not work under any conditions. A few would abandon their children regardless of the effects. At present, no one can tell which are which. Almost all uniformly founder in the green tide we call generosity.

He stands at Joe's Grocery on the corner watching the street for action. He wears a handsome new hat of many-shaded blue suede, but his black fur-lined coat has begun to tear at the shoulder and his proud platform boots are down at the heel. A wino wanders toward him up the street. His teeth are gone, his lower lip hangs askew and shows pink, one hip is shot, and he has to twist his whole body to walk. His eyes are dull. His urine-stained trousers scratch on the street. He stinks of rotten liquor. Sam reaches into his pocket and gives the man a dollar from the ten I had left him. The man bows and shuffles in servile gratitude. Sam waves him on. He walks away. Sam looks up and down Clinton. Nothing seems to be happening. So he strides back around the corner to Concord Avenue to find a card game at P.K.'s or Tommy Joe's. Perhaps he can parlay those $9—that spiffy new hat, that warm, mellow smile, that Marine Corps cool, that Sam Beau swash—into something big. A butcher shop? A new car? A good woman? A family? A retirement pension? Or a real sense that the world needs him. It does, you know. Ask Buddy. On Clinton Avenue a good man is hard to find. I stayed in my car and watched him walk into a house on Concord Avenue, waving back at me as he went.

Then suddenly in the car's other window framed a face, fumed a smell, spoke a bitter sentence. "What you lookin' at. Git out of here. You got no right to look at me. Git." I suddenly recognized him. It was the same old man I had met almost two years before, on my first visit to Clinton Avenue, when I blundered into his unkempt room. They had been bad years for him. It was a face like a broken bottle, a fiasco of a face, ready to cut and to hate, dripping with bad drink, caked with old blood, lined with scars, a face of losses, endlessly cut, until there was nothing but his mud-shot eyes sinking back into the venom of his own sodden brain, his own debilitated death, a loss already cut to nearly nothing. Who, I wondered, had poisoned that face, that life? Why?

I looked coolly back. He would have liked to cut me, I suppose; but he lacked the strength or the will. So he spat at the car and stumbled back to his seat, among the brown paper bags with drained bottles, sucked dry, on the once grand steps up to the sad house, with its once proud pediment above the door, intricately sculpted, hardly worn by the years, yet grimly wrought of irony now over the cluttered stoop, from which the man could rise and labor across the sidewalk only by a gout of venom and racial hatred.

But who had cut that man? It was not me, I said to myself angrily as I drove away. And I would look, I said, because I did not want it to happen again, happen to Sam. We cannot for another generation allow our victims to fester as invisible men, while we preen on our idealism and charity. And mere visibility is not enough. We must look deeper, I thought, or we will not know what we are doing, why they are dying, what kind of hell we pave with our fine generous intentions in these grandly imagined houses, in the shadow of the imperially erected Mall of a government that pretends to be generous and great.

Postscript

Mitchell Brewer did not fare well on the Albany streets. A few years after we left him, he was convicted of another rape and sent to Dannemora with a twenty-year sentence. His daughters and a later son passed through foster homes and were finally adopted. The adoptive parents report a series of episodes so violent and deranged that they sued the adoption agency for falsely assuring them that the children had been well treated.

About the Author

George Gilder is a senior fellow and director of high technology and public policy studies at Discovery Institute, in Seattle, and a founding editor of *ASAP*, the bimonthly technology supplement to *Forbes* magazine. He is a graduate of Harvard University and has been a fellow at Harvard's John F. Kennedy School of Government, chairman of the Lehrman Institute's Economic Roundtable, and program director at the Manhattan Institute. Gilder is the widely known author of *Wealth and Poverty* (ICS Press, 1993), *Recapturing the Spirit of Enterprise* (ICS Press, 1992), *Men and Marriage, Microcosm*, and *Life after Television*. *Wealth and Poverty*'s economic message on the moral sources of capitalism grew directly out of the author's experiences in the writing of *Visible Man*.

DISCOVERY INSTITUTE

Learning from the Past, Learning from the Future

What We Do. Discovery Institute sponsors a wide variety of research and policy programs which proceed from the sound principles of representative democracy, individual liberty, free enterprise, technological advancement, regional cooperation, and internationalism.

The Institute is established to identify public issues and to find the connections among them; to subject these issues to factual, philosophical, and historical analysis; to discover the best means for addressing these issues and finding synergies among them; to submit the ideas that are developed to private consultations among fellows and Institute members and through public dialogue in seminars, conferences, debates, and media presentations; to publish reports, articles, and books that contribute to improved public understanding of the Institute's ideas; to devise applications of the Institute's long-term proposals that elected officials and other policy makers can use even in the short term; and to show in diverse ways how 21st-century humanity can benefit from the principles, policies, and practices advocated by the Institute and its fellows.

How We Do It. Discovery Institute is a distributive community of public policy scholars and writers, with a headquarters in Seattle and an office in Washington, D.C. Fellows are multidisciplinary in background and approach. A research and advocacy project is selected when it is in harmony with Discovery's vision and mission, when the Institute can make an original and significant contribution to the issue's development, and when it is within the Institute's resources. Most issues selected are of national or international scope. The Institute's Cascadia project promotes cooperation between Western Canada and the Northwest United States as an example of the future of binational regionalism.

Financially, the Institute is a nonprofit educational foundation funded by philanthropic foundation grants, corporate and individual contributions, and the dues of individual members.

Discovery's Vision. The Institute is guided by a belief in God-given reason and the permanency of human nature; the principles of representative democracy and public service expounded by the American Founders; free market economics domestically and internationally; the social requirement to balance personal liberty and responsibility; the spirit of voluntarism crucial to civil society; the continuing validity of American international leadership; and high technology's potential to promote decentralized power sharing for individuals, families, and communities. We consider that the best means of applying these principles in practice arise through wide consultation and debate and a creative determination to link many people's aims in common goals.

ICS PRESS

INSTITUTE FOR CONTEMPORARY STUDIES

The Institute for Contemporary Studies is a nonpartisan, nonprofit public policy research organization. The Institute was founded in 1974 on the principle that men and women have the capacity, right, and responsibility to make the fundamental decisions that affect their lives and their communities. ICS Press was established in 1975 as the publishing subsidiary of the Institute.

ICS promotes self-governing and entrepreneurial ways of life in the United States and around the world. To further this mission, the Institute is dedicated to making the ideas of self-governance known, understood, and used as widely as possible among individual citizens, community groups, scholars, and policy makers at all levels.

ICS Press has published some of the most influential, innovative, and readable books on public issues, including the writings of eight Nobel laureates and more than 250 books and monographs in four languages. ICS publications have enjoyed considerable recognition and success over the years in the development of critical issues of national interest. Through the Classic Edition Series, ICS Press also reissues influential books from many sources on themes of self-governance.

Institute for Contemporary Studies programs include the Center for Self-Governance, the International Center for Self-Governance, and the International Center for Economic Growth.

The Center for Self-Governance (CSG) is dedicated to the study of self-governing institutions, drawing on the best available research in economics, political science, anthropology, psychology, and sociology. The projects of CSG are focused on cultivating national, state, and local policies and programs that foster citizen initiative to build strong communities, with particular emphasis on public housing communities.

CSG regularly sponsors the publication of important books on entrepreneurship, schools, governance and leadership, and social policy.

The International Center for Self-Governance (ICSG) is dedicated to promoting self-governing and entrepreneurial ways of life around the world. Working primarily in developing countries, ICSG assists individuals and groups at all levels of society in organizing themselves, setting their own rules, pooling their talents, and managing their own resources in order to enhance their own and their country's well-being. ICSG's activities are focused on three functions: producing practical training materials, building an international participatory network of nongovernmental organizations, and disseminating the ideas of self-governance worldwide.

ICSG sponsors the production of multilingual books, videos, and other publications, which are in wide use around the world and are in great demand among development scholars and practitioners.

The International Center for Economic Growth (ICEG) facilitates economic growth and human development in developing and postsocialist countries. To accomplish this ICEG sponsors a wide range of activities—including research, publications, conferences, seminars, and special projects advising governments—through a large network of correspondent institutes worldwide. ICEG is committed to assisting nongovernmental organizations to develop local responses to economic and social problems, consistent with local values and informed by global experiences with economic and social reform.

ICS Press publishes the work of these programs.

The experience of the Institute for Contemporary Studies has been that strong ideas ably presented have a significant influence on the conduct and progress of human affairs.

INSTITUTE FOR CONTEMPORARY STUDIES
720 Market Street, 4th Floor
San Francisco, CA 94102
E-MAIL icspress@hooked.net
FAX 415-986-4878 TEL -415-981-5353
1-800-326-0263